AF076977

not a stage!

AC SS | Adolescent Cultures, School & Society

Joseph L. DeVitis & Linda Irwin-DeVitis
GENERAL EDITORS

VOL. 60

This book is part of the Peter Lang Education list.
Every volume is peer reviewed and meets
the highest quality standards for content and production.

PETER LANG
New York • Washington, D.C./Baltimore • Bern
Frankfurt • Berlin • Brussels • Vienna • Oxford

not a stage!

A Critical Re-Conception of Young Adolescent Education

PRINCIPAL AUTHOR & EDITOR
mark d. vagle

PETER LANG
New York • Washington, D.C./Baltimore • Bern
Frankfurt • Berlin • Brussels • Vienna • Oxford

Library of Congress Cataloging-in-Publication Data

Not a stage!: a critical re-conception of young adolescent education /
Principal author and editor Mark D. Vagle.
p. cm. — (Adolescent cultures, school and society; v. 60)
Includes bibliographical references and index.
1. Middle school education—United States. 2. Teenagers—Education—
United States. 3. Educational sociology—United States.
I. Vagle, Mark D. (Mark Dennis).
LB1623.5.N68 373.236—dc23 2011052996
ISBN 978-1-4331-1633-9 (hardcover)
ISBN 978-1-4331-1634-6 (paperback)
ISBN 978-1-4539-0528-9 (e-book)
ISSN 1091-1464

Bibliographic information published by **Die Deutsche Nationalbibliothek.**
Die Deutsche Nationalbibliothek lists this publication in the "Deutsche
Nationalbibliografie"; detailed bibliographic data is available
on the Internet at http://dnb.d-nb.de/.

For Nicole, Maya, Rhys, and Chase—a beautiful contingent, recursive crew

Acknowledgements

I would like to thank the educators of young adolescents for remaining tirelessly committed to helping young people learn and grow in and through the day-to-day complexities of life. This book was written, in part, to recognize the importance of everydayness—to continually find ways to draw out contexts and to try to stay focused on what is happening in the here and now.

This book was also written to draw attention to the innumerable contexts and messy conceptions of growth and change that researchers, theorists, teacher educators, and policymakers must consider as they tend to broad, overarching issues and problems. I wish to thank the people who are drawn to this type of work. I hope you find this text helpful.

Writing and editing a collection is only made possible when all sorts of folks are responsive and supportive. I feel most fortunate to have received such support from the staff at Peter Lang Publishing. I thank the series editors, Joseph DeVitis and Linda Irwin-DeVitis, for including this book in the *Adolescent Cultures, School, and Society* series. I wish to give a special thanks to Chris Myers and Sarah Stack. Their patience and openness was remarkable and most appreciated.

I also wish to thank Jaye Thiel, a doctoral student at the University of Georgia, who spent many hours formatting and proofreading the manuscript in preparation for publishing.

Finally, I want to extend my appreciation to the scholars who wrote chapter responses to my anchor essay. The contributors in this volume are doing smart, beautiful work that will make a difference in the lives of young adolescents and those who educate them.

Table of Contents

Introduction

Being a Bit Disruptive

Mark D. Vagle

For over half a century, it has been commonplace—natural, an "of course"—for those who focus on the education of young adolescents to draw on developmental psychology and, in particular, the accompanying "developmental stages" which have served—and continue to serve—as the dominant conception of young adolescent growth and change. Although stage developmentalism has brought attention to the needs of young adolescents in the name of developmental responsiveness, it also has proceeded without careful enough consideration of critical theoretical perspectives regarding issues related to power, interest, agency, gender, race, class, culture and so on. The primary purpose of this edited volume is to help *re-orient* the discourse on young adolescent growth and change and in turn *re-conceptualize* the education of young adolescents.

To those who are skeptical (for any and all possible reasons) of these sort of re-orienting and re-conceptualizing projects, I want to make clear, from the start, a set of assumptions that I have about such work.

> **Assumption #1:** Re-conceptualizing knowledge, assumptions, structures, theories, ideas, philosophies, goals, aspirations, practices—to name a few—is a given. That is, I assume all scholars and practitioners in any and all fields (disciplines) should always be re-conceptualizing what they do. Although I realize this could be read as a naïve statement of the obvious, I think the obvious must be tended to and opened up. This volume might, in part then, be read as an opening up of at least one of the most *vexingly obvious* aspects of what we should be doing in fields of study—*constantly re-conceptualizing them.*

> **Assumption #2:** Building off the first assumption, such re-conceptualizing should not only be reserved for matters related to application or implementation of theories, ideas, philosophies, and the like (which, in my opinion, receive the most attention because they are the most readily accessible), but also for the very foundational theories, ideas, and philosophies themselves. This is important because the theories, ideas, and philosophies are often woven through the fabric of our applications and implementations. Some-

times they are woven so tightly, that we cannot see or feel their influence on our actions, language, questions, and answers. It is only when we scratch and gnaw at them a bit that we can see how they are working on (framing, constraining, limiting, allowing) our actions and implementations. This volume might also, then, be described as a *scratching, gnawing* text.

Assumption #3: This also means that I assume gnawing and scratching will take place between you (the reader) and this text. I sincerely want the ideas forwarded in this volume to be poked, prodded, and wrestled with. I want it to serve as a discursive space where ideas are played with in a seriously thoughtful way. Finally, then, this volume might be read as a *playful* text.

Situating the Contingent, Recursive

Guided by these particular assumptions, this volume is designed to incite a discourse around young adolescent growth and change. At the close of her powerful book, *Act Your Age! A Cultural Construction of Adolescence,* Nancy Lesko (2001) calls for alternative (to developmentalism and socialization) conceptions of growth and change. She writes:

> I think that if we assumed that growth and change are *contingent,* we would need to specify the contingencies and that would lead us to examine and document multiple microcontexts. I also think that a conception of growth and change as *recursive,* as occurring over and over as we move into new situations, would reorient us. Rather than the assumption of cumulative and one-way development that is now in place in both science and popular culture, a recursive view of growth and change directs us to look at local contexts and specific actions of young people, without the inherent evaluation of steps, stages, and socialization. (pp. 195-96)

Breaking free of dominant discourses (such as stage developmentalism) is no simple task—as per their dominant nature, it is difficult to imagine different discourses without using the dominant as (at the very least) a reference point, and more likely as the very rubric by which all conceptions are judged. The task, then, requires a critical theoretical approach—that is, it requires an approach that aims to disrupt norms on both the individual and social level. One must carefully watch both the larger social matters that constrain some things and make other things possible. Such a project needs an approach that sees who ends up privileged and who ends up marginalized—and examines the social conditions that made (and continue to make) this happen.

Critical theorists have been committed to this work, as Pinar (2009) states, for over 40 years. Although Pinar recognizes what motivates critical theorists (pedagogues), he is concerned that there is an assumed ideological freedom in which critical folks do not critique their own ideologies. For Pinar, this will always limit what can be accomplished using critical theory. He writes:

> what stultifies the educational Left is not only the reproduction of power 'outside' but also within us, the incapacity to imagine resistance against ourselves and with others.... Without subjective reconstruction of one's own ideological interpellation (subjugation in Butler's parlance) the split-off 'I' asserts itself as a unitary context-free cohesive self, reserving for itself the agency evidently eluding everyone else. (p. 193)

Though I find Pinar's critique a bit sharp, I do not want this critical project to fall into the same trap. I want for this text to be read as a critically oriented project in which the critical theory that is put to use is also marked by a healthy dose of humility (Vagle, 2011). This project is meant to be both an advocacy and a contemplation. It is a contemplation of ourselves as humans who are growing and changing as young adolescents are growing and changing; a contemplation of how power and agency circulate through all relations; a contemplation of how developmental frames of growth and change provide the very rules of the playground and are enacted in particular micro-contexts by living, breathing human beings.

In this book, the problem of preserving "young adolescence" is described as a reification of dominant, oppressive structures—it needs to be disrupted, yet also needs to be the starting point. This seeming contradiction is one of many that will be taken up, debated, considered, amplified—but not settled. In fact, this book is specifically designed to incite a discourse that tries to draw out and preserve complexities. It is tantalizing to craft texts—in this case a book—that try to "answer" questions. Unfortunately the questions posed here do not lend themselves to simple answers.

I also feel it is necessary to acknowledge that having this "developmental stage" foregrounded has accomplished significant political, fiscal, and practical changes on the ground—in schools and classrooms. It has done important things. This book is not about denying or denouncing positive actions. Second, though, it is necessary to look at what is not so positive. Who is left out (intentionally or unintentionally) when the development stage of young adolescence is talked about, described, and enacted as a neutral platform for all other decisions regarding schooling practices? Who is privileged when this happens? What are the ends and aims of such discourses? What is lost when a conception such as stage developmentalism is not questioned?

I also want this book to be situated in the present—in real political contexts. Two recent texts convincingly make the case that the "Accountability Movement" has wielded profound power (and control) and inflicted significant damage on U.S. schools. Dianne Ravitch's (2010) *The Death and Life of the Great American School System: How Testing and Choice Are Undermining Education* is a particularly powerful indictment, as is Sharon Nichols and David Berliner's (2007) *Collateral Damage: How Highstakes Testing Corrupts America's Schools.* This book, therefore, is written at a time when students and teachers are under immense pressure to perform on tests that are far from the contingent, recursive realities of their day-to-day lives. I remain hopeful that the contingent, recursive conception asserted in this volume can, at once, inform the day-to-day(ness) of schooling and the larger societal issues (struggles, practices, policies) that frame what is even possible in schools.

The Project

With these commitments in mind, the book aims to do the following:

1. To infuse, following Lesko, a contingent (profoundly contextual and dependent) and recursive (occurring over and over again in and over time) conception of adolescent growth and change into the discourse around young adolescence by making three theoretical pleas to those interested in the schooling of young adolescents (10-15 year olds):
    - To move away from a developmentally responsive vision to a contingently and recursively relational vision;
    - To move from "characterizing" young adolescenCE to "particularizing" young adolescenTS; and
    - To move from a "sameness" curriculum to a "difference" curriculum.

2. To have these three pleas, collectively, contribute to a theoretical basis for more particularized, critical work regarding issues including but not limited to race, class, gender, sexuality, power, and struggle.
3. To bring multiple responses to these pleas together in the same textual space, creating opportunities for readers to engage in and theorize what contingent, recursive growth and change might look and feel like. Scholars invited to respond represent different fields such as adolescent literacy, middle grades education, urban education, foundations, curriculum studies, comparative education, policy studies, and teacher education.

To these ends, I authored a theoretical essay (Section 1 of this volume) that serves as the "anchoring" text for the book. The anchor essay was sent to invited contributors. Potential contributors were asked to read the essay and based on their reading craft a response to one or more of the three theoretical pleas I made in the anchor essay, with the understanding that it would become a chapter length contribution in this volume.

I emphasized that the goal was to have the pleas seriously and thoughtfully considered (extended, stretched). To this end, I suggested that contributors might primarily discuss the plea(s), connect something from their own scholarship to one or more of the pleas, point-counterpoint particular arguments embedded in one or more of the pleas, or open up a plea wider (or extend its reach) for further "critical" consideration than I had done. In these cases (and other possibilities) a related goal was always to incite a discourse regarding contingent, recursive conceptions and the accompanying pleas. The goal was *not* to settle matters, as this would counter the very contingent, recursive conceptions that need to be imagined. When crafting their responses, contributors were asked to spend limited time (10-15% of the chapter) discussing the pleas and most of the time connecting somehow to their own work.

Twenty scholars collectively contributed thirteen sole and co-authored chapters "in response" to the anchor essay. What follows includes my anchor essay (Section 1); my editorial grouping of the chapters—in three subsequent sections, including my introductions to each section; and my concluding remarks. Again, the anchor essay is designed as a disrupting discourse, by which all the other contributions extend, expand, and—at times—push back. For instance, some contributors (e.g., Brown; Conklin) felt that my pleas might set up unnecessary binaries, and could be more nuanced. Although they are in favor of disrupting stage developmentalism, they do not want the "alternative" to create a juxtaposition that then needs to be disrupted. The nuance of their arguments preserves complexity in powerful ways.

Collectively, then, the anchor essay and each individual response are intended to accomplish what one perspective (written by one scholar) cannot—put multiple perspectives into play. After authoring the theoretical anchor for the book and having edited the thirteen responses, it is also clear to me that the theory forwarded in the anchor essay *comes to life* in the particular responses. Finally, and perhaps most importantly, I am hopeful that this volume is merely the beginning of an effort to use innumerable "micro-perspectives" of "micro-contexts" to re-conceptualize young adolescent growth and change contingently and recursively.

How One Might Read This Book

I realize that I do not get to decide how readers choose to read (or find themselves reading) this book. That said, I have some suggestions that might be useful. Of course, reading this volume cover to cover is perhaps the most desirable option! At the least, though, I suggest beginning with the anchor essay. As just described, the anchor essay is a starting point for all subsequent chapters and is, therefore the most logical place to start reading. I anticipate that reading the anchor essay first will allow for deeper connections with and extensions of each contributing author's response. In fact, some contributing authors' arguments consistently pivot off the anchor essay, making it necessary to have read the anchor essay.

After reading the anchor essay, I think it would be interesting for readers to pick and choose chapters depending on their interests—the sections are organized thematically, but that doesn't mean they necessarily have to be read in tandem. Also, the sections do not build off one another—that is, they (and the chapters themselves) are their own entities in relation to the anchor essay.

An Invitation to Messiness

When I first proposed this volume, what follows served as the proposed closing for the book. The book now has a new closing and its proposed closing is now here—to close the introduction. I begin (this closing) with a few slivers of stories from my childhood.

Sometime during the 1978-79 school year, my first grade teacher said to my mother at parent-teacher conferences, "Mark is doing really well in school, but his desk is very messy." At the end of my first year teaching (1995), my principal spent at least 30 minutes talking about how great a teacher I was and then when we got to the *what to work on for next year* portion of the meeting she stated, "your classroom is really messy and it could distract students from learning." This of course came on the heels of being told that students were learning a great deal in my classroom. Fast forward to the spring of 2001. During my first evaluation conference as a middle grades assistant principal, the principal carefully walked through a host of glowing comments about my organization, insightfulness, calm demeanor, clear vision, and thoughtful follow-through—all important attributes of a good leader. The closing *what I want you to work on*, predictably, was "your office is awfully messy. I'd like you to keep it cleaner." I do not recall my response. Since joining the faculty at the University of Georgia in 2006 I have had at least seven different people give me the same (unsolicited) feedback about my office.

I am pretty messy. The feedback is warranted. Unfortunately, I do actually try to be neat. I clean my office and can actually get it to the point that even "neat people" might say that it looks fairly neat. However, it doesn't last very long and I think I know why. There is a part of me that *gravitates to messy*. I think I find myself in-the-messy, in part, because one is not supposed to necessarily be messy in public settings. The more that I am told that it is distracting or unprofessional, I wince momentarily and then settle into some conflicting sense of satisfaction-guilt. There is some degree of comfort in the mess for me. This is not to say that I never get frustrated with my messiness. Rather, I think there is a larger, overarching *messiness ethos* that animates me, that makes me feel alive.

Perhaps this is one reason why I find myself resisting developmentalism (tidy) and being drawn to contingencies and recursivity (messy). That said, it is still difficult to not close this introduction with some type of tidy final setup. Although this is clearly the way most academic writing operates, I want to do something a bit different. I don't want to make things tidy, because they are not. I don't want to say anything more than I already have about what you are supposed to learn because, again, I don't get to decide. There is nothing tidy about trying to poke holes in a dominant discourse and then attempting to re-orient toward discourses that are contingent and recursive.

To say that growth and change (and schooling practices related to this growth and change) depend on micro-contexts and that they change over and over again through these contexts is saying something wild and messy. It means that we cannot chart "meaning progressions." This is not to say that people do not get older and that getting older cannot be marked by time. It is to say that what these markings come to mean is highly situated in contexts that are ever-moving and ever-changing. This is unsettling. If one is looking for a clean conception this project is not for them. However, if one is looking for messy conceptions that try to get fleeting holds on the innumerable ways in which folks grow and change, then this project is exciting. So instead of closing this introduction cleanly, I end with the following:

Consider yourself formally invited to a messy conception. Come on in, find a chair, move some piles of paper around and let's talk about contingent, recursive relationality, particularizing young adolescen(TS), and a difference curriculum. I promise you the messiness will not distract from learning or become unprofessional—in fact, I cannot think of a better way to act as a professional learner than to resist clean explanations and get after the messy stuff.

References

Lesko, N. (2001). *Act your age: A cultural construction of adolescence.* New York: Routledge/Falmer.

Nichols, S. L., & Berliner, D. (2007). *Collateral damage: How high-stakes testing corrupts America's schools*. Cambridge, MA: Harvard Education Press.

Pinar, B. (2009). The unaddressed 'I" of ideology critique. *Power and education, 1*(2). 189-200.

Ravitch, D. (2010). *The death and life of the great American school system: How testing and choice are undermining education*. New York: Basic Books.

Vagle, M. D. (2011). Lessons in contingent, recursive humility. *Journal of Adolescent and Adult Literacy, 54*(6), 362-370.

Section 1

The Anchor Essay

Trying to Poke Holes in Teflon: Developmentalism; Young Adolescence; and Contingent, Recursive Growth and Change

Mark D. Vagle

Educators interested in the academic, social, and emotional needs of youth 10-15 years old most often base their advocacy on developmentalism and in particular the developmental stage of young adolescence. In this theoretical essay, I argue that by relying solely on developmental discourses and not allowing critical perspectives equal play, these same educators (which I consider myself) run the risk of not achieving their (our) primary goal—creating the best schools possible for young adolescents.

To make this argument, I use Nancy Lesko's (2001) call for a contingent (profoundly contextual and dependent) and recursive (occurring over and over again in and over time) conception of growth and change to analyze three seminal texts in U.S. middle grades education—a field dedicated solely to the education of young adolescents. Based on my analysis, I make three theoretical pleas—that educators of young adolescents move away from a developmentally responsive vision to a contingently and recursively relational vision; from "characterizing" young adolescen(CE) to "particularizing" young adolescen(TS); and from a "sameness" curriculum to a "difference" curriculum.[1] My ultimate hope is that, collectively, these three pleas might contribute to a theoretical basis for more particularized, critical work regarding issues including but not limited to race, class, gender, sexuality, power, and struggle.

Introduction

> To say that adolescence is a social and cultural construction is to recognize, first of all, that adolescence meant something very different in the past and that it may mean something very different in the future. It is also to recognize that the meanings assigned to adolescence are not arbitrary but rather relate to broader material and symbolic power struggles. Social

> meanings embedded in the construction of adolescence grow out of the particular sociohistorical, economic, and political realities from which they emerged. (Saltman, 2005, p. 17)

In keeping with Saltman, it is reasonable to assume that one of the central questions for those interested in the education of young adolescents should be: How might adolescence be socially constructed in the future? However, responding substantively to this question first presumes that educators of young adolescents believe that adolescence is indeed a social construction. Unfortunately, at least in the leading field dedicated to the education of young (10-15 year olds) adolescents, *middle grades education*[2], a socially constructed adolescence has yet to be fully acknowledged. In fact, *developmentalism* and the resultant developmental stage of young adolescence, has served as the primary justification for the existence of middle grades education since its conception in the United States (in the early 1960s) and throughout Canada, Australia[3], New Zealand, and Europe over the past 40 years[4]. Young adolescence as a developmental stage seems to have been treated more like a discovery of the "natural" progressive order of growth and change, rather than a social construction imbued with politics, power, and struggle.

I argue that when a perspective such as developmentalism is elevated to the status of "fact" or "the given", other—especially critical—perspectives are muted. Furthermore, I suggest that amplification of these muted perspectives is particularly important at this point in time as the education of young adolescents in the United States, within and across disciplines, has been and continues to be indelibly marked by high-stakes testing throughout the No Child Left Behind (NCLB) era—and will most likely continue with President Obama's *Race to the Top* initiative. It is difficult to keep young adolescents at the forefront of policy and practice when their test scores become the primary way they are talked about and educated—and equally difficult when the young *adolescent* gets obscured by the developmental stage of young *adolescence.*

What I am suggesting here has been present for some time in early childhood education—a field with similar commitments as middle grades education in that both fields center on the "whole child," a particular developmental stage, and are interdisciplinary. One difference however is the presence of alternatives to developmentalism in early childhood education. For instance, some early childhood scholars have dedicated their work to reconceptualizing the field by challenging common sense assumptions about developmental appropriateness.

Over fifteen years ago, Mallory and New (1994) edited a book entitled *Diversity and Developmentally Appropriate Practice: Challenges for Early Childhood Education*. In it, Lubeck (1994) argues that cross-cultural research can be used to challenge the presumption that all children develop in the same way. Bloch, Tabachnick, and Espinosa-Dulanta (1994) take this a step further when asserting that concepts of readiness and assessment are in and of themselves social constructions rather than "objective" entities. Later, with regard to the guidelines for developmentally appropriate practice in early childhood education, Lubeck (1998) asks leaders in the field to focus less on standards and more on conversations regarding the contextualized nature of practice over time.

The strong presence of traditional and critical perspectives continues today as there is, for example, an American Educational Research Association (AERA) Special Interest Group (SIG) dedicated to *Early Education and Child Development* and another dedicated to *Critical Perspectives on Early Childhood Education*. While there are AERA SIGs dedicated to *Adolescence and Youth Development* and *Middle-Level Education Research* there is no SIG dedicated specifically to critical perspectives on young adolescence or middle grades education.

A commitment to a variety of traditional and critical perspectives is, however, present in the field of adolescent literacy. For instance, in a special issue of *Harvard Educational Review*, leading scholars in the field were brought together to provide their perspectives on what editors Ippolito, Steele, and Samson (2008) describe as the "urgency of adolescents' literacy needs and to the distinctive challenges posed by those needs" (p. 3). The perspectives in this special issue include, for example, research on content area literacy, including a focus on multiple disciplines (Shanahan & Shanahan, 2008), on promoting mastery of intellectual discourse in particular disciplines (Draper,

2008), and on advanced cognitive strategies that help prepare students for disciplinary and workplace thinking (Conley, 2008).

These perspectives are joined by others that focus on the contextual nature of adolescent literacy. For instance, Moje, Overby, Tysvaer, and Morris (2008) point to how adolescents use literacy as a way to negotiate social capital through their social networks. Tatum (2008) presses educators to think about the raced and classed nature of literacy in schools, as it marginalizes African American male adolescents in impoverished communities. Although these perspectives do not directly interrogate stage developmentalism, they do suggest that considering what literacy means for adolescents in contexts in and over time is an essential aspect of understanding adolescent literacy.

Although critical perspectives have been present in early childhood education and adolescent literacy, they have been noteably absent in mainstream middle grades education scholarship (Brown & Saltman, 2005). Instead, critical perspectives such as those published in a special issue of *Theory into Practice* dedicated to rethinking the education of young adolescents (e.g., Gay, 1994; Lesko, 1994) have remained on the perifery. Fortunately, Brown and Saltman have recently brought critical perspectives on young adolescence to light in their edited book, *The Critical Middle School Reader*, and therefore have renewed opportunities for critical dialogues about the future of educating young adolescents. This critical reader, the first of its kind in middle grades education, could not have come at a better time.

I fear that by continuing to rely solely on a linear, uni-directional, and time-bound conception of development and without serious consideration of critical perspectives regarding young adolescence, those interested in the education of young adolescents will fail to achieve their ultimate goal—to create the best schools possible for youth 10–15 years old. More importantly, if all educators dedicated to young adolescent learners are not collectively challenging themselves to bring all possible perspectives to bear, in the end, the young adolescents will suffer.

One of the most promising critical perspectives that can be used to re-envision the education of young adolescents is the call Lesko (2001)—an author in Brown and Saltman's (2005) reader—makes for a reoriented discourse around adolescence, one that strives to capture what she describes as the contingent (profoundly contextual and dependent) and recursive (occurring over and over again in and over time) nature of growth and change. Lesko's perspective challenges educators of young adolescents to consider the simultaneity of what may appear to be contradictory identities such as adolescents being mature and immature and learning and learned at the same moments in time, as opposed to being immature and learning at one point in time and necessarily moving toward a state of maturity and learnedness in adulthood. Lesko also stresses the need to think about the *blizzard* of social factors that influence the lives of adolescents, rather than a straight line in which one factor occurs after another. The challenges Lesko offers can influence what, as Saltman (2005) stresses, young adolescence might mean in the future and in turn how the education of young adolescents can be re-envisioned.

To this end, I use Lesko's (2001) reoriented discourse to analyze issues regarding the education of young adolescents that are found in three seminal texts in the field of middle grades education—*This We Believe: Keys to Educating Young Adolescents* (NMSA, 2010), *Research Summary on Young Adolescent Development* (Caskey & Anfara, 2007), and *Turning Points 2000* (Jackson & Davis, 2000). I selected the texts because they are often cited in the field best known for its focus on the needs of young adolescents, and I see the texts and the field of middle grades education, therefore, as the best places to start re-envisioning the education of young adolescents.

I use these texts as vehicles to bring Lesko's critical perspective to bear on the education of young adolescents. I do not read them as based on critical theory. Rather, I believe they contain openings (i.e., opportunities) for critical work. That said, critique of these texts and the present state of the education of young adolescents is inevitable when I use Lesko to identify and proceed through the openings I have identified. My hope is that these critiques are viewed by educators of young adolescents as an incitement to a discourse that continually re-envisions what (generous, loving, complicated, conflicting, contextual) schooling for young adolescents might be like.

I begin by articulating a set of theoretical perspectives that explicate a distinction that Brown and Saltman (2005) make between critical and traditional perspectives and then identify Lesko's (2001) reoriented discourse around adolescence as one particular critical perspective worth using. In addition, I articulate a theoretical image of developmental and critical perspectives that I have tried to utilize in my own theorizing and teaching and in turn the crafting of this essay. I proceed by describing the way in which I used Lesko's perspective to analyze the three texts. I then make three theoretical pleas to educators of young adolescents and close by reflecting on the broader implications of this work.

Theoretical Perspectives

Critical and Traditional Perspectives

For Brown and Saltman (2005), what makes a particular perspective critical is its aim to *challenge oppression and promote emancipation*—and such perspectives center on a belief that knowledge and truth are multiple and contexually situated. Critical perspectives are motivated by issues of power, politics, interests, and material practices. There is no goal of determining what is "best" or "right" or "appropriate" in any sort of absolute or final way. In fact there is a consistent and deliberate commitment to interrogating any practice, policy, belief, or knowledge; especially those that purport to be the "best." I add then that critical perspectives are by definition partial and forever deferred. In this way, all perspectives (critical included) must remain doggedly committed to turning themselves on themselves.

Conversely, traditional perspectives according to Brown and Saltman (2005) do quite the opposite—they reinforce "existing relations of power, by blindly accepting and transferring unexamined bodies of knowledge as factual information" (p. 1). This reinforcement becomes dangerous when such factual information becomes the pervasive belief among those who make decisions regarding schooling practices. In fact, when beliefs become facts, I would argue that the traditional perspective is no longer even a perspective, but rather a rule or a law. In my estimation, young adolescence as a developmental stage has become a rule.

By "chipping away at the Teflon coating" (Lesko, 2001, p. 192) that blankets developmentalism, Lesko has in effect softened developmentalism a bit. This softening makes it possible for me to in turn use the following image in this essay. I picture a box with a lid placed on top of it. Inside the box is where innumerable critical perspectives reside. The lid is developmentalism. It is very thick—designed to keep all of its contents safe and controlled. Although the lid has been softened, it still does not have many (if any) holes to allow for air, like a hamster cage might. The critical perspectives are suffocating. I hope to poke some holes in the lid, thus allowing critical perspectives to get some air; with the long term goal of prying the lid away from its conflated relationship with adolescence—making it one of the innumerable possible perspectives on adolescence instead of the dominant one. Lesko's conception of contingent and recursive adolescence is one perspective that needs more air.

Contingent, Recursive Growth

Lesko's (2001) call for a remade adolescence is based on a rigorous, thoughtful sociohistorical analysis about how adolescence in the U.S. has come to mean something over the past century. It begins, as most historical accounts of adolescence, with G. Stanley Hall's (e.g., 1904) thoughts in the early 1900s. Hall's views are laced with concerns for protecting the nation, and as such, focus on making sure uncivilized white boys are taught to be civilized white men who can lead the nation. While the women's rights and civil rights movements have presumably changed the political and cultural landscape of the U.S. over the past century, it is reasonable to concur with Lesko's assertion that our social construction of adolescence has not changed all that much from the days of G. Stanley Hall.

Of equal importance is that the education of young adolescents continues to launch from the assumption that young adolescence is a distinct developmental stage—an assumption that in effect "freezes" students in time and space without agency, context, politics, or power. Lesko is particularly concerned that a developmental depiction of growth and change, while seemingly intended to be a generous act designed to locate and define what is unique about people at various points in life, actually limits and determines the individual more than it emancipates that individual. Moreover, Lesko believes that by constructing adolescence as a distinct time period, adults in schools and government are allowed to control, study, measure, anticipate, and redirect the individual. Therefore, contrary to common-sense assumptions about the emancipatory aims of policies and practices for educating young adolescents, constructing and re-constructing a developmental adolescence can be read as serving the adults and society more than the adolescents.

Lesko (2001) is equally concerned with the absence of context in developmentalism. Characterizing adolescents one way or another void of context reflects Lesko's concern that adolescents are often described "as 'oversocialized,' passive, [and] without critical awareness or active agency" (p. 195). In response to the dominate *development* and *socialization* discourses of adolescence, Lesko offers a discourse that captures, again, the contingent (profoundly contextual and dependent) and recursive (occurring over and over again in and over time) nature of growth and change. This discourse moves the conception of adolescence away from either-or logic and aims to preserve the complexity of living as an adolescent. "Somehow a remade adolescence must take up the contradictions of being simultaneously mature and immature, old and young, traditional and innovative" (Lesko, p. 196).

Lesko's (2001) use of the word *remade* suggests that adolescence is something that has been, is, and will continue to be constructed (made). This social construction, Saltman (2005) argues, is part of a critical project aimed at a more substantive democratic society, where democracy is "struggled over by different groups with competing material and ideological interests" (p. 19).

Taking a critical stance on adolescence allows for such arguments in that it "acknowledges that there are multiple contextually derived perspectives and sources of truth, many of which have been and are subjugated in order to maintain existent relations of power" (Brown, 2005a, p. 4). In this respect, adolescence should not be treated as a clearly defined stage in life. However, it does not mean there is nothing scientific or biological about adolescence. Instead, a socially constructed adolescence is one that recognizes "that the meaning of biological and psychological realities do become meaningful or relevant in different ways in different social contexts" (Saltman, 2005, p. 16). Using Lesko's notion of a contingent and recursive growth and change opens up the possibility to see *adolescence* in particular ways and therefore opens up the possibility of seeing individual *adolescents* in these same ways.

Conceptual Analysis

As previously mentioned, I chose to analyze three seminal texts often cited in the field of middle grades education—*This We Believe: Keys to Educating Young Adolescents* (NMSA, 2010), *Research Summary on Young Adolescent's Developmental Characteristics* (Caskey & Anfara, 2007), and *Turning Points 2000* (Jackson & Davis, 2000). I read each text with the goal of first locating potential openings to use Lesko's perspective. Then, I interrogated each opening by asking myself the question, *How might Lesko's notion of contingent and recursive growth and change be given more air through this opening?* Based on my analysis I have articulated three theoretical pleas to educators of young adolescents—one stemming from each of the three texts. To elucidate each plea, I begin by briefly and somewhat generally describing it. I then identify the opening I analyzed, followed by the analysis itself.

Making Pleas to Educators of Young Adolescents

Plea #1—To Move from a Developmentally Responsive Vision to a Contingently and Recursively Relational Vision

The phrase *developmentally responsive*—"using the *distinctive nature* of young adolescents as the foundation upon which all decisions about school organization, policies, curriculum, instruction, and assessment are made" (emphasis added, NMSA, 2010, p. 13)—is described in *This We Believe* —now in it's 4th edition—as the first of four essential attributes for what successful schools for young adolescents should look and be like. Although this phrase is intended to accomplish the opposite, it can be read as limiting. First, the word "responsive" has the potential to reinforce a binary relationship between adults and young adolescents. The adults are to monitor the young adolescents and then determine how to respond. Second, the responsiveness is directed toward the young adolescent's development and the "distinctive nature of young adolescents". At first read, this would appear to be a generous and loving act as the description of this particular developmental stage is marked by hyper-variability among individual young adolescents and has brought much attention to the needs of 10-15 year olds. However, a more careful reading points to the possibility that the developmental stage is treated as a neutral (natural) platform, without consideration of how the stage itself has been socially constructed (made).

Conversely, I argue that the phrase "contingently and recursively relational" can free up educators to spend less time seeing young adolescents in a developmental (natural) frame and more time seeing young adolescents in innumerable, lived (de-naturalized) contexts. I also argue that, in practice, it may not matter what a list of developmental characteristics says a boy or a girl should or should not be able to do at a particular time —especially when the list is not implicated as being based on a raced (white), classed (middle), gendered (male), and sexed (heteronormative)[5] developmental stage. What does matter is how adults and young adolescents find themselves in relation to one another as they struggle (mightily perhaps) to continually learn and grow with and from one another.

To these ends, I ask those interested in the education of young adolescents to move away from developmental responsiveness in favor of contingent and recursive relationality, as the latter may more accurately capture the intent of educators—to be profoundly present with and for the young adolescent.

Opening. *This We Believe* (NMSA, 1982, 1995, 2003, 2010) is written as National Middle School Association's (NMSA) position paper on what successful schools for young adolescents should look and be like. The core of the latest version is organized around 4 essential attributes—developmentally responsive; challenging; empowering; and equitable—and 16 characteristics, 5 of which focus on curriculum, instruction, and assessment; 5 on leadership and organization; and 6 on culture and community.

The most recent edition of *This We Believe* (NMSA, 2010) has made some important moves toward particularizing and contextualizing development. For instance, the end of the book contains lists of developmental characteristics that are foregrounded by the ways in which gender, race, ethnicity, and culture (to name a few) influence growth and change; how various types of development (i.e., physical, social-emotional) are interrelated; and how characteristics

> should be understood as...reasonable generalization[s] for most young adolescents, one that is more or less valid for particular young adolescents in particular situations...variations in race, ethnicity, socioeconomic status, sexual orientation, immigration history and language usage, and physical and mental abilities, among other factors, can influence how young adolescents experience their development, and the resulting implications for educators. (p. 54)

These moves are meaningful as they provide rich opportunities for critical theoretical work to be done. That said, as I discuss throughout this and the second plea, I would like to see the very foundation (i.e., developmentalism) itself be directly troubled, rather than continuing to describe "factors" as "variations" of an assumed norm. I also would like to see such troubling front and center (i.e., as essential attributes), rather than at the end of the document. With this in mind, I focused my analysis on one paragraph taken from the introduction.

> Young people undergo more rapid and profound personal changes between the ages 10 and 15 than at any other time in their lives. Although growth in infancy is also very extensive, infants are not *the conscious witnesses of their own development*. Early adolescence is also a period of tremendous variability among youngsters of the same gender and chronological age in all areas of their development. Changes occur irregularly, *as young adolescents enter puberty at different times and progress at different rates*. Individual differences proliferate, making dubious such assumptions as, 'All seventh graders are...' *Socioeconomic status, privilege, and ethnicity are among factors that add to the diversity of students*. (emphasis added, NMSA, 2010, pp. 5-6)

It is difficult to determine precisely what it means to be a conscious witness of one's development. I am not sure that people are all that aware of their own growth and change, as much as they are aware of very specific experiences they might have as they grow and change. This could be what the authors intended when they crafted this statement. Nevertheless, let me take this a bit further.

Here is a point at which linear developmental discourses may do more harm than good. As young adolescents encounter experiences that trouble them and may trouble others around them, a developmental discourse that states whether "now" is the "right" time to experience something not only does not help the student, it may in fact hurt the student. A contingent and recursive conception of growth and change locates the growth and change directly in the experiences, not in an abstracted construction of what should be happening. The particular experiences are not, then, compared to anything—the experiences are the points of consciousness. Furthermore, the recursive nature of growth and change signals that the growth and change occur over and over again through various and sometimes competing contexts. Lesko's (2001) use of the term "blizzard" to describe this effect is helpful. When a young adolescent has an experience (troubling, satisfying, etc.), the growth and change that might accompany the experience is not necessarily progressing toward a more enlightened state of being. Subsequent and previous experiences may contradict the present experience.While this might not be so difficult to imagine when reflecting on one's own life, it may be more difficult to live out in schooling practices. Lesko stresses that

> the evolutionary roots of adolescence impose a strong interest in *the future* over the present or the past; one eye is always on the ending, which spurs the documentation of movement or lack of it toward the desired characteristics. The temporal movement into the future is understood as linear, unidirectional, and able to be separated from the present and the past. (p. 191)

A contingent and recursive conception of growth and change allows one to spend less time dividing time into past, present, and future and instead locates the growth in particular contexts. This does not mean that young adolescents do not exist in time. Rather, their growth and change is marked more by what is happening now. In other words both eyes (i.e., the conscious witnessing) rest squarely on the here and now.

This leads to a second entry point in this opening—how puberty and a developmental construction of adolescence are conflated. Clearly, people experience particular biological changes that are unique to this time in life. What is at issue is the degree to which the biological developmental progression is used to chart all other progressions (e.g., cognitive, emotional, social). It appears that the excerpt above treats the biological progression of development as the rubric by which all other aspects of one's growth and change is measured. It would make sense, then, that in schools educators create a developmental map for what students should know and be able to do at different moments in time; for when it is acceptable to teach sex education (not to mention what is included in such education); or for when it is time for students to make choices about what they learn. I am not suggesting that educators do not need to make these determinations. Rather, I am trying to interrogate what is being used to make such determinations. By making decisions based on being developmentally responsive, educators assume that they have somehow discovered a natural order to living, and that this natural order tells them the proper times and ways to do things. Unfortunately, people rarely live this way.

A contingent and recursively relational discourse would locate the determination in the contexts that are experienced in relationships. And as the contexts change so do the determinations. I acknowledge that it may be difficult to imagine growth being something that occurs over and over again, rather than being progressive and moving toward a fixed target that in essence is a desired state. Letting go of the notion of a desired state—which in the case of adolescence is described as reaching a "civilized" adulthood—can be frightening. At the same time, maybe we can reflect on some of the situations we have encountered as adults. Perhaps we can then come to grips with the fact that adulthood is not some desired state—that we are not necessarily any more "civilized" than we were as children, and in some cases acknowledge that we are probably less civilized as adults than we were as children. Once we commit to this activity we may then be ready to consider an even more uncomfortable notion—that not all people want to move to the same desired (civilized) state, that the dominant desired (civilized) state is not a universal truth, and that in many contingent situations it is more desirable to be *unruly* (Shor, 1996). Lesko (2001) reminds us that "adolescent theory has been about developing people according to raced, classed, and gendered experiences and criteria formulated in the West...this means that 'adolescent development' has been about creating and endlessly re-creating whiteness and developing masculinity" (p. 191).

When NMSA (2010) says that socioeconomic status, privilege, and ethnicity are among factors that add to the diversity of students, they may be obscuring the complexity of the issue. From a critical theoretical perspective, socioeconomic status, privilege, and ethnicity are not "factors" that influence a universal definition of development. As Lesko (2001) states, the notion of development itself is a raced (white), classed (middle), gendered (male), and I add sexed (heterosexual) construct. It was never and will never be a neutral and natural criterion for how all people grow and change. Moreover, race, class, gender, and sexuality are not factors; they are the very ways we "are" in the world with one another. We are constantly being raced, classed, gendered, and sexed just like the developmental discourse.

To be developmentally responsive is to be complicit in perpetuating and strengthening a discourse that is raced, classed, gendered, and sexed toward what has historically been assumed to be "good" and the most "civilized"—white, middle class, male, and heterosexual. Lesko (2001) highlights how just 100 years ago theorists believed in recapitulation theory—"that each individual child's growth recapitulated the development of humankind" (p. 31). Moreover, it was believed that humankind had "evolved" to its most civilized state in white middle class men. Adolescence was in turn determined to be a critical time in development because it was a time in which individuals (that is white boys) would either reach their most desired state of being (become civilized) or not (remain as savages).

Although it may appear that human development is not seen in exactly these terms today, the echoes of this history are still strong and therefore must be continually disrupted. Lesko (2001) even feels that some of the important work with regard to alternative sets of developmental stages does not do enough disrupting. For example, Lesko stresses that

> to argue...that girls may develop moral reasoning in distinctive terms is to challenge the universalizing discourse of developmental stages with a minoritizing one, which states that particular minority groups have different needs or patterns of growth. Under this critical stance various 'minority'

differences flourish, but the universal stance remains untouched. (pp. 191-192)

Again, the latest version of *This We Believe* does move toward what Lesko (2001) might see as an effort to articulate "minoritizing" developmental stages. Although a positive move, it still implicitly preserves a universalizing norm. Those interested in the education of young adolescents could significantly disrupt this untouched universal developmental perspective by breaking away from a developmentally responsive vision in favor of a contingent and recursively relational vision.

Plea #2—To Move from Characterizing Young Adolescen(CE) to Particularizing Young Adolescen(TS)

From a policy perspective, it feels reasonable to spend time creating lists of general attributes that help others make some sense of what to expect when working with young adolescents. However, any list of this kind will not only fall short, but will also reinforce the untroubled developmental discourse that suffocates the innumerable perspectives that lie beneath it.

It would be impossible to describe all the possible contexts and microcontexts in which young adolescents find themselves. However, continuing to open up these contexts through a variety of texts (e.g., critical, narrative, ethnographic, phenomenological, feminist, post-structural) that aim to breath life into what it means to experience the world may be possible. Capturing the contingent and recursive particulars could then move the construction of adolescence away from describing young adolescents as developing creatures who, if different, are viewed as variations of the norm—as if the norm itself is somehow not a construction—toward a social construction of adolescence that views young adolescents as "whole" people living in contexts, in time. Such time is marked by multiplicity rather than simplicity. These particulars cannot be generalized or characterized, and this perhaps is what makes Lesko's perspective scary. Because as soon as we write something about what it is like to be a young adolescent, that same young adolescent is experiencing something new (and so are we). The beauty of this, however, is that such a project opens up the particular so that we, instead, see a realm of possibilities that can be constantly pursued.

Opening. In addition to *This We Believe,* National Middle School Association publishes a number of research summaries on topics important for the education of young adolescents. One such summary focuses on research related to young adolescent developmental characteristics (Caskey & Anfara, 2007) and also contains good openings for critical theoretical work[6]. The summary begins with a defintion of young (i.e., early) adolescence.

> Early adolescence is a distinct period of human growth and development situated between childhood and adolescence. During this remarkable stage of the life cycle, young adolescents (10 to 15-year-olds) experience rapid and significant developmental change. Recognizing and understanding the unique developmental characteristics (traits associated with human growth) of early adolescence and their relationship to the educational program (i.e., curriculum, instruction, and assessment) and to the structure of the middle school (e.g., flexible block scheduling, advisory programs, and team teaching) are central tenets of middle school education. (p. 1)

Caskey and Anfara (2007) highlight the history of young adolescence, beginning with G. Stanley Hall (1904) in the early 1900s and extending through the work of psychologists such as Piaget (1952, 1960) and Flavell (1963). They then articulate sets of developmental characteristics beginning with physical and continuing with intellectual, moral/ethical, emotional/pschological, and social characteristics. The summary also includes two important cautions for the reader, both of which constituted the openings for my analysis.

> First, while the developmental characteristics of young adolescents include physcial, intellectual, emotional/psychological, moral/ethical, and social domains, these characteristics are *interrelated and overlap. Depending on who is writing about young adolescents, the categories can vary and be somewhat arbitrary* (Scales, 2003). Second, although educators, academics, and researchers often use these categories to portray youth ages 10 to 15, they need to be *mindful of generalities and oversimplification* (Kellough & Kellough, 2007). (emphasis added, Caskey & Anfara, 2007, p. 1)

Caskey and Anfara's (2007) warnings provide helpful starting points for critical work—I extend their warnings here. From critical theoretical perspectives, being mindful of generalities and oversimplification means to also mindfully critique how any act of characterizing almost inevitably leads to generalization and oversimplification and is never neutral. In other words, if one aims to describe something "generally speaking" he or she does in fact characterize that thing in one way or another and such characterizing is always, already a social construction. While characterizations can make some rhetorical sense, they quickly become problematic when they lead to categorical thinking.

Reading this from a critical theoretical perspective, the reasons categories can vary and be somewhat arbitrary is due to the reality that when categories are constructed they are built with particular aims in mind. These are not neutral acts. For instance, it means something to say, "young adolescents are often keenly aware of flaws in others, but are reticent to acknowledge their own" (Caskey & Anfara, 2007, p. 3). This statement might be read as assuming that younger children and adults are not as keenly aware of the flaws of others and are more reticent to acknowledge their own flaws—not to mention that the idea of something being "flawed" is socially constructed. My experiences as a father would lead me to believe that my young children and my willingness to acknowledge my (our) own flaws has more to do with the particular situation, my (our) mood, and what is at stake, than whether I (they) have (or have not) "developed" morally and ethically. Young people 10–15 years old experience the same situations. At one point they might appear extremely mature and at another point not all that mature. As a 40 year-old white, middle class, heterosexual male I see myself the same way.

In like fashion, I thought about a number of situations throughout my life as I read another statement. "Emotionally-charged situations may trigger young adolescents to resort to childish behavior patterns, exaggeration of simple occurrences, and vocalization of naïve opinions or one-sided arguments" (Caskey & Anfara, 2007, p. 4). Again, I can think of some recent situations in which I have exhibited such behavior. I also have seen this behavior in young adolescents recently. My point is not necessarily to negate the presence of particular attitudes, behaviors, actions, and beliefs that are used to characterize young adolescents. Rather, I want to pull these attributes away from general characterizations and situate them in particular situations. In some cases it is quite appropriate, maybe even expected, to resort to childlike behavior. In other cases it might not be.

For this reason, I think it is necessary to talk about young adolescents in present terms, rather than in past/future terms. Young adolescents are living as people in moments—and educators must do whatever they can to enrich these moments. Recursive growth and change means that growth and change occurs over and over again. None of us are done vocalizing naïve opinions or one-sided arguments. We are all prone to this, depending on the situation and the context. The same holds true for young adolescents. They can be incredibly sophisticated one moment and incredibly not the next. This is not because they are "all over the place" and are simply "being" an adolescent—it is because they are human. The situations they and we (as adults) find ourselves in allow us to try on our sophistication. We all learn and grow through these situations, whether we anticipate them or not.

Moving away from characterizing adolescents also means to resist characterizing adulthood in the same manner. Static definitions of all stages of development are limiting. Although imagining a particularized adulthood is beyond the scope of this essay, it is important to remember that adolescence has been constructed to meet specific demands that must be realized in order for adulthood to in turn be realized. Hence, adulthood is treated as a definitive state of being as well, with its own set of characteristics by which to measure people.

Amplifying Caskey and Anfara's (2007) warning—to characterize young adolescents (and adults for that matter) is not only to remind ourselves that their characteristics should not be oversimplified, but it is also to acknowledge that we are in fact oversimplifying young adolescents each and every time we characterize them. It is inevitable. This is one reason why Lesko's (2001) contingent and recursive conception of adolescence is so important. We must force ourselves to see, for example, the boy in poverty and the pregnant girl in their particular situations, and more importantly we must see these situations as saturated with politics, power, struggle, and possibility. It does the pregnant girl no good to be told she is not ready to be a mother, when she in fact is going to be a mother. Being "developmentally" ready to be a parent does not mean she will not parent. This particular situation demands that she parents.

My sense is that by continuing to characterize young adolescence, we run the risk of losing the young adolescent in the process. I ask those interested in the education of young adolescents to take Caskey and Anfara's (2007) warnings a step further and actively resist characterizing in favor of particularizing so that the platform (i.e., young adolescence) itself becomes individualized.

Plea #3—To Move from a "Sameness" Curriculum to a "Difference" Curriculum

In the wake of President Clinton's *Goals 2000* initiative and presently in the *No Child Left Behind (NCLB)* and *Race to the Top* eras in the United States, it is perhaps difficult to imagine a curriculum that does not center on standards—or what I term sameness. Although I do not care to engage in a debate over whether or not there should be standards in the first place, I do want to press on how standards (however they are written) limit as much as they make possible. Moreover, standardizing the curriculum feels counterintuitive when educators of young adolescents have long advocated for a curriculum that centers on the individual young adolescent's interests and desires. To this end, I propose a difference curriculum which does not dismiss standards, but does take hold of the standards. I use *take hold* here to signal that the agency be displaced from outside authority and (re)placed into the hands of young adolescents and their teachers.

Opening. *Turning Points 2000* (Jackson & Davis, 2000) contains seven separate yet interrelated design elements that all center on *Ensuring Success for Every Student*. The design elements focus on all aspects of schooling such as curriculum, instruction, and assessment, as well as on issues related to interpersonal relationships inside and outside of school. One such design element focuses specifically on curriculum and provided an appropriate opening for my analysis. For Jackson and Davis, an appropriate curriculum for young adolescents should be

> grounded in rigorous, public academic standards for what students should know and be able to do, relevant to the concerns of adolescents and based on how students learn best. Considerations of both excellence and equity should guide every decision regarding what will be taught. Curriculum should be based on content standards and organized around concepts and principles. (p. 23)

When reading the design element itself I, like Brown (2005b), was concerned that an integrated (Beane, 1997), problem-posing (Freire, 1970/2002) curriculum would be difficult to enact given the focus of the design element. Why are standards the centerpiece? My initial assumption—that this was a direct reflection of the national standards movement (Brown) and was yet another example of the power nation-making (Lesko, 2001) has on curriculum—led me to reflect on more substantive questions. Who writes these standards? Who decides what is rigorous? Why is there a need to insert the word academic? Why is relevance to adolescents' concerns second to public standards? Are adolescents' concerns by definition not as academic or rigorous as the standards that adults write?

My initial concerns were assuaged, to some degree, after reading the expanded description of the design element.

> We call for teaching a curriculum grounded in, *though not strictly limited to,* rigorous public standards for what students should know and be able to do, recognizing that *standards should be flexible to reflect changes in society*. We also recommend that the curriculum be *tied to adolescents' concerns,* in a call for relevance missing from the original notion of a core. (emphasis added, Jackson & Davis, 2000, p. 26)

The statement, *though not strictly limited to,* in reference to rigorous public standards is one example of an opening for Lesko's (2001) contingent, recursive adolescence. Where else might the curriculum be grounded if not in standards that are in large part if not solely determined through a large bureaucratic process? Who gets to determine the other things that young adolescents will learn? Might this be a space for the problem-posing education that Freire (1970/2002) advocates? It seems inevitable that today's young adolescent will continue to be surrounded and defined by standards. Some of the future teachers I teach talk about how important standards are for equity in education—how else could we be "sure" that all students are receiving the education they deserve? This seems to imply that determination of curriculum cannot possibly reside with teachers or students. There must be an outside force (i.e., standards) controlling what is to be learned. In this way, the sameness curriculum becomes some "thing" that is wielded for particular material and symbolic purposes.

A curriculum grounded in Lesko's (2001) contingent, recursive adolescence concerns itself with difference rather than sameness. It is impossible to know what students can learn without meeting and living with them. Our best attempts to create a standardized education will always fall short of what a curriculum focusing on difference can accomplish. This does not mean that I think what is contained in standards is worthless; it simply means that I think it should be *worth less* than it is now.

Jackson and Davis (2000) remind educators of young adolescents that *standards should be flexible to reflect changes in society*. Might one take this to mean that a teacher and his or her students can attack the very (raced, classed, gendered, sexed) assumptions that undergird the standard and if not satisfied with the outcome adjust the standard accordingly? This seems plausible with language such as the curriculum should be *tied to adolescents' concerns*. In fact, what if the language was opened up a bit more to include adolescents' concerns as the very basis of the curriculum? The standards would then become the thing to be "tied." New language for the design element might read something like this.

> *We call for teaching a curriculum grounded in young adolescents' concerns and tied to rigorous public standards, recognizing standards should be flexible to reflect changes in the particular situations in which students find themselves in and over time.*

This statement might make the standards more fluid and malleable—able to be troubled, deconstructed, and read critically. Standards would no longer serve as targets that define what is happening. Instead, they would be something larger by which to connect one's learning. Public standards (when conceived as monolithic targets) cannot capture the innumerable contingencies that exist in all classrooms. A curriculum that values a contingent, recursive conception of growth and change would not set a standard and then assess where students reside relative to the standard. A contingent, recursive (difference) curriculum would instead begin with the student and then proceed to set, not a target, but a direction—a way to proceed that is not predetermined, but is profoundly connected to present moments. Such curricula would operate under an assumption that young adolescents always, already are growing and changing in multiple directions at multiple moments in time—like Lesko's (2001) blizzard of social factors. Moreover, a contingent, recursive curriculum assumes that young adolescents already have what it takes to live, learn, and theorize their world. What young adolescents need is not standards to tell them what to learn and teachers to make sure they get there. Rather, they need teachers to recognize the multiple contingences and then to facilitate their growth recursively through these contingencies.

A difference curriculum would turn standards on their head, but would not ignore standards. Leading with the needs, desires, and interests of young adolescents, giving young adolescents agency in determining what to do with standards, and in turn bringing standards to life through blizzards of contingencies (no matter how messy) might soften the sameness and sharpen the difference.

Broader Implications

It is challenging to open up a dominant discourse in ways that allow other perspectives to be seen. When analyzing the texts I found it desirable to try to shed the dominant discourse. This was impossible. Developmentalism is strong, clean, and dependable. It lines up with time. It can be measured and tracked. This is most likely why it was constructed in the first place. This also reminded me that my goal was not to get rid of developmentalism. It was to trouble developmentalism just enough so that other perspectives can be more fully considered.

I hope this consideration is evident in my three pleas. Moving from developmentally responsive to contingently and recursively relational; from "characterizing" young adolescen(CE) to "particularizing" young adolescen(TS); and from a "sameness" curriculum to a "difference" curriculum is an attempt to deflate developmentalism from a rule to a perspective and, in turn, to elevate Lesko's notion of contingent and recursive growth and change to equal footing. This effort is worth pursuing because, to me, it more closely reflects the messy realities where young adolescents live. This also means that Lesko's call for *a* contingent, recursive conception can be re-cast as forever partial and plural. That is, it would not be possible to come up with one contingent, recursive conception—by definition there would be multiple conceptions that would be built in and over time. If those interested in the education of young adolescents truly want to make schooling for young adolescents the best it can be, then it is necessary to bring all possible perspectives on the matter to bear on substantive issues regarding curriculum, instruction, assessment, and relationships. The continued assumption that developmentalism is the untouchable foundation for young adolescence will limit what educators hope to accomplish. Although I have started this project by analyzing texts in the field of middle grades education, I conclude by suggesting broader implications for this work and its potential for hopeful intersections with ongoing conversations in other fields such as early childhood education and adolescent literacy.

The timing of this work is important because schools for young adolescents, like all U.S. schools, again, have become high-stakes testing environments. I fear that educators run the risk of losing sight of the young adolescent under this testing regime. In other words, the incessant focus on testing where a student should be at a particular moment in time calcifies a time-bound conception of development that forces young adolescents to be learned at certain points in time. If the young adolescent is not deemed learned based on the test, he or she, his or her teacher, and perhaps his or her entire school receive a failing grade. It is a prime example of Lesko's concern that we have set up a system that is designed primarily to test, measure, and control young people. It is difficult to keep the young adolescent and their learning at the forefront of policy and practice when their test score becomes the primary way they are talked about and educated.

Fortunately, as mentioned at the beginning of this essay, there have been scholarly conversations taking place in other fields that can intersect with potential conversations in the fields that focus on young adolescence. In early childhood education the notion of developmentally appropriate practice appears to parallel middle grades education's commitment to developmental responsiveness. However, in early childhood education there has been a robust debate among scholars about the limits of stage developmentalism and the promise of critical perspectives. In middle grades education, this debate has yet to ensue (Vagle & Parks, 2010). One implication of what I suggest is that such a debate in middle grades education not only has the potential to influence the conception of young adolescence and in turn the schooling of young adolescents, but also how schooling from early childhood through young adolescence can be re-envisioned (perhaps even prompting a name change from *middle grades* to *young adolescent education*). As it stands, the debate—and in turn its benefits—between developmental and critical perspectives is limited to early childhood.

A similar implication is possible when turning to recent work in the field of adolescent literacy. As an advocate for the education of young adolescents, I am pleased to see the needs of adolescents at the center of these important conversations. That said, I find one aspect of Ippolito, Steele, and Samson's (2008) rationale for dedicating a special issue of *Harvard Educational Review* to adolescent literacy both promising and concerning.

> A second distinctive challenge of adolescent literacy instruction lies in attending to *adolescents' developmental needs as they mature from children into young adults.* To engage adolescents, literacy instruction must capture their minds and speak to the questions they have about the world as they contemplate their place within it. It must allow them to interact with intellectually challenging content even as it sharpens their ability to derive meaning from texts. (emphasis added, p. 2)

I resonate with Ippolito, Steele, and Samson's desire to make sure educators of adolescent literacy help their students use literacy as a way to question their world and to contemplate their place in it. Like Lesko, however, I grow concerned that critical (literacy) practices aimed in this direction will have limited value if adolescents are described in a developmental frame with particular developmental needs. The perspectives—including the more critical—in this special issue do little to assuage my concern in this regard as most of them seem to assume a developmental adolescent. In fact, Moje et al. (2008)

are the only contributors who explicitly consider the question—What is an adolescent?

Perhaps all fields that focus on young adolescence can benefit from what I have suggested in this essay. Contingent, recursive conceptions of growth and change open up possibilities for young adolescents and spawn important questions: How is adolescence and the adolescent constructed in the scholarship across fields? Are dominant developmental discourses the norm? Has the adolescent come to mean something so "normal" that it seems unnecessary to conceptualize growth and change? If so, how might critical perspectives of adolescent growth and change disrupt this notion?

The important point to remember is that when educators and researchers aim to study young adolescence or indvidual young adolescents they must take the time to conceptualize young adolescence rather than assume it is conflated with a developmental stage. Contingent, recursive conceptions may in fact serve as theoretical foundations for more particularized, critical work regarding issues including but not limited to race, class, gender, sexuality, power, and struggle. Each of these innumerable particulars can then in turn continually inform these ever-changing contingent, recursive conceptions—conceptions that need more air and can simultaneously breathe air into all scholarship that is dedicated to the needs of young adolescent learners.

References

Beane, J. A. (1997). *Curriculum integration: Designing the core of democratic education.* New York: Teachers College Press.

———. (2005). Foreword. In E.R. Brown, & K. J. Saltman (Eds.), *The critical middle school reader* (pp. XI-XV). New York: Routledge.

Blackburn, M. V., & Smith, J. M. (2010). Moving beyond the inclusion of LGBT-themed literature in English Language Arts Classrooms: Interrogating hetero-normativity and exploring intersectionality. *Journal of Adolescent & Adult Literacy, 53*(8), 625-634.

Bloch, M. N., Tabachnick, R., & Espinosa-Dulanto, M. (1994). Teacher perspectives on the strengths and achievements of young children: Relationship to ethnicity, language, gender, and class. In B. L. Mallory & R. S. New (Eds.), *Diversity & developmentally appropriate practices: Challenges for early childhood education.* (pp. 223-249). New York: Teachers College Press.

Brown, E. R. (2005a). Introduction. In E.R. Brown & K. J. Saltman (Eds.), *The critical middle school reader* (pp. 1-14). New York: Routledge.

———. (2005b). The middle school concept and the purpose of education. In E.R. Brown & K. J. Saltman (Eds.), *The critical middle school reader* (pp. 151-158). New York: Routledge.

Brown, E. R., & Saltman, K. J. (Eds.). (2005). *The critical middle school reader.* New York: Routledge.

Caskey, M. M., & Anfara, V. A., Jr. (2007). *Research summary: Young adolescents' developmental characteristics.* Retrieved May 24, 2010, from http://www.nmsa.org/Research/ResearchSummaries/DevelopmentalCharacteristics/tabid/1414/Default.aspx

Conley, M. (2008). Cognitive strategies for adolescents: What we know about the promise, what we don't know about the potential. *Harvard Educational Review, 78*(1), 84-106.

Draper, R. J. (2008). Redefining content-area literacy teacher education: Finding my voice through collaboration. *Harvard Educational Review, 78*(1), 60-83.

Flavell, J.H. (1963). *The developmental psychology of Jean Piaget.* Princeton, NJ: Van Nostrand Reinhold.

Freire, P. (2002). *Pedagogy of the oppressed.* M. B. Ramos (Trans.). New York: The Continuum International Publishing Group Inc. (Original work published 1970).

Gay, G., (1994). Coming of age ethnically: Teaching young adolescents of color. *Theory into Practice, 33*(3), 149-155.

Hall, G. S. (1904). *Adolescence: Its psychology and its relation to physiology, anthropology, sociology, sex, crime, religion, and education.* New York: Appleton & Company.

Ippolito, J., Steele, J. L., & Samson, J. F. (2008). Introduction: Why adolescent literacy matters now. *Harvard Educational Review, 78*(1), 1-6.

Jackson, A. W., & Davis, G. A. (2000). *Turning points 2000: Educating adolescents in the 21st century.* New York: Teachers College Press.

Kellough, R. D., & Kellough, N. G. (2007). *Teaching young adolescents: Methods and resources for middle grades teaching* (5th ed.). Upper Saddle River, NJ: Prentice Hall.

Lee, K., & Vagle, M. D. (Eds.). (2010). *Developmentalism in early childhood and middle grades education: Critical conversations on readiness and responsiveness*. New York: Palgrave Macmillan.
Lesko, N. (1994). Back to the future: Middle schools and the turning points report. *Theory into Practice, 33*(3), 143-148.
———. (2001). *Act your age: A cultural construction of adolescence*. New York: Routledge/Falmer.
Lubeck, S. (1994). The politics of developmentally appropriate practice: Exploring issues of culture, class, and curriculum. In B. L. Mallory & R. S. New (Eds.), *Diversity & developmentally appropriate practices: Challenges for early childhood education* (pp. 17-43). New York: Teachers College Press.
Lubeck, S. (1998). Is developmentally appropriate practice for everyone? *Childhood Education, 74*(5), 283-292.
Mallory, B. L., & New, R. S. (1994). *Diversity & developmentally appropriate practices: Challenges for early childhood education*. New York: Teachers College Press.
Moje, E. B., Overby, M., Tysvaer, N., & Morris, K. (2008). The complex world of adolescent literacy: Myths, motivations, and mysteries. *Harvard Educational Review, 78*(1), 107-154.
National Middle School Association (NMSA). (2008). *Affiliate organizations*. Retrieved May 18, 2010, from http://www.nmsa.org/AboutNMSA/AffiliateOrganizations/AffiliateWebLinks/tabid/332/Default.aspx
National Middle School Association (NMSA) (2010). *This we believe: Keys to educating young adolescents*. Westerville, OH: National Middle School Association.
Piaget, J. (1952). *The origins of intelligence in children*. New York: International University Press.
———. (1960). *The child's conception of the world*. Atlantic Highlands, NJ: Humanities Press.
Saltman, K. J. (2005). The social construction of adolescence. In E.R. Brown & K. J. Saltman (Eds.), *The critical middle school reader* (pp. 15-20). New York: Routledge.
Scales, P. C. (2003). Characteristics of young adolescents. In National Middle School Association, *This we believe: Successful schools for young adolescents* (pp. 43-51). Westerville, OH: National Middle School Association.
Shanahan, T., & Shanahan, C. (2008). Teaching disciplinary literacy to adolescents: Rethinking content-area literacy. *Harvard Educational Review, 78*(1), 40-59.
Shor, I. (1996). *When students have power: Negotiating authority in a critical pedagogy*. University of Chicago Press.
Tatum, A. W. (2008). Toward a more anatomically complete model of literacy instruction: A focus on African American male adolescents and texts. *Harvard Educational Review, 78*(1), 155-180.
Vagle, M. D. (2011). Lessons in contingent, recursive humility. *Journal of Adolescent and Adult Literacy, 54*(6), 362-370.
Vagle, M.D. & Parks, A. (2010). A schismatic family and a gated community? In K. Lee & M. D. Vagle (Eds.), *Developmentalism in early childhood and middle grades education: Critical conversations on readiness and responsiveness* (pp. 213-231). Palgrave McMillian: New York.

Acknowledgements

I would like to thank JoBeth Allen, Hilary Conklin, and Bob Fecho for their helpful comments on earlier versions of this essay.

Section 2

Locating and Opening Up Some Obscured Micro-Contexts in Order to Do More LEARNING FROM (rather than Teaching) Young Adolescents

Mark D. Vagle

Central to a contingent, recursive re-orientation, is a dogged commitment to identify and examine as many micro-contexts as possible—and to discuss these microcontexts while resisting the gravitational pull toward the dominant (decontextualized) developmental perspective. The chapters in this section aim to do just that. Whether considering the value of 19th century adolescent authors, Hmong immigrant girls, English Language Learners, or the gendered constructions of boys and girls, these chapters insert important particularities (micro-contexts) into the larger conversation. Ngo, Zenkov, Moore, Hughes-Decatur, and Crowder, at times delicately and other times forcefully, remind us to see young adolescents as incredibly active agents in the here and now—and not constrained by whatever broad characterizations of their developmental stage might suggest. Such particularization is also, collectively, located in an interrogation of what one might assume is a problem or crisis, or a gender, or a discourse, or a writer. This contemplative work is necessary, because it can puncture assumptions about who is (or should be) teaching whom.

Drawing on some of her earlier ethnographic work with immigrant youth, Ngo, in *Constructing Immigrant Adolescent Identities: Exploring the "Magical Property" of Discourses*, carefully unravels some of the complexities surrounding young adolescent identities. She argues that adolescent identities are deeply contextual and continuously in-the-making. She goes so far to suggest that rather than whole and complete, adolescent identities are temporary, contradictory and unresolved (Ngo, 2010). Ngo's point is well taken, relative to a contingent, recursive conception of growth and change. Because adolescent identities are so fleeting and ever-changing, charting these changes is not only a futile effort, but it is also a damaging one. As one moves, shifts, and contradicts through adolescence (and life, I would add), having to compare (and be compared) to a normal, stable pattern of identity development can be mighty discouraging. Ngo's work reminds us that these comparisons are often amplified for immigrant youth trying to navigate unfamiliar terrain, while deficit-oriented discourses perform their magic. Ngo reminds us that these magical properties have very real material consequences for young people. As she demonstrates throughout the chapter, discourses that categorize and stereotype have the power to literally tell people who they are or should be and whether they are successful or not. Stage developmentalism tends to be put to use in categorical ways (e.g., now is the right time, too early, too late, not yet), and thus contains the same sort of magical properties that can have the same negative consequences.

Zenkov, Ewaida, Bell, and Lynch in, *Seeing School and Learning English: Recent Immigrant Youths' Insights into Adolescents, Young Adolescence, Learning, and Teaching,* also eloquently describe the lived experiences of immigrant youth, through the use of photo elicitation methodologies. Here, we are able to move back and forth between compelling photos taken by young adolescents and their articulations of how these images capture some of their perceptions of the purpose of school; what helps one to be successful in school; and what gets in the way of one's school success. Reflecting on my plea for a "difference" curriculum, Zenkov et al. convincingly argue that such a project is not all that meaningful without some explicit awareness of just what those differences are. They suggest that it is only with these differences in mind that we should modify our curricula and pedagogies. This is one example of how my call for a difference curriculum comes to life—it is here that the theoretical plea begins to permeate the particularities that young adolescents live with and through. Zenkov et al. want us to consider how immigrant youth are continually constructing themselves as resistant in order to deal with all of the cultural material they are encountering—often making them more and more acutely aware how far they still have to go before "arriving" as culturally competent. The implications for teachers are significant, as oftentimes this resistance is perceived negatively instead of as a rather astute (and necessary) strategic move by immigrant youth—suggesting that teachers perhaps have more to teach than to learn in this regard.

Chapter 3 (Moore) and 4 (Hughes-Decatur) turn to matters of gender. Here we see just how important it is to systematically peel away layers of common-sense assumptions about what it means to be (and see) boys and girls.

Moore in *Putting 'Boy' in Crisis: Seeking an Education of Gender Rather than in Gender,* helps us see how those layers are built up and reified through pop psychology and biological explanations that have an almost insidious resonating quality. That is, they continually reinforce what seems normal—that there are in fact natural differences (rather than constructed) between males and females. Moore is particularly concerned that static, essentialized, binaried understandings of gender, as male and female, permeate curriculum, classrooms, and reform movements. She situates her argument in the test-driven, hyper-accountability discourses which reign supreme today, and argues that the rhetoric and reforms surrounding test results exemplify the dominant gendered discourses that are operating in education, and reveals the way in which adolescents are receiving an education *in* gender. This is one particularly powerful influence of Moore's work—her call for a difference curriculum *of* gender, rather than *in* gender is not a subtle play on prepositions. She advocates a particularized curriculum that does not turn to and pathologize boys as 'in crisis', rather it turns to a curriculum which is responsive to students within context. Moore's use of "of" then is about making gender an explicit subject within the classroom rather than a hidden force. Ultimately, she asks educators to call attention to the ways in which pedagogical talk, interactions, and media and curricular resources are always already gendered.

In *Always Becoming, Never Enough: Middle School Girls Talk Back,* Hughes-Decatur is also concerned about normalized constructions of gender—this time with young adolescent girls. Concerned by society's incessant desire to keep young adolescent girls "too young" to talk about their bodies, Hughes-Decatur strongly advocates for an adult reflexivity of our own assumptions about what young adolescents can not, should not, or shall not. Hughes-Decatur's work is a particularly poignant example of how one might heed Pinar's (2009) concern that critical theory does not implicate itself in the very assumptions it hopes to disrupt. This chapter not only helps us see young adolescent girls differently (as ready, as enough, as able, as better), it also helps us see how important it is to contemplate *as* we advocate. It reminds us to check our own assumptions so we can see young people differently. It is a reminder to check our "savior" mentality at the door and consider that we are the one's who might need the saving—and that young adolescents are the ones who can momentarily do so. This reminder is amplified in Hughes-Decatur's creative use of a multi-voiced found poem to visually represent a conversation she had with her young adolescent research participants. Here, we have the opportunity to read our way through the complexities of the young adolescent girls' voicing of their thoughts, feelings, and opinions—and how Hughes-Decatur tried to navigate these complexities.

The final chapter in this section, *Reappraising "Juvenilia" as a Means of Re-Conceptualizing "Adolescence"*, provides a unique glimpse into a field not often considered in educational discourse—literature. Drawing on literary theory and in particular *juvenilia,* a literary term used to describe literary works that have "not yet reached" maturity, Crowder argues that the connotations associated with juvenilia fit as neatly as *adolescence* into a linear, chronological timeline. He convincingly asserts that developmentalism pervades this construction of young authors as yet to arrive, just as it does in the field of education. Crowder's use of examples from various authors who first published their writing when they were children helps those in education get "outside" of education in order to gain a new perspective about what is happening inside. In addition, he makes the case that the juvenilia model emphasizes an *evolutionary trend toward perfectibility* that privileges the assumption that growth and change is lived in a straight and unobstructed path. That is, the absence of difference and context and problem and possibility not only limits the validity of the conception, but it can in turn literally limit what we can learn from young adolescents in the here and now. Ultimately, the juvenilia (in literary theory) and developmentalist (in educational psychology) models calcify, for Crowder, a *permanent deficit model* of childhood—

and limit important things that can be learned *from* children *when* they are children.

References

Ngo, B. (2010). *Unresolved identities: Discourse, ambivalence and urban immigrant students*. New York: State University of New York Press.

Pinar, B. (2009). The unaddressed 'I" of ideology critique. *Power and education, 1*(2), 189-200.

Chapter 1

Constructing Immigrant Adolescent Identities: Exploring the "Magical Property" of Discourses

Bic Ngo

I ask Ananh what his parents think about his tattoo and he tells me, "They know. They don't care." But then he adds that this isn't his first tattoo, and he doesn't tell his parents until afterward. He then pulls up the sleeve of the white shirt again, this time to show me a smaller tattoo on the shoulder of the same arm. He explains that a friend also gave him this first one, three years ago when he was fourteen. When I ask him if anything was used to help with the pain, Ananh says, "No. It don't hurt much." I say "Wow" and shake my head at his bravado. Ananh then suggests that I also get a tattoo. I respond with a laugh and tell him that I don't like pain, so I could never do it. Ananh laughs with me, becomes quiet for a brief moment, and then declares that people are "stupid" because they think that if you get a tattoo, you're a "bad person" and "into gangs." (FN, 2/26/02, Chemistry)

Immigrants come to the United States to take welfare. Immigrants take jobs from Americans. Immigrants are a drain on the economy. Immigrants bring crime to communities. Immigrants do not want to learn English. These are some of the most prevalent discourses about immigrants in the U.S. (American Civil Liberties Union, 2011). These discourses have fueled anti-immigrant sentiments and recent legislation in states such as Arizona, Georgia and Alabama. In the most restrictive legislation to date, Alabama's anti-immigrant law sums up these discourses in this way: "The State of Alabama finds that illegal immigration is causing economic hardship and lawlessness in this state and that illegal immigration is encouraged when public agencies within this state provide public benefits without verifying immigration status" (American Immigration Lawyers Association, 2011). Among other extreme measures, it requires public schools to determine the immigration status of all students beginning in kindergarten.

My work with immigrant adolescents has revealed the nuances of these discourses in educational experiences and outcomes. I found that discourses about what it means to be immigrant youth have the tendency to simplify and constrain the identities and experiences of immigrant adolescents (see, e.g., Ngo, 2010). As Ananh insightfully notes in the above ethnographic fieldnote, identity constructions of adolescents with a tattoo include a "bad person" who is "into gangs." Significantly, adolescents such as Ananh are keenly aware of the ways in which dominant discourses construct identities of immigrants as delinquent, welfare-dependent, and foreign Other. The power of discourses—language—is real, with the capacity to create identities, make policies and build worlds.

In order to attend to the power of discourses in the lives of adolescents, I consider and extend Vagle's (this volume) first *plea—to move from a developmentally responsive vision to a contingently and recursively relational vision* of adolescence. I draw on my work with Southeast Asian immigrant youth to elaborate on the social construction of adolescent identities. I discuss the primary role of discursive practices in the relational process of understanding and constructing adolescent identities. Following discourse analysts and poststructural theorists (see, e.g., Davies, 1993; Gee, 2005; Weedon, 1987) I suggest that discourses have the "magical property" of creating identity and reality. I illustrate the ways in which discourses about immigrant adolescents construct dominant, deficit understandings (i.e., reality) about what it means to be an immigrant youth.

The Magical Property of Discourses

Identities are contextual (i.e., contingent) and recursive (i.e., continually constructed) because of the central role of discursive practices in identity formation. Rather than naturally occurring through a developmental process, identity is produced and negotiated through discursive practices that are mediated by social, political, and historical contexts (Davies, 1993; Hall, 1996; Weedon, 1987). As Hall (1996) cogently put it, "identities are constructed within, not outside discourse, [and that] we need to understand them as produced in specific historical and institutional sites within specific discursive formations and practices, by specific enunciative strategies" (p. 4). From this perspective, issues related to race, ethnicity, and gender are not simply "factors," but play a significant role in the ideological positioning of immigrant adolescents (and their families). Discourses that characterize immigrants as criminals and economic burdens produce a specific immigrant identity within a specific sociopolitical context.

Further, because identities are formed within discursive relations, they do not follow a linear path, but are temporary, contradictory and continually changing. This relational and recursive process provides opportunities for discourses to be repeated and naturalized (institutionally, ideologically) as well as openings for resignification and new, alternative discourses. Put another way, the relational process of identity construction has the potential to exacerbate as well as alleviate deficit visions of adolescence.

Specifically, discourse analysts such as Gee (2005) suggest that we use language to create and enact identities. Activities involving language make up "little d" "discourse" and "big D" "Discourse." "Little d" "discourse" is comprised of language-in-use, while "Discourse" with a capital "D" reflects a broader world view and includes "ways of combining and integrating language, actions, interactions, ways of thinking, believing, valuing, and using various symbols, tools, and objects to enact a particular sort of socially recognizable identity" (p. 21). According to Gee (2005) identities such as "being a type of middle-class American, factory worker, or executive, doctor or hospital patient, teacher, administrator, or student, student of physics or of literature, member of a club or street gang, regular at the local bar . . . . are all Discourses" (p. 27).

Through repeated use and circulation, some D/discourses become so established that they become "natural" and conceal the existence of competing, alternative discourses (Weedon, 1987). Discourses thus have the power to legitimate and create knowledges, identities and realities. For Gee (2005), language has a "magical property" because it "always simultaneously reflects and constructs the situation or context in which it is used" (p. 97). He suggests that "language and institutions 'bootstrap' each other into existence in a reciprocal process through time" (Gee, 2005, p. 10). We saw this happening in the late 1960s with the emergence of the discourse of Asian American success that emphasized the role of hard work, family support, and "cultural" values in the achievements of Asian Americans (Lee, 1996). Formed within the contexts of the racial discontent of the Civil Rights movement, discourses of Asian American success created and legitimated identities of Asian Americans as "model minorities" (see Lee, 1999; Osajima, 1987). Because identity is reflective of power and takes place within discursive relations, discourses about immigrants as illegal aliens or resistant to assimilation reflect political positions, values, and social practices.

At the micro level of the day-to-day experiences of immigrant adolescents, the contingent and relational nature of their identities includes the presence of multiple discourses – dominant deficit discourses as well as alternative discourses about their identities as immigrant adolescents. Adolescents do not fit into neat identity categories such as "good student" *or* "bad student." Their identity work draws on a multiplicity of discourses that have the (material and ideological) power to shape their lives. The next section draws on ethnographic research with urban, immigrant high school students to illustrate the temporary, contradictory—complexity—of immigrant adolescent identities.

Immigrant Adolescent Identities as Contingently and Recursively Relational

My research with immigrant youth has helped me to understand that adolescent identities are deeply contextual and continuously in-the-making. In particular, my research suggests that rather than whole and complete, adolescent identities are temporary, contradictory and unresolved (Ngo, 2010). This conceptualization of adolescents shifts from a linear developmental understanding to one that highlights the ways in which adolescent identities are continuously shaped and reshaped by discourses. In this section, I share the ways in which discourses constructed the identities of Ananh and Kett, two Lao American eleventh grade students I came to know during a year-long ethnographic study at Dynamic High School.

The Power of Discourses

For the first half of the year during my time at Dynamic High (see, e.g., Ngo, 2010) the school faced escalating gang activity inside and outside of the school. After a couple of months of pulled fire alarms that emptied the school, and arrests of Asian American males outside and inside the school with weapons ranging from guns, knives, crowbars to baseball bats, administrators offered teachers and staff a training about gangs. This training included an overview of gang names, gang characteristics (e.g., colors, signs), as well as photos of gang members who were recently arrested inside and outside of Dynamic High. In an interview I asked Ms. Preszler (pseudonym), a Chemistry teacher at the school, to recount this time period. Her account highlights the ways in which the language-in-use within the context of these activities (coupled with broader societal discourses about gangs) informed teachers' construction of the identities of male immigrant students.

For example, consider what Ms. Preszler said regarding the questions some teachers asked after learning about indicators for whether or not students were involved in gangs:

> *Ms. Preszler*: We tried to find out as much as we could. Like it got to the point where they were telling us things to look for. But we're not trained really in that. Officer Thomas tried to help us with some pointers. But it got to the point where people were saying, "Well I saw an African American student with 05 on his jersey, on a jersey that he was wearing. Does that mean that he's now in the OMBs?" I'm just using that as an example. I can't remember what the numbers were for who. But they would see an African American student with a number that signified the OMBs, "Does that mean they're in, in?" . . . . The people who knew that they were from Laos would say, or knew that they're family was from Laos would say, "Well what about those students? Are they starting to get into the Hmong gangs?" Officer Thomas said again, "You might see it but it's probably unlikely that they would join the Hmong gangs. But they *may*!"

This excerpt points to the way that context and language-in-use may construct adolescent identities as gang members. Ms. Preszler points out that language-in-use that provided teachers with information about gangs also made available discourses to construct the identities of *any* adolescent with similar characteristics as gang members. The power of discourses in the construction of identities is reflected in remarks about whether an African American student wearing a particular number was a member of the OMBs (Oroville Mono Boys, a Hmong gang) or whether a student from Laos was part of a Hmong gang.

For Lao immigrant adolescents such as Ananh, the ways in which he looked and behaved as an Asian male provided teachers with discourses to identify him as an adolescent who may be a gang member. Ms. Preszler shared her experiences with Ananh in this way:

> *Ms. Preszler:* Ananh got very upset with me because after that all happened [training about gangs] I had folders that had to be taken away because of possible gang-looking graffiti. And Ananh's was one of them. And he was *very* upset about that, like, "No, I'm not in that activity. Just because I'm Asian you're assuming that." I said, "I'm not assuming anything. I looked at some of these folders. I saw some stuff that was a little bit scary and had Officer Thomas look at it, and he took the three folders." And it wasn't just their group. It was two other groups, but it all was in the same class. So one of the students in that class was a part of one of the Hmong gangs. So I mean I did it for a reason.

Significantly, the "possible gang-looking graffiti" that Ms. Preszler learned from the gang training were part of the images and ideas that have the "magical property" to construct adolescent identities as gang members. The context of Dynamic High coupled with discursive practices about gang characteristics worked together to create very specific identities for Asian American male adolescents (Gee, 2005).

As I noted earlier, adolescents such as Ananh are not oblivious to these deficit discourses. Ms. Preszler shared Ananh's reaction to his identification as a possible gang member in this way:

> *Ms. Preszler:* But unfortunately Officer Thomas saw Ananh's folder in his group. I mean his whole group was just stunned by it. But he was the only Asian student in that group and so was just like, "You're just attacking me because of that. And I'm not Hmong." And I was like, "I'm not saying that. But this is what I had to do. I saw some things on there that were potentially gang signs. I brought them to Officer Thomas. He felt the same way, he kept it. End of story. I'm sorry you're offended, but it looked like it and right now we have to be very careful."

For Ananh, he was perceived to be a potential gang member by discourses that included images that he made—things on his folder that "were potentially gang signs" as well as the ways in which he *looked* as an Asian American male. Given the predominance of Hmong students at the school and the OMB Hmong gang, Ananh's identity was constructed to be Hmong (even though he was Lao) and a potential gang member. Indeed, as Ms. Preszler went on to share, suspicion of Ananh was also enhanced because his handwriting also reflected that of gang graffiti style: "If you've ever seen the way he writes. He has the very common block graffiti style of writing."

While dominant discourses may simplify and misrecognize the identities of urban, immigrant adolescents, their identities are much more temporary and contradictory. In the next section, I focus on this aspect of their contingent and recursive identities.

Temporary, Contradictory Identities

In one of my first encounters with Kett, he asked me if I believed in Jesus and invited me to attend his church. This eagerness to promote his Christian faith earned Kett the reputation of "a Godly man." As he shared:

> *Kett*: Yea, they all know I'm like a Godly man. 'Cause I always tell them about me, like I changed and I don't do this and that. And I just talk about God and Jesus. Everybody in class knows, most of the people. They all know me from middle school and how I did change a lot. And I like crack jokes, but not like bad things. I'm pretty known.

During my time at Dynamic High, I witnessed Kett "talk about God and Jesus" as he engaged in discursive practices that emphasized his identity as a Christian. He preached the greatness of God and the transformative impact of Christian faith on his life:

> *Kett*: I experience life differently from then to now. It's just like way different how it's before when I don't know Christ and now. And that's why I want to be a pastor just to show them all things are possible when you call on God . . . . I used to cuss and joke around and saying bad things . . . . Just be clowning like joking in a bad way. And don't think at all. And don't do nothing for other people like care about them and stuff. I don't, I'm not into that. I really didn't care about family, and now I care about everything, the things that I do and other people too.

Kett shared with me that since the end of his freshman year, he stopped "clowning" at school and dedicated his life to the Christian faith. He was extensively involved in the activities of his church, including living in the home of the pastor, leading the youth group, playing drums in the church band, helping to recruit new members, and providing transportation to enable community members to attend Sunday service. Kett described some of his responsibilities in this way:

> *Kett*: And Sundays, get up in the morning at eight. Get ready. Call people, some of the people and then go in the service. If I don't go in to the adult service before the youth service I just go pick up people and, you know, call them, 'Y'all coming?' Like ask them if they coming. If they coming we go pick them up. But most of the time I'm always in the service. And after the service I call people again, if they coming or not, go pick them up.

On the occasions that I attended service at his church, I observed Kett in leadership activities such as leading prayers and greeting members of the congregation. As Kett explained, these activities are important because "I want our church to grow to see kids and stuff coming to church, praise the Lord together and making community in peace." Further, his engagement with church allowed him "to serve the Lord and to show [members] how to be the Light, the Light to others – a role model."

Kett's attempt to be the "Light" and role model for others included changes to his school behavior and outlook. He shared: "I was praying, praying God know I want to take school seriously and I want to serve him more and to keep myself praying at home." Indeed, his changed attitude toward school resulted in making the B Honor Roll in his sophomore and junior years. Getting good grades was important because he wanted to be a good role model. He explained, "If I don't pass and stuff, and if I show a bad example, you know getting bad grades—How I'm supposed to be a leader to others?"

While Kett's discursive practices construct his identity as a Christian and a "good student," Kett's identity is neither seamless nor complete. In the contingently and recursively relational process of identity construction, identities are always open to change, recognition and misrecognition. Within the context of Dynamic High School, Kett's adolescent identity confused some teachers:

> *Ms. Anderson*: Kett is a great example of a kid who has no clue what his identity is. I mean he sometimes does stuff that's representing for a gang. He'll walk around with a rag hanging out of his pocket, and yet then he'll, I mean in his journals last year he used to write about church *all the time*. Like he's *really*, seemingly really religious or he has this part of his identity that's like really religious. Yet, he obviously has this other pull of potentially get-

> ting kind of drawn into gang-related stuff, and kind of trying to be this cool [person]. I don't know. He just strikes me as a kid who's *really* having some serious identity issues and not really knowing what direction he's going to go.

As an adolescent who wore baggy jeans, oversized t-shirts, closely shaved his head and sometimes walked around the school "with a rag hanging out of his pocket," Kett reflected dominant images and understandings—discourses—of a gang member. However, because identity is continually informed and constructed by discourses, Kett's discourses about God and Christianity disrupted what it meant to be a "gang member," "Christian" and "good student."

For teachers such as Ms. Anderson the continual process of identity construction was perceived as Kett being pulled on one hand by a Christian identity and on the other hand by a gang identity. His identity options are reduced to two paths, where, according to Ms. Anderson, Kett did "not really know what direction he's going to go." From this perspective adolescent identity development is supposed to proceed on a linear path—in this case between two presumably competing ends of a binary, Christian and gang member. However, given the role of discourses in identity construction and the magical property of language, Kett's identity will never be complete, but continually shaped and reshaped.

For immigrant adolescents such as Kett, his contingent and recursively relational identity involved trying to be consistent about how he behaved in the contexts of church and school. Although he reported that he was no longer "clowning" around and wanted to "take school seriously" his identity was much more complex than a linear developmental progression can explain. Kett explained the importance of context on his identity in this way:

> *Kett*: *In church I'm more adult and stuff,* everywhere I go. And in school it's just – I'm trying to be mature – and its hard. . . . It's just other kids want to draw you into the things they be doing. But I know that *I have to get myself away from that*. And, it's just different 'cause *I could be way, way better here [church] and not that much in school.* (my emphasis)

In this comment, Kett suggests the ways in which his identity shifts across the contexts of church and school. At church he was "more adult and stuff", whereas at school it was difficult for him to be mature. Similar to Ms. Anderson, Kett wanted to choose "one path" of a unitary identity. However, because his identity is contingent and relational, Kett's identity was shaped by competing discourses of "gang-related stuff" as well as what it means to be a Christian. The identities of adolescents such as Kett can never be as simple as choosing one discourse, one direction.

Conclusion

Discourses of what it means to be an immigrant adolescent are neither linear nor harmless. As we saw in this chapter, the identities of urban immigrant youth are multiple, contradictory and fluid. This conception of adolescence significantly shifts from a developmentally responsive understanding to one that is grounded in contexts and continual relations. Significantly, I suggest that a contingently and recursively relational vision of adolescence particularly needs to attend to the power—"magical property"—of discourses. For educators of young adolescents, this means paying attention to language-in-use. As we saw in Ananh's case, language-in-use within the contexts of Dynamic High helped to construct his identity as a gangster, as teachers worried about escalating gang activities. Further, Kett's experiences suggest that young adolescence is informed by multiple, contradictory discourses. Rather than finalize or categorize—that is, stereotype—adolescents, educators need to introduce adolescents to rich, abundant discourses as a way to open possibilities for their identities and lives. This is critical, because discourses have the power to tell adolescents *who they are or should be,* assign responsibility for school success and failure, and influence educational expectations, policies, and practices.

References

American Civil Liberties Union (2011). Immigration myths and facts. Retrieved June 18, 2011 from http://www.aclu.org/immigrants-rights/immigration-myths-and-facts

American Immigration Lawyers Association (2011). HB56. Retrieved June 18, 2011 from http://www.aila.org/content/default.aspx?bc=1019|25668|35536|35850.

Davies, B. (1993). *Poststructuralist theory and classroom practice.* Geelong, Australia: Deakin University Press.

Gee, J. (2005). *An introduction to discourse analysis: Theory and method (2nd ed.).* New York: Routledge.

Hall, S. (1996). Introduction: Who needs 'identity'? In S. Hall & P. du Gay (Eds.), *Questions of cultural identity* (pp. 1-17). Thousand Oaks, CA: Sage.

Lee, R. (1999). *Orientals: Asian Americans in popular culture.* Philadelphia, PA: Temple University Press.

Lee, S. J. (1996). *Unraveling the "model minority" stereotype: Listening to Asian American youth.* New York: Teachers College Press.

Ngo, B. (2010). *Unresolved identities: Discourse, ambivalence and urban immigrant students.* New York: State University of New York Press.

Osajima, K. (1987). Asian Americans as the model minority: An analysis of the popular press image in the 1960s and 1980s. In G. Y. Okihiro, S. Hune, A. A. Hansen, & J. M. Lie (Eds.), *Reflections on shattered windows: Promises and prospects for Asian Americans studies* (pp. 166-174). Pullman: Washington State University Press.

Vagle, M. D. (this volume). Trying to poke holes in Teflon: Developmentalism; young adolescence; and contingent, recursive growth and change. In M. D. Vagle (Ed.) *Not a stage! A critical re-conception of young adolescent education* (pp. 11-38). New York: Peter Lang Publishing.

Weedon, C. (1987). *Feminist practice and poststructuralist theory.* Oxford: Basil Blackwell.

Chapter 2

Seeing School and Learning English: Recent Immigrant Youths' Insights into Adolescents, Young Adolescence, Learning, and Teaching

Kristien Zenkov, Marriam Ewaida, Athene Bell, & Megan Lynch

Snapshot

Figure 1: My Name Is Short

"My Name Is Short"

What makes me unsuccessful in school is language....My name has caused me many problems in America. In Sri Lanka, my name is short and everyone can pronounce it. However, in America, my name is long and difficult to pronounce so nobody can say it correctly. When I do an assignment for class, I have to make sure there is a space provided for my name. Otherwise I need to add a space so people will know it is my name and not just a word....Sometimes I cannot understand what Americans are talking about because there are a lot of differences between American English and British English. I have to use American English....Sometimes the teacher just says, "Read the book." I can read, but I cannot understand everything I read....English is hard and can make me unsuccessful in school.

—Anuruddha

Anuruddha was an extraordinarily bright young man and a dedicated student. He was generally proficient in his British version of English, but he struggled in the middle school language arts class where we worked with him. We are all full- or part-time teachers working with English language learning (ELL) youth, and we have encountered an increasing number of ELL students facing similar difficulties. Like so many of his peers, Anuruddha was challenged by the structure and vocabulary of the English language on which we relied. As his image and reflection above indicate he had already come to understand that his success with school-related activities was dependent on his ability to navigate expectations that were more foreign to him than the language he thought he had learned in his native Sri Lanka.

Over several months of working with Anuruddha in this "English Speakers of Other Languages" (ESOL) class, we discovered that he engaged best when we considered more about him than the fact that he represented the changing demographic changes of our ex-urban community—a commuter region beyond the first ring suburbs filled with workers who serve our urban locale. Like almost all of our recent immigrant students, Anuruddha was able to accomplish his academic tasks when we oriented our pedagogies around the unique qualities of these young adolescents, evolving notions of young adolescence, and ongoing inquiries into their relationships to school. Our critical, inquiry-oriented approach relied on literacy practices that called on our students to depict and describe just what school meant to them. In their visual and written responses—and in the very process of these inquiries—we discovered both a notion of a "difference" curriculum (Vagle, this volume) and solutions to serving these students in our language arts classes.

Contexts and Questions

Our small community represents a different present and the certain future of U.S. schools. Our mid-Atlantic ex-urban city has experienced considerable demographic shifts in the past decade, at what seems like lightning speed, from 5% to almost 50% ESOL students. Further complicating these changes is the fact that our city borders one that has been deporting citizens perceived to be illegal immigrants, making ESOL youth difficult to track, since many families don't send their children to school for fear of drawing the attention of truancy officers. These families are arriving from as close as our major city's inner-ring suburbs—where housing costs are increasingly unaffordable—and as far away as Guatemala, El Salvador, Korea, Russia, and many other nations.

While these rapid demographic changes seem extraordinary, they are representative of the shifts in constituents, their relationships to school, and their language and literacy capacities that virtually every U.S. middle school teacher will face in the future. These students arrive in our classrooms with developing English proficiencies and introductory knowledge of an *academic* English language. While they share physical and overall maturity levels with their U.S.-born counterparts, it has become obvious that they are faced with a steep acculturation curve with regard to the very structures of the U.S. public school system. School and its foundational language simply don't *mean* to these youth and their families what it does to us—their teachers—who are almost universally White, native English speakers.

Of course, these different, generally less appreciative views of school, are not unique to our ELL students. Across our years of teaching diverse—typically urban—youth, we have become ever more aware that the very social contract of schooling is increasingly in question. Like many teachers working with young people who have not known much school success—whether students whose first language is English or those who are being introduced to the language—we have encountered what can appear to be an impenetrable indifference to school. While public school critics and youth advocates alike might dismiss these laments as an adolescent right of passage, we believe these incidents are reason for serious concern. Perhaps the most obvious evidence of this large-scale shift in our communities' relationships to school is the fact that the high school dropout—or "pushout"—rate has hovered near 50% amongst non-White students in almost every major U.S. city for four decades (Alexander, Entwisle, & Kabbani, 2001; Balfanz & Legters, 2004).

The dropout or "pushout" picture for ELL youth is both strikingly similar to and different from what we see in our diverse, but U.S.-born adolescents. ELLs in the US disappear from high school at this same astonishing, nearly 50% rate (NCES, 2009; Somers, Owens, & Piliawsky, 2009). But the causes behind this percentage seem to be even more distressing. ELLs have only comprised such a large percentage of our middle and high school population for the past decade or so, but already their relationship to this most foundational U.S. institution—our schools—already seems in question. They are *rejecting* schools before—or perhaps *because*—they have yet to develop any substantial knowledge of it.

For us, these phenomena ultimately relate to *literacy* issues. "Literacy" in our world means something entirely different than it did for us as K-12 students and the educational institutions by which we are employed. Numerous scholars have documented the expanding nature of "literacy" in the early 21st century, where "texts" are as diverse as music, Web-based media, texting, and social networking tools (Christenbury, Bomer, & Smagorinsky, 2009; Moje, Overby, Tysvaer, & Morris 2008). We are attempting to serve young people who have very different *literacies* in the English language and the media through which it is communicated.

Given these various contexts, we have been driven by the question of what we—middle-level language arts teachers and teacher educators—do to stem the tide of this seemingly unavoidable school rejection. We now believe that we must rethink just who these young adolescents are and what "adolescence" means. In an effort to address these questions over the past several years we have used a photo elicitation project to explore students' perspectives on school. Our inquiries were born out of desperate personal and professional needs to gain a responsive perspective on our ELL young adolescents.

Our Framework and Recent Research

All of these contextual factors have led us to a critical pedagogy framework as the foundation for our work as teachers and researchers serving ELL young people. Our visually based English language arts instruction and the study on which we report in this chapter rely on the foundational assumption that educational practices should address how to construct institutional conditions in which the lived experience of empowerment for students is a defining quality (Ayers, Michie & Rome, 2004; Darder, Baltodano, & Torres, 2002). We recognized that critical perspectives on the disengagement issues—and young adults' and family and community members' relationships to school—that we were encountering might be discovered through the use of alternative, visually oriented research methods (Gold, 2004).

Fortunately, in an effort to understand diverse youths' perspectives on school and engage them in meaningful school activities, some researchers are considering these students' perspectives on school (Easton & Condon, 2009; Yonezawa & Jones, 2009). These studies have helped us to understand factors related to the success and failure of these young people in our language arts classes (Cook-Sather, 2009; Zenkov & Harmon, 2009). And, while many studies of youths' perceptions of school have been language-focused inquiries, some of these research efforts have looked to the visually oriented media with which youth are familiar (Zenkov, 2009).

Thus, we relied on theoretical and research bases that recognize the value of youths' perspectives in research methods, literacy pedagogies, curricula, and school reform (Kellett, 2009). Recognizing that young adults' literacy development plays a significant role in their decisions to remain in school (Morrell, 2007; Strickland & Alvermann, 2004), we appealed to current concepts of literacy for a more responsive framework and set of texts to engage these often alliterate and detached youth (Kist, 2005; Lankshear & Knobel, 2006). These visually oriented processes reveal that image-based tools motivate students to develop an awareness of and share—through complex writings and presentations—personal insights related to their school experiences (Doda & Knowles, 2008; Marquez-Zenkov & Harmon, 2007).

Methods

These perspectives on diverse adolescents' literacies and school experiences evoked the tools of our photovoice project, through which we hoped to help middle level students consider their relationships to school—to inform themselves, us, and our broader communities about these connections—and become better writers (Kress, 2006; Streng et al., 2004). For this chapter, we worked with twenty-one middle-level ELLs and used their digital photographs and related reflections to consider, illustrate, and describe the purposes of school, the supports for their school achievement, and the obstacles to their success. Our school's community was composed of working-class families and the majority of their parents had not completed high school.

In the three versions of this project from which we have data we were supported by grants from the university where Kristien (first author) was based. We provided all participants with digital "point and shoot" cameras and we instructed them in the basics of camera operation. We then led them on "photo walks" around our schools and their neighborhoods, modeling the photo elicitation process and how to consider camera angles and composition. We conducted each version of the project in weekly or bi-weekly sessions in our language arts classes for two to four months, with each participant taking an average of 100 images in response to the three project questions:

1. What is the purpose of school?
2. What helps you to be successful in school?
3. What gets in the way of your school success?

Each youth shot a minimum of 10 images prior to each class session, where we worked with students to examine, discuss, and write about their photos. We then reviewed photographs with participants in small group and one-on-one gatherings, discussing images as a part of the elicitation process—asking questions like "What do you like about this photograph?" and "What does this photo mean to you?" We transcribed their oral reactions to images and helped them to edit their reflections on the photos that they felt best answered the project questions. Collectively these project participants shot more than 2200 images and after multiple draft reflections, these young adults wrote about approximately 40 of these in paragraph-length reflections.

We have engaged in an ongoing data analysis process during and after our completion of this project in each of the three versions on which we report. In the 1:1 and small group interactions with participants, Kristien and Marriam (second author) began to recognize that youth often described notions of adolescence that we found striking and elements of our English language arts pedagogies that they appreciated or perceived as troubling. This informal review process represented the first stage of our analysis. At the conclusion of these three small projects, we analyzed the content of the images and writings youth had identified as the most compelling responses to the project questions, tracking and coding prevalent and visual and descriptive themes in youths' visual and written data (Patton, 2002; Rose, 2007). As a result of this content analysis, we confirmed that notions of young adolescence and examples of effective English language arts pedagogies were predominant themes in students' work.

The final stage of analysis involved a framed content analysis of the entire set of approximately 40 images and accompanying reflections (Van Leeuwen & Jewitt, 2001). We each reconsidered our general content analysis notes and these visual and written data through the lens of what these suggested about the following broad questions: 1) Who are "young adolescents"?; 2) What is "young adolescence"?; and 3) What are some of the pedagogical practices that these young people believe would serve them most effectively? After sharing and discussing our final analysis notes we came to a consensus about the ideas—and related illustrative students' images and writings—that we share below. We believe each theme offers critical concepts of young adolescence and curricula, as well as instructional practices that can serve ELL youth.

Findings

Recognizing that we were almost desperate to gain some insight into who this new population of students were, we not only engaged in a consideration of their ideas about school, but we focused our analysis on the three questions that we most urgently needed answered. The responses we share here are by no means exhaustive, but they represent important and perhaps startling insights. We briefly detail and discuss these perspectives, and conclude this chapter with reflections about the nature of visual inquiries for learning about and serving diverse young adolescents.

Who Are Young Adolescents?

One of the outcomes of the visual sociological inquiry in which we engaged these ELL young people was a richer picture of who they are, of some of their most unique characteristics. Given the often large cultural gap between us and them, it now seems imperative that we lead a very intentional exploration of the details of these youths' lives. A "difference" curriculum (Vagle) or stance is not meaningful without some explicit awareness of just what those differences are. Ultimately it is only in light of these differences—the everyday traits of our students—that we should modify our curricula and pedagogies. In their images and writings, these young adolescents revealed a range of qualities, including the fact that they are often not explicitly aware of their difficult, complex places in a new society, and that they are challenged in subtle and overt ways by their native English-speaking peers to engage with school.

Unwittingly Complicated Positions. One of the best illustrations of the challenging, complicated roles these young adolescents play in a society that is still foreign was represented by De'Andre, with his image and writing below. He was practically a poster child for the complex and even seemingly incongruent demographics of these diverse young people. He was a recent immigrant to the United States, but he did not come from one of the homes most Americans believe are those of these recent arrivals.

Figure 2: My Life

"My Life"

If someone is trying to attack you, you can use [this gun] for protection. The gun reminds me of my dream and goal, which is to become an air force officer. I want to be an air force officer because they don't always go to war or die, but they still help the country. I want to protect the United States because there are a lot of bad people in the world and we need to stop them. For example, I want to help stop illegal immigrants from coming to the United States....Even though I am originally from Panama and came to the United States three years ago, I still want to serve the United States. In order to reach my goal, I need to become a good reader and writer. Reading and writing are my protection, just like the gun. When I read and write, I gain the knowledge and feel smarter than other people. I am no longer ignorant, but I know more information.

—De'Andre

De'Andre arrived in our northern Virginia community under quite different conditions than what most stereotypes about immigrants suggest. His family was well educated in a formal schooling sense, and he was very much a *legal* immigrant. He had come from Panama, which meant that he was both Black and of Latino origin—again, not a combination that most people in the U.S. are accustomed to seeing.

De'Andre was also aware of the immigration controversies in the U.S., and his professional goal was to help ensure that future "illegal" immigrants would not so easily enter his adopted country. Of course, many of the youth by whom De'Andre was surrounded in our class were ones who he would not have allowed into the U.S. He saw no tension in this fact, but he did appreciate that reading and writing would help him to achieve this objective. More often than not our young immigrant adolescents fail to fit into the narrow traditional roles that our society and schools have offered them. This unwitting complexity—and even these seemingly contradictory roles—represent some of the most important traits of which we must be aware.

Challenged by Their American-Born Peers. Much research and even our own experiences with our traditional, American-born students suggest that it is young adolescents' peers who play some of the most significant roles in their lives and in determining their relationships to school. It is likely true, too, that our immigrant youths' appreciation for school is similarly influenced—positively and negatively—by their immigrant peers. But we have encountered in these young folks' images and reflections more subtle and challenging impacts of U.S.-born students on the immigrant youth who are their peers. Julio's writing and image below offered a poignant illustration of these effects:

Figure 3: Guns and Racism in the United States

"Guns and Racism in the United States"

> Guns make me unsuccessful in and out of school. For example, if my parents knew that I had a gun, they would kick me out of the house or they would send me to the correctional center until I am eighteen or more....I am scared of getting into fights with other kids in the school, because some of them are racist towards Hispanic students. One time my friends and I were walking in the hallway and a group of kids approached us. They said, "Get the @#$% out of America, you stupid Hispanics!" I was very upset, but also scared. These students had knives on them.
>
> —Julio

We are conscious of and cautious about the fact that we have chosen these youths' perspectives on violence to represent who they are. We count this first as evidence of their quick learning: the U.S. culture to which they are being introduced normalizes aggression, in both overt and discreet forms. Most importantly, these images—representative of numerous other pictures and reflections that addressed our students' heightened awareness of the threats to their safety inside and outside of their new schools—are troublingly informative of who our young adolescents are and the issues with which they are concerned.

What Is Young Adolescence?

These immigrant adolescents' images and writing revealed something more than a laundry list of their unique traits. As a result of this project and study we now have insight into what "young adolescence" is for these early teens who have arrived from around the world and are trying to make their ways in our classrooms and communities. This notion of adolescence might be similar to or strikingly different from what it means for our U.S.-born and native English-speaking young adolescents; we offer a few key features of this version of adolescence here not as a point of comparison, but to help readers better serve these immigrant youth.

A Time of Reluctance Rather than Resistance. Contrary to what teachers and observers of this population might perceive, young adolescence for our ELL students represents a time of *reluctance* toward school, rather than a period of *resistance* to its structures or tasks. Archana illustrated and described this quality of this period with the following image and reflection:

Figure 4: What Is Your Name

"What Is Your Name?"

> Some things that make me unsuccessful in school are teachers [and] assignments....I don't always understand the [homework] directions or the assignment, so I fall behind. Sometimes the teachers get mad at me and yell, so I am sad and feel like they don't like me. Some of the assignments I do in school seem boring to me. I don't feel motivated to finish them, so I don't learn as much as I'd like to. Then I fail the test because I didn't learn the way I should have....I moved to the United States in 2006. When I arrived, I only knew how to answer the question, "What is your name?" Since then, I have learned a lot more English, but sometimes I still get confused when I hear long words that I don't know the meaning of or when people talk too fast.
>
> —Archana

Archana was practically mute in our language arts class and, yet, she sat up straight in class and was motivated to at least simulate the behaviors of an engaged student. While she made incomplete efforts to finish her assignments in our class, she both did not seem to have the English proficiency to achieve in the way she and we hoped, and she appeared inconsistently but occasionally resistant to our efforts and assignments. Or at least that is what we believed until we began to meet with her in one-to-one conferences—one youth, one teacher, and a dedicated if brief private interaction.

Archana's confusion was echoed in the writings and conversations we had with almost every one of the students in this project. While they often may not even attempt to complete assignments in our classes and are even less likely to finish a daily homework activity, the reason is that they are most often confused by our directions or the task itself—they simply are not confident in their ability to intelligently express their questions. Or because they are paralyzed by what we recognize as a very natural adolescent pride—a reluctance to *appear* even more uncertain about how to engage in school and with adults than most adolescents already seem to *feel*.

Young adolescence in the U.S. may, by its very nature, involve adults or teachers and their students in an ongoing game of impressions and judgment. But it is clear to us now that these immigrant youth have many more reasons and perhaps even an unavoidable need to present a resistant facade toward teachers and school, given the significant nature of the cultural learning curve they are confronting. It behooves us as teachers of these diverse youth to approach them with a recognition of and respect for their very sensible caution.

A Time When They Play Complicated Family Roles. As veteran city teachers we have worked for a combined six decades with diverse U.S.-born youth, and we have grown accustomed to recognizing and responding to the fact that these young adolescents and young adults often face very complicated family responsibilities that we did not during our own school years and that often keep them from concentrating on our school tasks. But our immigrant students face not only the additional duties that come with poverty, including parents who need to work long hours, leaving the child care to these older siblings, but they also encounter family roles and responsibilities that grow out of a very difficult cultural connection to school, a very different history with these still new institutions. Lucelly's reflection and the image below of a collection of over-the-counter drugs offered a poignant illustration of these complicated roles that we now count as a core element of young adolescence for our students:

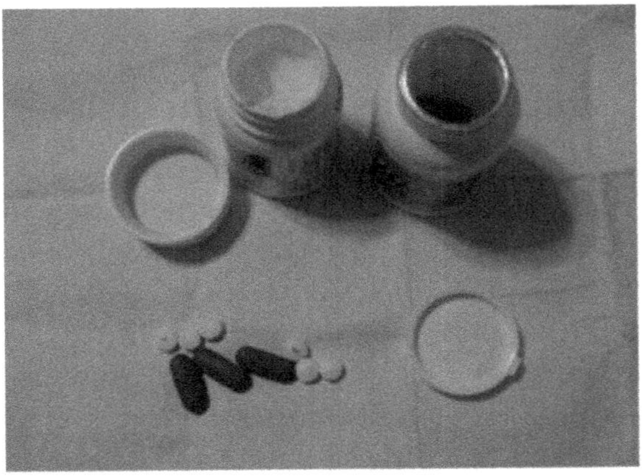

Figure 5: Home

"Home"

What makes me unsuccessful at school is my home environment and drugs because at my house my brother uses drugs and that makes me unsuccessful....Sometimes he tells me if I call the police or I say something to some-

> body, he says he will go and do something bad to me and I start crying. My mom says don't pay attention to him....When it is time to eat dinner, I need to put the food on the table for him. If he doesn't like the dinner, he throws the food in my face. If I do something to him, my mom says she will ground me. Every day I need to clean my brother's room, the kitchen, and my mom's room. When this happens at home, I don't come to school because I don't want people to see me crying or sad, and I don't finish my homework.
>
> —Lucelly

Still learning English after arriving from Guatemala a few years prior, Lucelly not only socialized with many of her classmates—in Spanish, of course—but she was friendly with us, revealing a mature sense of humor and a wisdom well beyond her thirteen years. Lucelly's performance in our class was uneven, though: she would often work diligently to complete her assignments, and then other times she would appear to be unabashedly disengaged. She was a capable English writer, but we did not always see this ability play out with positive results in school. And when we read the above writing—and numerous others from her and her peers—we recognized just how their family roles, relationships, and responsibilities, carried with them from their native country to their new one, were impacting their school engagement and success.

Implications and Conclusions

We have shared only a handful of the insights about young adolescents and young adolescence in this chapter. The youth with whom we have worked on dozens of versions of this project have offered numerous other details and perspectives with which we—their teachers—should be concerned. In addition to the new information and novel perspectives that our project has provided, perhaps the most important outcomes are the curricular and pedagogical implications we have drawn from these young folks' images and writings. We highlight two of these—regarding our responsibilities to pay attention to the realities of young adolescents' lives and keep them safe in our classrooms and schools, and the extent to which we must share specific expectations for them in our classrooms—with two final examples of students' reflections, which are echoed by other recent research on ELLs.

Help Youth to Be Safe in Our Classrooms and Share the Realities of Their Lives

Emmanuel was an eighth grade student in our language arts class for English language learners last year. He often struggled to engage with school and our literacy activities, but he found some of the greatest success when we appealed to his proficiency with multimodal tools as starting points for our writing assignments. These activities called on him to share his experiences with school and English class as a foundation for his literacy and school engagement. His reflection and photograph below powerfully addressed his trepidation:

Figure 6: How the Police Work

"How the Police Work"

This picture of a police car reminds me of feeling safe. I feel safe in the United States more so than I did in Mexico. In Mexico there are a lot of gangs and not enough police, but in America, there are police everywhere. In America, I feel safe going to school because there are police officers in my school and it is not dangerous. Reading and writing for me is safe inside school because the teachers help me and tell me to read. When I go home, I read and write, but not all the time. I feel unsafe reading and writing because I don't have a lot of help at home.

—Emmanuel

Based on Emmanuel's and many other students' writing and pictures, we now know that we must explicitly invite students' lives into our classrooms, into these literacy class activities. Orienting our curriculum around these invitations and centering our pedagogies on visual tools like the ones we used in our project allow us to mitigate some of the fear our English language learning students feel (Green, et al., 2008; Jimenez & Rose, 2010).

This approach contrasts greatly with many standard English class activities that fail to honor ELL youths' cultures, their often frustrating experiences with school, and the contemporary concepts of literacy with which most teachers operate. As literacy educators and teacher educators we have learned over the past decade how we might challenge teachers' narrow concepts of adolescence and literacy and these educators' often, unfortunately negative, perceptions of youths' reading, writing, speaking, and listening abilities.

Explicitly Explain the Assumed, Everyday Rules of School and Our Classrooms

Perhaps the most the frequently mentioned and straightforward desire for our curricula and pedagogies that these youth illustrated and articulated was for an absolute clarity in our assignment guidelines and with the general rules of school operation. Complementing a photograph he took of a soccer trophy he had recently been awarded, Juan articulated these wishes in almost painful terms:

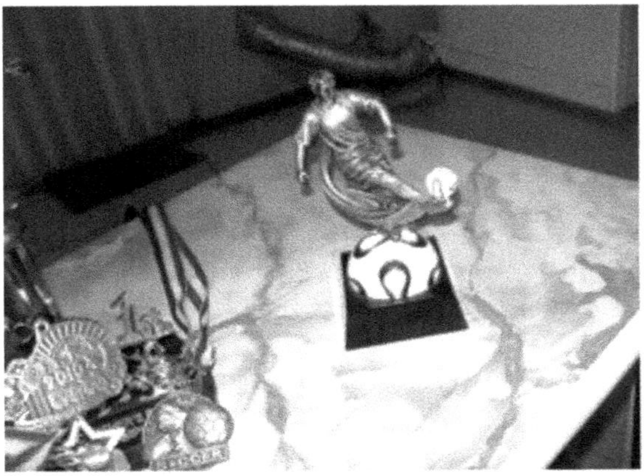

Figure 7: The Effort that I Put

"The Effort that I Put"

I am a soccer player. I work really hard to be a successful soccer player. I won this first place medal at a tournament in Virginia Beach last year. In order for me to be a good forward, I have to practice at least twice a week. I enjoy practicing and feel proud of my success as a soccer player. At school, however, I don't always feel successful. I feel successful in math class because I understand the rules and how to do the homework. But in my other classes, I am not a good reader and writer....It takes a lot of time and effort and sometimes I don't know the rules in writing. I know that I need to practice and work hard to get a medal in soccer and I also know I need to work hard at reading and writing if I want to be successful in school.

—Juan

In our review and analyses of their photographs and writings we found that almost every one of our middle-level ESL students echoed the need for explicit support to maneuver the expectations of school and our language arts class. When we worked closely enough with these young people to recognize that it was this lack of clarity that was impeding much of their school achievement, our students wrote more proficiently than ever before (Ozer, Wolf, & Kong, 2008; Suarez-Orozco, Pimentel, & Martin, 2009). And we recognized that our language arts classes were part of an institution that they simply did not understand, even after a few months or even years.

We discovered numerous other suggestions for ways we might alter our pedagogies and curricula to serve these young adolescents better, and to honor the "difference"-oriented notions of young adolescence with which we now try to operate. Yet we are left with the distinct impression that our exploration of this critical perspective on adolescence is, necessarily, an ongoing affair. Adolescence for the newest members of our society and the youth who struggle most to understand the English language and the traditions of our classrooms and schools is not a static entity.

Young adolescence has long been defined as a period of identity formation and role challenges. But for these English language learning young people the school engagement and achievement stakes are so very high and the nature of their questions about our educational practices, curricula, and institutions are rooted in a cultural learning curve that has perhaps never before been appreciated—at least not systematically, by our school districts, teacher training methods, or societal traditions. A critical, "difference"-driven curriculum may, then, only be developed and sustained through continued explorations of these young folks' ideas about school and their places in it. These inquiries call on us to use tools that do not rely on a language—English—that these young people do not yet know, to consider media that really *are* universally understood—photographs—and to begin with an intimate, relationship-based pedagogical stance.

References

Alexander, K.L., Entwisle, D.R., & Kabbani, N. (2001). The dropout process in life course perspective: Early risk factors at home and school. *Teachers College Record, 103*(5), 760-822.

Ayers, W., Michie, G., & Rome, A. (2004). Embers of hope: In search of a meaningful critical pedagogy. *Teacher Education Quarterly, 31*(1), 123-130.

Balfanz, R., & Legters, N. (2004). *Locating the dropout crisis: Which high schools produce the nation's dropouts? Where are they located? Who attends them?* Baltimore, MD: Center for Social Organization of Schools, Johns Hopkins University. Retrieved September 18, 2011 from http://www.csos.jhu.edu/crespar/techReports/Report70.pdf

Christenbury, L., Bomer, R., & Smagorinsky, P. (Eds.). (2009). *Handbook of adolescent literacy research.* New York: Guilford Press.

Cook-Sather, A. (2009). *Learning from the student's perspective: A methods sourcebook for effective teaching.* Boulder, CO: Paradigm Publishers.

Darder, A., Baltodano, M., & Torres, R. (2002) *The critical pedagogy reader.* New York: Routledge Falmer.

Doda, N., & Knowles, T. (2008). Listening to the voices of young adolescents. *Middle School Journal, 39*(3), 26-33.

Easton, L., & Condon, D. (2009). A school-wide model for student voice in curriculum development and teacher preparation. In A. Cook-Sather (Ed.). *Learning from the student's perspective: A secondary methods sourcebook for effective teaching* (pp. 176-193). Boulder, CO: Paradigm Press.

Gold, S.J. (2004). Using photography in studies of immigrant communities. *American Behavioral Scientist, 47*(12), 1551-1572.

Green, G., Rhodes, J., Hirsch, A. H., Suárez-Orozco, C., & Camic, P. M. (2008). Supportive adult relationships and the academic engagement of Latin American immigrant youth. *Journal of School Psychology, 46*(4), 393-412.

Jimenez, R. T., & Rose, B. C. (2010). Knowing how to know: Building meaningful relationships through instruction that meets the needs of students learning English. *Journal of Teacher Education, 61*(5), 403-412.

Kellett, M. (2009). Children as researchers: What we can learn from them about the impact of poverty on literacy opportunities? *International Journal of Inclusive Education, 13*(4), 395-408.

Kist, W. (2005). *New literacies in action: Teaching and learning in multiple media.* New York: Teachers College Press.

Kress, G. (2006). *Reading images: The grammar of visual design.* New York: Routledge.

Lankshear, C., & Knobel, M. (2006). *New literacies: Everyday practices and classroom learning* (2nd ed.). Maidenhead, UK: Open University Press.

Marquez-Zenkov, K., & Harmon, J. (2007). Seeing English in the city: Using photography to understand students' literacy relationships. *English Journal, 96*(6), 24-30.

Moje, E.B., Overby, M., Tysvaer, N., & Morris, K. (2008). The complex world of adolescent literacy: Myths, motivations, and mysteries. *Harvard Educational Review, 78*(1), 107-154.

Morrell, E. (2007). *Critical literacy and urban youth: Pedagogies of access, dissent, and liberation.* New York: Routledge.

National Center for Education Statistics. (2009). *The condition of education: 2009.* Washington, DC: National Center for Education Statistics/Institute of Education Sciences.
Ozer, E.J., Wolf, J.P., & Kong, C. (2008). Sources of perceived school connection among ethnically-diverse urban adolescents. *Journal of Adolescent Research, 23*(4), 438-470.
Patton, M.Q. (2002). *Qualitative research & evaluation methods* (3rd ed.). Thousand Oaks, CA: Sage.
Rose, G. (2007). *Visual methodologies: An introduction to the interpretation of visual materials* (2nd ed.). Thousand Oaks, CA: Sage.
Somers, C.L., Owens, D., & Piliawsky, M. (2009). A study of high school dropout prevention and at-risk ninth graders' role models and motivations for school completion. *Education, 130*(2), 348-356.
Streng, J.M., Rhodes, S.D., Ayala, G.X., Eng., E., Arceo, R. & Phipps, S. (2004). Realidad Latina: Latino adolescents, their school, and a university use photo-voice to examine and address the influence of immigration. *Journal of Interprofessional Care, 18*(4), 403-415.
Strickland, D.S., & Alvermann, D.E. (2004). *Bridging the literacy achievement gap: Grades 4-12*. New York: Teachers College Press.
Suárez-Orozco, C., Pimentel, A., & Martin, M. (2009). The significance of relationships: Academic engagement and achievement among newcomer immigrant youth. *Teachers College Record, 111*, 5-6.
Vagle, M. D. (this volume). Trying to poke holes in Teflon: Developmentalism; young adolescence; and contingent, recursive growth and change. In M. D. Vagle (Ed.), *Not a stage! A critical re-conception of young adolescent education* (pp. 11-38). New York: Peter Lang Publishing.
Van Leeuwen, T., & Jewitt, C. (Eds.). (2001). *Handbook of visual analysis*. Thousand Oaks, CA: Sage.
Yonezawa, S., & Jones, M. (2009). Student voices: Generating reform from the inside out. *Theory into Practice, 48*(3), 205-212.
Zenkov, K. (2009). Seeing the pedagogies, practices, and programs urban students want. *Theory Into Practice, 48*(3), 168–175.
Zenkov, K., & Harmon, J. (2009). Picturing a writing process: Photovoice and teaching writing to urban youth. *Journal of Adolescent and Adult Literacy, 52*(7), 575-584.

Chapter 3

Putting 'Boy' in Crisis: Seeking an Education of Gender rather than in Gender

Shannon D. M. Moore

A normative discourse surrounding masculinity within popular culture, and certain educational research, claims a 'boy crisis' (Epstein, Elwood, Hey & Maw, 1998; Foster, Kimmel, & Skelton, 2001; Griffin, 2000; Sommers, 2000). Using standardized test results, dramatic personal narratives, and extremely public acts of violence committed by males, the media has created a moral panic about underachieving boys that reinforces biological essentialism (Titus, 2002). The theoretical premise of this popularized understanding is that 'boys' and 'girls' are biologically distinct, and in turn learn differently (Gurian, 2001).

While the 'boy crisis' has received much attention in academic and popular sources, it is supported by disputable statistics (Husain & Millimet, 2008), fueled by biological determinism (Foster, Kimmel, & Skelton, 2001), and driven by the understanding that masculinity is singular, fixed and heteronormative (Connell, 1995/2005). Even though this 'turn to boys' is upheld by pop psychology, the accompanying media-driven moral panic has created a fervor for funding and policy changes (Weaver-Hightower, 2003). Subsequently, this 'crisis' serves to re-establish dominant ideals of gender by manufacturing the belief that there are negative academic and social issues with boys in educational spaces. In response, resources and reforms are put towards boys in a way that fixes binaried, normative understandings of gender.

A Time-Honored Formula

To elucidate the ways in which naturalized gendered discourses dominate educational curricula and reform, I draw on the formula of the 'boy crisis'. This example reveals the way that biological categories inform, and operate within, education. Through this formula, gendered identities are fixed, bodies are regulated, and achievement is narrowly defined. I assert that the boy crisis, like developmental discourses, reifies a singular, static notion of identity; in this case, a predetermined notion of adolescent masculinity—boy. In the same way that the young adolescent gets obscured by the developmental stage of young adolescence (Vagle, this volume), the male body is obscured by hegemonic understandings of masculinity. Normative understandings of masculinities become the marker through which male bodies are read, understood, and therefore produced. This formula fails to question the way in which societal constructions of gender are aligned with the sexed body (Butler, 1990, 1993). Instead, standardized curricula and notions of achievement reify dominant narratives by focusing on individuals who do not meet the marker, rather than reflecting on the markers *of* gender and achievement. If our goal, as Vagle points out, is to provide the best education possible, how is this achievable when the theories that ground education are misguided? Or, as Lesko (2002) points out, guided in a very particular direction—to reinforce dominant social norms? Turning to Vagle's pleas for a contingently and recursively relational vision of education, a particularized view of young adolescence, and a difference curriculum, I look at the ways that schools could disrupt narrow understandings of gender by engaging with a Butlerian understanding of gender. This involves making gender a subject in schools, rather than something students are subjected to (Weaver-Hightower, 2003). I posit an education *of* gender rather than an education *in* gender.

Developing Gender

In the first section of this book, Vagle (this volume) speaks of the ways in which developmental discourses have become a rule in education. Similarly, gender reigns. Vagle makes reference to the alignment between developmental and gender discourses, declaring that "we are constantly being raced, classed, gendered, and sexed just like the developmental discourse" (p. 18). Drawing on Lesko (2001), he goes on to say that the developmental discourse is itself gendered, and as such complicit in reifying dominant understandings of male and female. Through this chapter, I take up this notion, outlining the ways in which developmental and gendered discourses are intertwined and mutually constitutive. In particular, I parallel Vagle's critiques of developmental discourses with the naturalized gender discourses that rule in education. By this I mean the ways in which static, essentialized, binaried understandings of gender, as male and female, underpin curriculum, classrooms, and reform movements.

Similar to Lesko's (2001) suggestion that developmentalism is Teflon, I argue that dominant understandings of gender in education are also protected, as the formula of the gender binary of boy and girl is so entrenched in our education system that it denies critique. Throughout this chapter, I thread elements of the 'boy crisis', such as the underlying epistemologies, standardized reforms, and statistical evidence, to reveal the way that normative gendered discourses operate in education to cover bodies in an invisible, synthetic, non-stick coating.

My Metal Spatula

The crux of Vagle's critique of developmental discourses, and subsequent pleas for education, relies on troubling dominant understandings of identity through Nancy Lesko's (2001) theorizing of adolescence. To challenge the developmental and gendered understandings that underpin education, I draw on Judith Butler's (1990, 1993) seminal texts on gender. Following Butler, we are always already subjects; however, we are not already gendered. The culturally enmired subject negotiates its constructions, even when those constructions are the predicates of the subject's identity. There is no mechanism that transforms the human subject into a gendered subject once and for all. Rather the subject is in constant negotiation with the discourses of gender. This is not automatic and cannot be presumed. Schools need to consider the ways in which they are actively constructing students according to the rigid binary of male/female at the expense of what could be otherwise.

Lesko's view of adolescence as contingent and recursive parallels Butler's view of gender as an iteration, never fully achieved rather constantly performed and dependent on repetition in order to be maintained. In particular, Lesko's notion of simultaneous, contradictory identities, at once mature and immature, old and young, learning and learned, parallels Butler's notion of gender as unfinished, at once but never fully 'male' or 'female'. In the same way that Lesko (2002) regards 'adolescence' as a social fact that is produced and regulated through educational and material practices, I view gender as a product of education subsequently used to justify gendered education and reform.

No Brainer

The notion that boys and girls learn differently, and should therefore be educated differently, stems from unquestioned biological notions of difference. Titus refers to this as a frame of biological destiny: "current popular wisdom is that men and women have different brains in terms of size, shape and function" (2002, p. 153). Gendered curriculum, predicated on essentialist declarations of 'how boys learn' (Gurian, 2001), and evidenced in boy-friendly activities, and boy-friendly books (Sommers, 2000), produce the very differences they supposedly serve. Notions of male and female not only limit and regulate bodies, they are complicit in upholding a heteronormative society. The 'reality' of gender is motivated and constrained by a heteronormative agenda which requires a society divided into men and women. Standardized curricula and definitions of achievement ensure that the rule of the gender binary is upheld. Conceptions of naturalized difference underpin education, and in turn construct male and female, a self-fulfilling prophecy at the expense of what could be otherwise. Echoing Vagle (this volume), I fear that by continuing to rely on a bifurcated notion of the student body, educators will fail to provide the best education possible. Instead, a Butlerian understanding of gender challenges the understandings of 'boy' and 'girl' that in/forms the education of young adolescence.

Butler Teaches Biology

According to Butler (1993), the very materiality of sex is constructed through the repetition of norms; sex is already gendered, already constructed, "already strained from the start" (p. 12). In recognizing that the body is actively sexed, the terms gender and sex are conflated (Butler, 1990); there is nothing "left of 'sex' once it has assumed its social character as gender" (Butler, 1993, p. 5). The notion of an essential sex is an attempt to hide the performative character of gender, and the possibilities for proliferating gender outside of these restrictive binaries (Butler, 1990). The heavily entrenched and pervasive understanding of sex as natural limits the way that bodies are understood, as the limits for how these bodies can be seen are set in advance. This does not dismiss the materiality of the body, rather, points to the ways in which the normative conditions, such as the assumption of heterosexuality and the necessary binary of sex, frame the conditions under which the materiality emerges (Butler, 1990, 1993).

It's Reigning 'Men'

The very category of sex, and the notion that there is a biological connection between bodies and natural ways of being 'male' and 'female' have remained prevalent in popular and academic discourse; this notion has been fiercely guarded and immortalized by major media, science, law and language (Connell, 2009; Fausto-Sterling, 2002; Lancaster, 2003). Likewise, schools reinforce normative understandings of gender through their structure, pedagogy, and curriculum (Connell, 1996; Mac an Ghaill, 1994). The bodies produced within these settings are then used as proof of naturalized differences between boys and girls.

Put simply, there is no biological basis for sex (Connell, 2009). Chromosomal variances contest the limited, binaried understandings of male and female; yet, the assertion that sex is 'natural' remains a widely held belief (Fausto-Sterling, 2002). Fueled by pop psychology and books about Mars and Venus, there is a common belief that the male and female brain are inherently different (Connell, 2009). Despite a lack of empirical evidence proving 'sex' based differences, Western culture remains so deeply committed to the 'natural binary' that language denies any other possibilities (Fausto-Sterling, 2002). This is echoed in a legal system that forces citizens to declare their gender within one of two boxes—an ironic 'defense of nature' (Fausto-Sterling, 2002). Profusions of gender performance are dismissed, policed, or degraded according to the supposed nature of sex. This policing is extremely evident within educational contexts in both the official and hidden curricula.

The Fix

Both gender and developmental discourses operate on a binaried understanding of identity, as male/female, adolescent/adult. This binary fixes identities, fixes bodies, within a linear construction. Yet, the way in which people perform their gender, or 'develop', is much more complicated than the binary.

Identities are fixed through developmental and gendered discourses, in every sense of the word— predetermined, secured, and repaired. These discourses are grounded in humanist understandings of identity that assume first there is an independent person who inhabits a particular identity. Physiological explanations are used to set identities prior to their entry into the education system. Predetermined notions of 'boy' are evident in statements that declare that schools are contributing to the feminization of boys, or ignore 'who boys really are' (Newcomb, 2000). These foundational ideas are fueled by researchers who assert that there are natural cerebral differences between boys and girls (Gurian, 2001). Such assertions are secured by reformers who use hyperbolic rhetoric to suggest that schools need to differentiate learning for boys and girls, otherwise male students are put at a disadvantage in 'feminized' educational spaces (Sommers, 2000). This has manifested in lists of pedagogical suggestions for teaching boys (as outlined in Weaver-Hightower, 2003). In turn, this ensures that a particular version of boy is maintained within the school system.

Lesko (2002) explains that at the turn of the twentieth century, the focus turned to adolescents—they were labeled in peril. These concerns for adolescents emerged amidst anxieties surrounding masculinity and dominance. Similarly, the current moral panic surrounding boys has emerged in unstable times of globalization, war and neo-imperialism (Weaver-Hightower, 2003). At the turn of the previous century, a focus on adolescents allowed for a particular version of masculinity and femininity to remain centered. The purpose of education became the production of young, masculine, Christians. Currently, the boy crisis is underpinned by the same motivations, securing a society that adheres to gender norms, educating students in the binary, and ensuring that a particular understanding of masculinity is privileged. As Vagle (this volume) and Lesko (2002) point out, these normative understandings are *already* white, middle class, male and heteronormative. Within this setup (fix) students are approached as in need of repair (fixing). This also secures (fixes) a normative version of gender.

Today, this notion of repair prevails, as there remain hegemonic understandings of what a boy and girl should be. These ideals have become so engrained that gender policing has been taken up by students who regulate one another according to the norms (Connell, 1995/2005; Dalley-Trim, 2007; Kehler, 2007; Martino, 2007). Connell (2009) states that by fourth grade boys have learned their gender. The unfortunate evidence she uses—homophobic insults begin and physical contact among boys becomes less common.

Something Much Butler

Rather than fixing identities, Lesko (2001) and Butler (1990, 1993) both assert the simultaneity and fluidity of identity. Lesko refers to the ways in which someone is at once old and young, mature and immature, traditional and innovative. Likewise, in Butler's understanding a person is never fully male or female, as gender is fluid and partial. Neither of these theorists deny that there is that which emanates from the body. Yet, all of these emanations, these desires, these matters of biology, are socially understood and assigned meanings within particular contexts. Unfixing gendered identities does not simply translate to engaging a catalogue of intersections, such as race, class, and sexuality. Fluidity is not found in a linear grid.

I've Always Hated Writing Lines

While the recognition of multiplicity ruptures singular, hegemonic assertions of *a* gender, the use of the term intersection presents discourses as linear, stable structures. Discourses of gender are themselves unstable as they are dependent on the subject: "There is no power that acts, only a reiterated acting that is power in its persistence and instability" (Butler, 1993, p. 9). Discourses of gender need the subject to perform them in order to be sustained. Further, the fluidity and simultaneity of identities to which Lesko and Butler are referring is not appeased by structuralist, linear crossings. Connell

(2009) outright rejects the use of the term intersection: "It is an unfortunate term, because it suggests social structures are rigid arrangements that can be understood by a kind of geometry" (p. 86). Butler (1993) concurs: "to say that there is a matrix of gender relations that institutes and sustains the subject is not to claim that there is a singular matrix that acts in a singular and deterministic way to produce a subject as its effect" (p. 8). There is no 'masculinity' that intersects with 'blackness' to produce plurality. Pascoe (2007) refers to this as an industry of cataloguing types of difference, which fail to recognize the fluidity *within* the categories.

These intersections fail to encapsulate the intricacy within an identity; or the *blizzard* that surrounds an identity (Lesko, 2001). Francis (2010) states that these approaches "risk diminution of gender analysis to simplistic typologies of different 'sorts' of masculinity or femininity" (p. 477). These discussions misrepresent identities in their failure to encapsulate the fluidity and multiplicity *of masculinities*. Masculinity is already plural and fluid before its contact with other discourses. These structural understanding of intersections dismiss the role of the subject in the reiteration of discourses. Gender itself is inconstant.

Without heeding these discussions, education is responsible for maintaining gender hierarchies, limiting students, and perpetuating heteronormativity, in seeking to produce bodies in particular ways.

Quite the Production

Proponents of the boy crisis argue that boys are underachieving in school, particularly in literacy, and that education contributes to the feminization of boys (Griffin, 2000). Solutions to the perceived achievement gap involve making curriculum and books more 'boy friendly', or increasing the amount of male teachers within schools (Griffin, 2000). Sommers (2003) furthers this hype by stating that boys are being systematically disadvantaged. She calls for a 'return' to developmental discourses claiming that a turn to child-centered, progressive practices has caused the boy crisis. This is an ingenious production, as it blames child-centered, progressive practices, which in my understanding are still underused compared to 'traditional' teacher/curriculum centered approaches. By blaming these approaches before they are even taken up, it reinscribes an already privileged practice and a privileged, idealized identity. In turn, the public panic surrounding this 'crisis' has led to a misappropriation of educational resources and curricular reform.

Understudy

Under the reign of gendered and developmental discourses, the particular student is ignored. Instead, students are educated according to fabricated ideas surrounding who the student is supposed to be. In turn, such discourses regulate and produce that which they use to fuel their own rationale. By that I mean, educating 'the boys' as such, potentially produces 'boys'. I am not suggesting that discourses are deterministic; Connell (1995/2005) declares that few men actually meet 'hegemonic standard'. However, the standard remains that to which all male bodies are viewed. These discourses obscure the way we see. Our readings of the body are always gendered; our recognitions are limited by gender norms. The way we see, and the performances we recognize as male or female, are impacted by dominant discourses. A male body acting masculine is not only recognized as such, but is used to uphold the discourses of masculinity. Alternately, a female acting 'masculine' may go unnoticed as we are unwilling to recognize these performances (Francis, 2010). I do not say this to suggest that all boys are successfully socialized as 'more active', rather their bodies are read as such, even when a female classmate beside them may be similar in character—these behaviors are noticed in the boys because they are expected. Such observations, in conjunction with the expectations placed on male bodies, reify the dominant notions about boys. This is limiting for both male and female students.

The result is privilege. Bodies that perform according to the marker are privileged, while others may be marked as unintelligible (Butler, 1990). The production of identities through these discourses can "do more harm than good" (Vagle, this volume, p. 22). Both developmental and gendered discourses regulate and produce that which they use to fuel their own rationale. The naturalized catch is that students are socialized according to these discourses, tested to see how well this has been achieved, and subsequently the results of the tests are used to make declarative statements about the nature of the groups.

Cookie Cutter

The proof of the supposed inequality between boys and girls rests in standardized tests; test scores are published in popular papers and websites fueling public cries for change (Weaver-Hightower, 2003). However, gender generalized statistics are extremely misleading as they ignore the fact that many boys do rank high. As Weaver-Hightower (2003) points out, the generalized way in which 'boys' are looked at in relation to test scores often results in a channeling of funds to the white, middle-upper-class boy. This is a striking irony since testing privileges those with cultural capital, which in the North American context means those who are white, male, middle class and straight (Lesko, 2001). Yet, as these are the parents who are most vocally responsive to the alarm of the boys 'underachieving', funds and resources are 'redirected' at a group that is already privileged, instead of looking at the particular boys who are underachieving. The generic category 'boy' is used to encompass a racially, ethnically, culturally, socioeconomically diverse group of students. These homogenizing statistics are misleading (Titus, 2004). As Connell (2009) declares of gender differences themselves, there is more overlap than difference in the test results (Epstein et al., 1998). Drawing on a plethora of authors, Titus (2004) states that any gender disparity in test scores may only be in relation to white boys and girls. Rather than gender, socioeconomic status, race and ethnicity are major factors that contribute to disparities in test scores. Misinformed cries of gender inequality ignore systemic privileges, such as the wage gap, classroom attention and access to jobs, that reveal that 'boys', writ large, are not underachieving in society (Weaver-Hightower, 2003). Unfortunately, these test results do nothing to interrogate the category of boy, or the very marker that is being used to define achievement—the tests themselves.

Too Sweet for Me

All of this is done without ever questioning the epistemological underpinning of 'boy', or by responding to the commonly asked question, *which boys?* Boys' underachievement is based on a developmental understanding of 'boy' and is reinforced by a standardized understanding of achievement—also reflective of developmental discourses. This 'boy crisis' is indicative of a larger issue with the naturalized notions of identity, and markers of achievement, that prevail in education.

Standardized tests are misleading as a marker of achievement as they uphold a particular understanding of intelligence and are culturally biased; in turn, particular identities and learning styles are privileged (Weaver-Hightower, 2003). Further, they do not represent particularities in relation to learning, as they place a final expectation on what all students should have learned at a particular point. The crisis should not be surrounding the students, rather the narrow definitions schools use to define intelligence. Within these standardized tests there is no room for multiple understandings of achievement or intelligence. In the particularly media rich context, it is shocking to think that an examination of rote knowledge still defines our understanding of intelligence. Beyond issues of validity in relation to standardized tests are the ways in which the statistics are read in order to provoke public reaction through misinformation about boys' achievement in schools. Differences between boys and girls are constructed by choosing to read the results according to this binary. A more critical analysis of the test statistics should consider intersections of identity such as race, class and sexuality—or rather challenge the validity of the tests themselves.

The rhetoric and reforms surrounding test results exemplify the dominant gendered discourses that are operating in education, and reveals the way in which adolescents are receiving an education *in* gender. Instead, the 'turn' in education should not be towards the boys, rather, as Vagle (this volume) suggests, towards a particularized curriculum. This entails responding to students within context, as opposed to an image of students. In particular, challenging the 'boy' that precedes curricular resources, pedagogical strategies, and statistics. While recognizing that we can never be fully cognizant of the subtle, mundane ways in which we produce gender, teachers and students need to make gender an overt subject within the classroom rather than a hidden force of regulation. This means calling attention to the ways in which our talk, our interactions, and the media and curricular resources with which we engage are always already gendered.

Monday Morning

Teaching is unpredictable and unknowable (Britzman, 2000). Following Loutzenheiser (2001, 2005) pedagogy should be messy and responsive to the uncertainties of the classroom. As is evidenced in the reforms suggested in response to the 'boy crisis', there is a rush to find practical solutions, or the 'correct technique'. This does not allow space for conflict, difference, or the unimagined. There is no singular theory for understanding the complexities of the classroom (Ellsworth, 1989). Standardized/gendered curriculum does a disservice to students as it imagines a generic student, ignores the diversity of responses that arise within each classroom, supposes we can dictate what students learn, and limits the possibilities for new iterations of gender.

Rather than creating curriculum for boys, Weaver Hightower (2003) suggests making masculinity a subject in the curriculum. I concur, and suggest that this should be a curriculum of gender. This would entail making overt, to the extent that we can, the subtle ways in which gender operates in our society. As I experienced with my own classroom, many students come to the pedagogical space with varying assumptions and understandings surrounding the term *gender*. For example, often when I sought to discuss gender norms in relation to the literature, media, or curricula with which we were engaging, students immediately confronted these discussions as 'feminist'. Some students heard the term gender as being only about/for women rather than a way in which to consider how normative understandings of gender operate in relation to all bodies. As I was unaware of these assumptions, this often intervened and curbed our conversations. It is important to begin any discussion of gender with the way in which students understand this very term.

My students' reading of the term gender, most certainly had to do with my own gendered identity, as female. The assumptions/alignments that we make as a result of bodies are also important to trouble within the classroom space. In my experience, I have found students resistant to the notion that male/female behaviors might not be natural. In these cases, I have found discussions of various cultural understandings of masculinities and femininities a productive way to engage with the notion of gender as a social construction rather than a 'natural fact'. In a very unscripted, messy moment in my Social Studies class, a student spoke of the way in which men in 'his culture' freely touched one another, held hands, and hugged. This prompted a deluge of other examples from students about performances and norms of masculinities and femininities in their various cultures. This example not only served to challenge naturalist understandings of sex/gender, but also the scriptability of teaching/learning and the authority of teacher. As is evidenced in the unscripted pedagogical example above, conversations of gender are never simply that. They are not only messy in their unpredictability, but also in the way that they are always also conversations of race, ethnicity, class and sexualities (Loutzenheiser, 2001).

As stated throughout this chapter, we should be working towards creating an education of gender rather than in gender. This reframes the 'boy crisis' as one that puts the term 'boy' in crisis. This is a direct challenge to developmental and gendered discourses that approach students as gendered beings on the path to adulthood. Fluidity, unknowability, and incompleteness, are terms that apply to both identities and pedagogy. It seems that if educators can acknowledge these three terms in relation to both their teaching and their students, we might create space for reimagining both.

References

Britzman, D. P. (2000). "The question of belief": Writing poststructural ethnography. In E. A. S. Pierre & W. S. Pillow (Eds.), *Working the ruins: Feminist poststructural theory and methods in education* (pp. 27-40). New York: Routledge.

Butler, J. (1990). *Gender trouble: feminism and the subversion of identity*. London: Routledge.

———.(1993). *Bodies that matter: On the discursive limits of sex*. London: Routledge.

Connell, R. W. (1995/2005). *Masculinities (2nd ed.)*. Berkeley: University of California Press.

———. (1996). Teaching the boys: New research on masculinities, and gender strategies for schools. *Teachers College Record 98*(2), 207-236.

———.(2009). Gender: In *world perspective* (2nd ed.), Cambridge, UK: Polity Press.

Dalley-Trim, L. (2007). 'The boys' present...hegemonic masculinity: A performance of multiple acts. *Gender and Education, 19*(2), 199-217.

Ellsworth, E. (1989). Why doesn't this feel empowering? Working through the repressive myths of critical pedagogy. *Harvard Educational Review, 59*(3), 297-324.

Epstein, D., Elwood, J., Hey, V., & Maw, J. (Eds.). (1998). *Failing boys? Issues in gender and achievement*. Buckingham, UK: Open University Press.

Fausto-Sterling, A. (2002). The five sexes: Why male and female are not enough. In C. Williams & A. Steing (Eds.), *Sexuality and Gender* (pp. 468-473). London: Blackwell.

Foster, V., Kimmel, M., & Skelton, C. (2001). "What about the boys?" An overview of the debates. In W. Martino & B. Meyenn (Eds.), *What about the boys? Issues of masculinity in schools* (pp. 1-23). Philadelphia, PA: Open University Press.

Francis, B. (2010). Re/theorising gender: Female masculinity and male femininity in the classroom? *Gender and Education, 22*(5), 477-490.

Griffin, C. (2000). Discourses of crisis and loss: Analysing the 'boys' underachievement' debate. *Journal of Youth Studies, 3*(2), 167-188.

Gurian, M. (2001). *Boys and girls learn differently! A guide for teachers and parents*. San Francisco: Jossey-Bass.

Husain, M., & Millimet, D. (2008). The mythical 'boy crisis'? *Economics of Education Review*, 1-11. doi:10.1016/j.econedurev.2007.11.002

Kehler, M. (2007). Hallway fears and high school friendships: The complications of young men (re)negotiating heterosexualized identities. *Discourse: Studies in the Cultural Politics of Education, 28*(2), 259-277.

Lancaster, R. (2003). *The trouble with nature: Sex in science and popular culture*. Berkeley: University of California Press.

Lesko, N. (2001). *Act your age: A cultural construction of adolescence*. New York: Routledge.

———. (2002). Making adolescence at the turn of the century: Discourse and the exclusion of girls. *Current Issues in Comparative Education, 2*(2), 182-191.

Loutzenheiser, L. W. (2001). If I talk about that, they will burn my house down. In K. Kumashiro (Ed.), *Troubling intersections of race and sexuality: Queer youth of colour and anti-racist, anti-heterosexist education* (pp. 195-215). New York: Rowman & Littlefield.

———. (2005). Working fluidity, materiality and the educational imaginary: A case for contingent primacy. *Journal of Canadian Association of Curriculum Studies, 3*(2), 27-40.

Mac an Ghaill, M. (1994). *The making of men: Masculinities, sexualities and schooling.* Philadelphia: Open University Press.

Martino, W. (2008) The Lure of hegemonic masculinities: Investigating the dynamics of gender relations in male elementary school teachers' lives. *International Journal of Qualitative Studies in Education, 21*(6), 575-603.

Newcomb, A. (August, 2000). Back seat boys. *Christian Science Monitor,* 92(175), 13.

Pascoe, C. J. (2007). *Dude, you're a fag: Masculinity and sexuality in high school.* Berkeley: University of California Press.

Sommers, C. H. (2000). *The war against boys: How misguided feminism is harming our young men.* New York: Simon & Schuster.

Titus, J.J. (2004). Boy trouble: Rhetorical framing of boys' underachievement' *Discourse: Studies in the Cultural Politics of Education, 25*(2), 145-169.

Vagle, M. D. (this volume). Trying to poke holes in Teflon: Developmentalism; young adolescence; and contingent, recursive growth and change. In M. D. Vagle (Ed.), *Not a stage! A critical re-conception of young adolescent education* (pp. 11-38). New York: Peter Lang Publishing

Weaver-Hightower, M. (2003). The "boy turn" in research on gender and education. *Review of Educational Research, 73*(4), 471-498.

Chapter 4

Always Becoming, Never Enough: Middle School Girls Talk Back

Hilary Hughes-Decatur

So there I was, sitting in this all-you-can-eat-pizza joint with six middle school girls at 6:00p.m. on a Tuesday night: a table full of teen magazines, caffeinated and sugar-filled beverages, and all the pizza and dessert one could ever want. Sounds like a dream date, doesn't it? It was for me. This would be the night, I decided, where *I*, the adult/researcher who was older and had more life experience than these twelve-year-old girls, would set the pace and tone of the *structured* bodytalk the girls and I would have—*not them*. Thinking I was being developmentally responsive to this group of girls who were participating in my research study, I would use magazines, food, and the camaraderie we had formed over the past few months to strategically manipulate them into some sort of bodied-conversation that had a protocol—a focus group, if you will, about how they experienced moments when someone or something told them they were not enough *of something* in their physical or lived bodies (e.g., not-pretty-enough, thin-enough, athletic-enough, English-speaking-enough, wealthy-enough, white-enough, smart-enough, feminine-enough, etc.). I would finally get these twelve-year-old girls, who seemed so astute at evading my previous attempts to interview them individually or in pairs, to participate in some kind of bodytalk about this phenomenon I had named and was researching, *bodily-not-enoughness.*[1]

I had been meeting with the six girls for over three months, once a week for about 2 hours each week as a writing group, and it was only after this night—or really, after *writing* about this night of pizza and bodytalk—that I realized just how *stuck* the traditions of adolescent developmentalism were to the bottom of my adult-teacher-researcher shoes. I was able to see that my "developmentally responsive"/manipulative ways were closing me off to learning both alongside and from the girls in my study. In the pages that follow, then, taking up one of Vagle's (this volume) three pleas to educators of young adolescents—*to move from a developmentally responsive vision to a contingent and recursively relational vision*—I share with you some *Aha* moments I experienced as I worked diligently to remain open to and understand the girls in my study. I describe some of the problematic origins of *adolescence* and how its traditions have become quite an adhesive that seems to be stuck to the bottom of America's shoes. I discuss *openness* as Gadamer (1960) refers to it and describe how I had to work doggedly to practice this openness when creating the multi-voiced found poem, "Ubiquitous Bodytalk" that I draw on in this chapter. Finally, I use the poem to illustrate the profound bodytalk the girls were always, already engaging in before any adult asked them to; and I suggest that if *we*—as adults, educators, and researchers—really begin interrogating our own assumptions about adolescent developmentalism like Vagle (this volume) asks of us, perhaps those constricted boxes 10 to 15 year-olds are commonly put in can be opened up and rethought so that *we*—the adults—can begin learning from and alongside *them*—the kids.

The Stickiness of Adolescence

In the early 20th century G. Stanley Hall published two volumes, each containing over 1300 pages, which proposed a working (and apparently sticking) definition of "adolescence," informed by "selective evolutionary and psychoanalytic ideas of Darwin and Freud" (Saltman, 2005, p. 16). Hall posited that adolescence was a crucial period of individual development "in which the individual's development replayed the development of the human species from primitive savage early humans to civilized White Europeans" (Saltman, 2005, p. 16). The phrase "storm and stress," when referring to young adolescents, came from Hall's argument that "all young people go through some degree of emotional and behavioral upheaval before establishing a more stable equilibrium in adulthood" (Arnett, 2006, p. 186). This is just one of G. Stanley's brilliant ideas that I spend much of my time trying to disrupt when working with preservice middle grades education students, because the notion that human beings only experience some degree of emotional and behavioral upheaval during the time period of *adolescence* has become such a 'truth' in education and popular culture discourse, that many think once they graduate from *adolescence,* they have no need to acknowledge their own continued "stormed and stressed" lives.

Hall's original notions of how youth moved through certain developmental stages (of course, with his added belief that some [white boys] would move up the 'chain of being' faster than others [white girls], while others [children of color] could *never* reach 'true' civility) were taken up by psychologists, sociologists, and education theorists over the past 100 years, leaving little room to think about *adolescence* as a social, historical, and cultural construction. This is how I envision adolescence as it is taken up in popular culture and a majority of educational discourses: time has shaped adolescence in a certain way, and adolescence has brought all of its encounters with it as it has continuously been shaped by those encounters over time. But *we*—educators, psychologists, social workers, parents, policy makers—are not privy to all of the encounters adolescence has had with various theorists in multiple fields over time, so we may not know all of the history (Gadamer, 1960) stuck to its surface, leaving little room for *adolescence* to have new encounters, to be considered in ways differently than it has been considered in years past.

Numerous scholars[1] have written about American youth in ways that disrupt existing bodies of knowledge that keep young adolescents and even more, young adolescents of color, boxed up in those confining and restrictive ways most familiar to G. Stanley and his motley crew of chauvinists. Lesko (1996), for example, has done fabulous work trying to re-envision how we construct youth by suggesting that adolescents are kept "socially young" because of the chronological ages assigned to them.

By encapsulating adolescents in this age-structuring system, Lesko (1996) argues we keep them timeless or "always becoming" during their adolescent years, so they are "both imprisoned in their time (age) and out of time (abstracted), and thereby denied power over decisions or resources" (p. 456). The work I did to understand the girls in my study differently—through contingent and recursive relational ways-of-being—constantly reminded and challenged me to not encapsulate them in the age-structuring system Lesko referred to; and it was extremely difficult, because developmentalism was always lingering over my shoulder, wanting me to shove the girls back into those developmental boxes from which they came.

Gadamer's Prejudice and My–isms of Development

Gadamer (1960) theorized beautifully about practicing openness to learn something new, to learn the 'otherness' of something. He posited that we "cannot stick blindly to our own fore-meaning about the thing if we want to understand the meaning of another" (p. 268). This does not mean we should try and forget all of the fore-meaning tied to our knowing, of course; just that we remain open to the meaning of the other person or text while always situating that meaning "in relation to the whole of our own meanings or ourselves in relation to it" (p. 268). Practicing openness is not an effortless act, mind you; it is actually a rather excruciating attempt to accomplish the impossible. And the consequences of practicing Gadamer's approach to openness are quite radical, even if it does not seem so on first thought, because we are "less emancipated from values and other pre-suppositions in our society than we would like to admit" (Dahlberg, Dahlberg, & Nystrom, 2008, p. 76).

Trying to remain open in order to understand the 'otherness' of something or someone, according to Gadamer (1960), involves the acknowledgement of one's own fore-meanings and prejudices, because "it is the tyranny of hidden prejudices that makes us deaf to what speaks to us in tradition" (p. 270). We have prejudices and fore-meanings which occupy our consciousness, and because they are not at our free disposal, we cannot separate in advance "the productive prejudices that enable understanding from the prejudices that hinder it and lead to misunderstandings" (p. 295). Until I did some thoughtful self-interrogation, I was not aware of the traditions that were taking up residency in my consciousness—traditions of developmentalism within the discourse of *adolescence*—so I could not separate the productive from the unproductive and I was temporarily stuck in misunderstanding. It did not occur to me, for example, to interrogate my actions or thinking when it came to putting developmentalism on the girls when I was with them, because I was no traditionalist! I had read and agreed with plenty of critical theorists who disrupted the developmental theories dominating educational discourse; and I had even published work trying to interrupt some of the grand narrative of developmentalism attached to young adolescent girls' bodies, so why would I need to check myself?

Foregrounding my own prejudice (i.e., thinking the girls were not capable of something because I was only seeing them through developmentalism) required suspending its validity for me; and as long as my mind was influenced by that prejudice, I could not consider it a judgment, so how could I foreground it if it was still influencing my consciousness? Gadamer (1960) argued that it is impossible for one to become aware of a prejudice while it constantly operates unnoticed; understanding begins only when that prejudice is *provoked*, when it addresses us. In order to provoke my own prejudice, to practice that level of openness, I had to write, re-write, talk, think, and question my way through all of my frustrations with not being able to "make" the girls talk about bodies how I thought they should talk about bodies, and I eventually came to understand that traditions of developmentalism were working on me.

"Ubiquitous Bodytalk"

To illustrate how those traditions of developmentalism sometimes worked on me, I created a multi-voiced found poem rather than using traditional data excerpts, because it allowed me to represent a more creative visual representation of the conversation at the pizza place. I strategically spaced the girls' lines apart from one another to create a visual representation of moments when multiple girls talked simultaneously and how many girls participated in the conversation at any given moment. For example, Paloma's lines are always on the far left margin of the right side of the page; Alice's lines are 5 spaces after Paloma's; Buttercup's 10 spaces after Paloma's, and so on. By placing myself on the far left side of the page, just on the crux of the girls' conversation on the far right side of the page, I aimed to visually represent how, as an adult and a researcher, *I* was many times on the margins of my own study. In a "multi-voiced" or "double-voiced" poem, the speakers' lines are set horizontally parallel on the right and left sides of the page if they are thinking/saying something at the same time; if there is a vertical space in between the lines on the right and left side of the page, then one speaker is saying/thinking something and 'right after' the other is saying/thinking something. In these first lines, for example, I am on the left side telling the girls I brought the pictures I took of them, and then Paloma said, "Oh, I hate that picture; I look so fat." Right after I said, "Look, pictures of you!

Look, pictures of you!	
	Oh, I hate that picture
	I look so fat
You're joking, right?	
	No
	I look so ugly
	I look
	I look
Who *ARE* You?	I look pale
	I like the second one
	I look like I'm only
	half of me
To the magazines then	
	J-14?
	But first I have to say some
	thing—
But not right now—	
I'm just sayin'	
we're not doing that right now	
...but... go ahead—	
	They just need me all
	through this magazine
	I like that shirt: "mind, body,
	spirit"—we're going to be talking
	about our mind and our bodies
	Girls, I notice, are comfortable
	talking about their bodies
	around girls their age
	or like, someone they trust,
	they know well
Wait, what now?	

	Girls, *most girls*, are comfortable talking about their bodies around girls their age or people they trust or are close to but no one else like, seriously. Or, older people who they trust.
I agree.	
	Are we a sorority? Are we the Purple Flowers sorority?
	But we're really close so we're OK with it-- But bring in somebody else somebody who's not close, it's like the conversation stops and we're like, *Nice weather we're having*
	We should go sign that wall as a sorority
What wall?	
	There, where other famous people have signed it Wait, are we famous now? I feel famous sometimes; I should be famous I will be famous one day We know We know We know
I'm going for seconds	
	I wish I could just get a plate and stop eating

<table>
<tr><td></td><td>I need to go running tomorrow
What are you talkin'
about?
I don't even have running shoes
I'm not a runner</td></tr>
<tr><td>And you have to go run?</td><td></td></tr>
<tr><td></td><td>I'm not a sports person
I don't like sweating</td></tr>
<tr><td>Then why do you have to run tomorrow?</td><td></td></tr>
<tr><td></td><td>I want to go for a run
I gotta go to Rack Room
and buy me some shoes</td></tr>
<tr><td>Why do you want to go for a run if you hate sports?</td><td></td></tr>
<tr><td></td><td>I know, I hate sports too
I just like to feel my heart
This is so buttery</td></tr>
<tr><td>This is buttery deliciousness</td><td>Really good
This food is deliciousness
because I like to eat
This is the most pizza</td></tr>
<tr><td>That's what it's for
it's an all you can eat buffet
you gotta get your money's worth</td><td></td></tr>
<tr><td>Mmmm, new kind of pizza to try:
veggie</td><td></td></tr>
<tr><td></td><td>I'm not a vegetable person-
only carrots and ranch
One of my 100 things to do before I die:
try every single food in the world
or at least America
Except for dog. I will never eat dog.</td></tr>
<tr><td>This little thing is probably my fa-</td><td></td></tr>
</table>

vorite	
	What? The butter?
Soaked in butter Cinnamon heart attacks	
	Now y'all got me scared to eat 'em
Just don't eat a whole pan of them you'll have a heart attack— If you eat four you'll be just fine	
	Man, she ate more than four that girl, she ate like thirteen of 'em I'm good. I'm done.
I was making that number up I've had like *twenty* so you're fine and you're resilient your hearts are just *pumpin'* that blood	
	OK, let's begin our session now
Our *session*?	
	But let me say something—
Actually, can I? Since I never really get to say any- thing? Can I have a turn? These magazines— they're to start some kind of conversation	Can we have the posters?
Huh?	Can we have the posters? I was going to ask you that question.

Yeah, but not right this second—	
for now—what I'd like to do—	
maybe you could close those for a	
second?	
I thought we could talk about body	
stuff—	
we can look through the magazines	
and just have a conversation about—	
like—	
what kinds of bodies are what kind	
represented—	
what kind of images—	
what type of bodies—	
Know what I mean?	
	You know what I've noticed?
No, no, hold on—	
So what I want y'all to do is just look	
through them--	Do you see what she's
see what you notice	wearing in here?
Listen, listen	
Who's in [the magazine]?	
Who's not?	
How does it all affect you?	
Does it?	
Like do you ever look at some of	
those pictures and think	
Oh, I wish I looked like that	Oh, I wish I was her, *sure*
	Yes, yes, *of course*
	Or, I hope I *don't*
	look like that
And we'll have a serious	
conversation so if one person is talk-	I wouldn't want that dress
ing just allow her to talk,	Do you see her
don't interject—	hair?
A protocol,	Horrible

we can try a protocol just letting one person talk— no side stories	I hate Justin Bieber I am so with you— he's so— Yeah, Justin Bieber looks good but he has a squeaky voice-- He sings like a girl—Oh my gosh, the first time I ever heard Justin Bieber…
You're in a side story right now	
	Oh right, you'll have to tape my mouth shut, sorry.
No, you can talk, as long as it's about what's— Did y'all watch the Oscars the other night?	
	That's a side story
Well, it was about bodies	
	Oh, right.
"Kim Kardashian's personal story about her struggle to be proud of her booty"	
	Oh, I love Kim Kardashian I know, I love her
She has issues with her butt?	
	Yeah, she got it smaller she used to have like— a big butt
She had surgery to get her butt smaller?	
	Yeah, she just had, like a butt, you know, a butt Y'all know Nicki Minaj gets shots, like steroids injected into her butt,

	makes it bigger
So, what could be wrong with that?	
	She used to have, she had, she still, that's why J-Lo has a bigger one than her, She used to have, Like, you don't wanna see that thing
But why? What's wrong with that?	
	I don't know Who, Nicki? getn' steroids injected into her butt to make it bigger Oooo, I heard Nicki got um— AIDS Yeah
	Every time they take pictures of girls they're always posing it's fake they're never just hanging out in a little kid photo. No, they're posing, like— and they have impossible clothes. Would you wear that?
But that's like the model pose	
	They pose in every maga- zine Well it's not natural I wish I were her
You wish you were her?	
	Yeah, because every time she gains weight she goes on a diet she loses it

So what, she gains weight and then loses it quickly?	
	Yeah, you don't even see it
Well then how do you know she gains weight?	
	Because of the pictures
So this is pretty cool: it doesn't seem like magazines do much for y'all, like with not-enoughness	
	And they rarely show people eating; you rarely see pictures like this unless they're advertising some food then they're eating stuff
Or they ask celebrities about their favorite foods	
When you're looking at all of this, do you ever look through and go, ewwww…	
	Of course, but then what? Yes, but I keep my opinions to myself I think a lot about the subject I do, when I'm in a bad— when I'm goin' through somethin' when I'm upset
But what about positive?	
	Oh, especially when it comes to hair I'll be like, my hair is so much better than hers.

	Everybody compliments my hair- that's why I always do the hair pose
You go through those pages and do what?	
	I only go through these pages Look at, compare the outfits think about how they would look on me
Do you?	
	Yeah Yeah Yeah Yeah, I would do that and second of all, I would be like that *does not* go with her body those shoes *do not* go with her skin Then I'll say, I'll never be caught dead in that dress that dress wouldn't complement my skin -my body Yeah, my body it wouldn't complement the shape of my body
Do you really? Are you just saying that?	
	I'm not just saying that I'm for real
I mean, I do that too	
	Whenever they show legs and stuff they're so skinny they make mines feel fat
Their legs?	

	Yeah, the legs some people have scars and stuff—me and my little sister other people have perfectly smooth—like they've never got a cut or never got bit by mosque- toes it's just not real
They're not real. Y'all know about airbrushing?	
	Yeh.
Everyone in here is probably not the original— If they took a picture of me and I had a zit they could just airbrush it out— they can change your whole body shape	
	Last year when we took our pictures if we wanted to buy them, they could take out your pimples, your, zits *Every* *thing*
Really?	
	Yeah, they take out your pimples and zits but if you have a cut across your face they won't take it out- what's the difference?
I've never heard of that for school pictures	
	And not only that they can take away a tiny little hair sticking out Yeah, take away all the hairs sticking out- It's called *retouching* They let you look at them first then you can go back and tell

	them what to fix I'm like, what's the point? To make me look normal?
What *is* normal for a body? What is that? What would that be?	
Earlier you asked how come they always talk about people gaining weight and not los ing—but my question is, How come they talk about people's weight *at all*? Why do we have to have conversa- tions about people gaining or losing weight? Like Jessica Simpson	I don't think there is a normal
	People sometimes be proud of their weight— if somebody a little out of their weight they proud of it so they wanna go and tell everybody
Sure. But in general, as a society, what do y'all consider a normal body?	Like not too fat, not too skinny
But what does that mean?	I think my body is nor- mal Like perfect, you know, on the scale from the doctor But if you're perfect, you're not normal, you're unique I wouldn't reflect it on weight I know Yeah

	Someone's own, like personality How you choose to be How they show people who they are
Like their sense of being in the world?	
	Yeah, how they show people how they are If they carry, like if they're depressed they carry themselves like— I think normal is basically, something, a normal body— they eat more, I guess, or sometimes less A normal body something that has unique stuff it has flaws it has everything flaws and the good stuff it's like positive and negative stuff if it has a mix of both, that's normal
Beautiful.	yeah because there is no such thing
But that's how you *want* bodies to be—where we live our culture and its obsession with bodies as you can see everywhere	That's why I'm going to Siberia

you go in every commercial	In every magazine, mmm-hmmm
If you watch TV for 30 minutes diet commercials beauty product commercials How come there aren't ever people who aren't considered— who aren't this thin?	
	Except for Precious, people big as Precious
I saw her on the cover of a magazine today	They're either going to have people that big or that small they don't have nobody normal except for Lane Bryant commercials
What do people say about Precious then?	She's big
I wonder if that will get to her soon	
	She don't understand they either like skinny people or big people they don't have normal people
Which is really normal	Yes They don't like that kind of size
...beautiful, curvy women	
	Yeah, curvy women They just leave stuff out they leave stuff out, man Or what about JC Pen- nys the women's sec- tion women's plus sizes that's the only time

	they'll show bodies like that I know, the plus size clothes, they make it ugly but they're making people who are overweight feel bad
In our country, the plus size is considered overweight in other countries that's normal a normal body go to Europe Mexico talk to people they say Americans are too thin we're obsessed with thin bodies	
	It's true Yeah, it is
Our plus sizes are other country's normal bodies	
	Plus size isn't really people who are fat I was thinking people are like walnuts people should think about other people like walnuts we should not only care about the shell we should think about what's on the inside
But how do we do that? when there's *this* everywhere— when people are obsessed and there are these magazines and people keep buying them	

over and over they keep seeing these types of bodies only these bodies represented they'll continue to think that's normal, some of them	
	Not me man it makes me feel horrible I mean, really seeing skinny bodies everywhere
Too skinny, really? Because all of you sitting at this table would be considered too thin	
	Me?
You? Yes, you are skinny.	
	I'm not too thin. I'm not even skinny.
	What if we did what she did in *13 going on 30*? You know, how she decides to change the image of her magazine—She uses the people she graduated high school with they are the models for her magazine *real* people with *real* bodies
So, do y'all ever hear your teachers talking about this stuff we're talking about in any way?	
	In P.E.?
Not P.E. Well, in any class— Do you read novels or talk about bodies in any way?	
	Not really

	I mean, the stu- dents do--like they'll judge peo- ple if they're fat or skinny like if they were fat they'd be like, I'm not gonna be your friend
What?	
	Exactly. There are some people that are *obsessed* with per- fection
Remember me telling y'all about the 8th grade girls I was hanging out with from your school who were cutting?	
	That's just going to make it worse I have had way too much sugar to- day I've had way too much food I've had too much Sprite— I'm *way* hyper! I don't feel too good...

Table 1: Ubiquitous bodytalk found poem

Contingent and Recursive Visions of Possibility

As I wrote different drafts of the poem, referring back to the transcripts, the recording of the meeting, and the notes from my research journal, I noticed that the words and phrases I was choosing directly from the data for the poem highlighted adequately just how inconsequential I was to the bodytalk that was always, already taking place when we met, needing no help from me or my developmentally responsive (or manipulative) ways. In the first few lines of the poem, for instance, I expected to 'tell' the girls about the magazines I brought and how *I* wanted them to talk about the magazines; but even before I tried to 'make' them stop talking (which I actually never did), they were already looking at and talking about the magazines, about the bodies in the magazines, and about their own bodies—all, of course, at the same time.

Buttercup acknowledged that "they needed her all through that magazine," while flipping through and observing the different teen models they had chosen for the magazine; Paloma spotted a shirt in another magazine ad that connected her to bodies and our bodytalk ("I like that shirt: mind, body, spirit: we're going to be talking about our mind and our bodies"); and Alice promptly began thinking out loud about how she was comfortable talking about bodies, only because she was in the safe-space the girls and I created together—that supplementary space we called our writing group. I want to point out, however, that Alice had to *repeat* what she said about how girls are comfortable talking about their bodies around other girls, because I was too busy trying to "make" the girls do what I thought they should be doing and did not hear her beautiful comment the first time: "Girls, *most girls*, are comfortable talking about their bodies around girls their age, or people they trust, or are close to, but no one else; like, seriously. Or, older people who they trust."

A similar scenario took place later in the conversation when I attempted a re-direct from the food-consumption-surveillance a few of us had just participated in about some cinnamon sticks to some kind of structured magazine conversation, and Blossom—to shift the attention away from Sunshine's comment about how many cinnamon sticks Blossom ate—said she was ready to begin our "session." This was the first time I heard the girls refer to my attempts at structured conversations around bodies as a "session," and I think the word, itself, illustrates fabulously how *inauthentic* those structured conversations could have felt for the girls. The fact that Blossom (and later others) referred to my attempts at structuring our bodytalk as "sessions" helped me (eventually) see that she (and the others) might feel as if she was in some kind of adult/child, therapist/patient, teacher/student power relation—a developmentally oriented power relation *I thought* I had worked so hard against when I met with the girls.

While I was busy telling the girls when to talk and not talk about bodies, they were having a brilliant discussion, reminding me later when I was typing the transcripts, that if I would have just stopped talking and listened *differently*, I could have heard so much more than I ever might have during some structured question/answer "session." From Kim Kardashian's 'booty reduction,' to Nicki Minaj's 'booty enlargement,' there was not much in between that the girls missed: all the while, I was on the margins either participating awkwardly or trying to manipulate the conversation, finding neither technique effective. Trying to be developmentally responsive and "make" the girls act in a way that I thought they *should* act (not interrupting each other; taking turns and listening to one another talk), or structure their talk how *I thought* it should be structured, I was assuming I knew the "developmental readiness, needs, and interests of young adolescents," a concept at the heart of middle level education (NMSA, 2010, p. 5).

I could not see the *adolescents* Lesko (2001) and Vagle (this volume) ask us to see when I was with the girls that night. Because my unchecked prejudice of developmentalism worked on my consciousness and blocked my understanding, I perceived the girls' actions as *just* adolescence, rather than taking up the contradictions of adolescence as being *simultaneously* "mature and immature, old and young, traditional and innovative" (Lesko, 2001, p. 196). I worked really hard, however, to practice Gadamer's (1960) openness later on while writing and re-writing my way through my analysis of the developmentalism I was putting on them so I could reach a *new understanding*. Vagle (2011) reminds us that Lesko's (2001) use of the word *simultaneously* to describe some of the contradictions young adolescents face is not intended to describe adolescence as a tumultuous time in life. "Instead, she was trying to dislodge a time-bound, unidirectional conception of growth and change and forward a contingent (i.e., profoundly contextual and dependent) and recursive (i.e., occurring over and over in and over time) conception" (p. 362). Remaking adolescence in this way, I was eventually able to 'see' how the girls were theorizing bodies, negotiating what "normal" bodies were for them, and how they understood so deeply how skewed the perception of bodies is in American culture. So many thoughtful ideas about what society does to bodies came from their bodytalk that night; and whenever I tried to "teach" them something about how bodies were disciplined or perceived, they in turn, taught me more, so that we were—in the poem—finding ourselves in relation to one another as we all struggled to continually learn and grow with and from each other (Vagle, this volume).

References

Aapola, S., Gonick, M., & Harris, A. (Eds.). (2005). *Young femininity: Girlhood, power and social change.* New York: Palgrave Macmillan.

Arnett, J. J. (2006). G. Stanley Hall's adolescence: Brilliance and nonsense. *History of Psychology, 9*(3), 186-197.

Brown, E.R., & Saltman, K.J. (Eds.). (2005). *The critical middle school reader.* New York: Routledge.

Dahlberg, K., Dahlberg, H., & Nystrom, M. (2008). *Reflective lifeworld research (2nd ed.).* Lund, Sweden: Studentlitteratur.

Fine, M. (1992). *Disruptive voices: The possibilities of feminist research.* Ann Arbor: University of Michigan Press.

Gadamer, H. G. (1998). *Truth and method (2nd revised ed).* (P. Siebeck, Trans.). New York: The Continuum Publishing Company. (Original work published 1960).

Giroux, H. A. (1998). Teenage sexuality, body politics, and the pedagogy of display. In J. S. Epstein (Ed.) *Youth culture: Identity in a postmodern world* (pp. 24-55), Malden, MA: Blackwell Publishers.

Giroux, H.A. (2009). *Youth in a suspect society: Democracy or disposability?* New York: Palgrave Macmillan.

Harris, A. (Ed.). (2004). *All about the girl: Culture, power and identity.* New York: Routledge.

Hughes, H.E. (2010). Fourteen is the new thirty: Adolescent girls, their bodies, and sexuality. In K. Lee & M. D. Vagle (Eds.), *Developmentalism in early childhood and middle grades education: Critical conversations on readiness and responsiveness* (pp. 149-156). New York: Palgrave McMillan.

———. (2011). *Phenomenal bodies, phenomenal girls: How young adolescent girls experience being enough in their bodies (Doctoral dissertation).* Available from ProQuest Digital Dissertations and Theses Database.

Lee, K., & Vagle, M. D. (Eds.). (2010). *Developmentalism in early childhood and middle grades education: Critical conversations on readiness and responsiveness.* New York: Palgrave Macmillan.

Lesko, N. (1996). Past, present, and future conceptions of adolescence. *Educational Theory, 46*(4), 453-472.

———. (2001). *Act your age! A cultural construction of adolescence.* New York: Routledge.

National Middle School Association (NMSA) (2010). *This we believe: Keys to educating young adolescents.* Westerville, OH: National Middle School Association.

Saltman, K. J. (2005). The construction of identity. In E. R. Brown & K. J. Saltman (Eds.), *The critical middle school reader* (pp. 237-244). New York: Routledge.

Vagle, M.D. (2011). Lessons in contingent, recursive humility. *Journal of Adolescent and Adult Literacy, 54*(5), 362-370.

———. (this volume). Trying to poke holes in Teflon: Developmentalism; young adolescence; and contingent, recursive growth and change. In M. D. Vagle (Ed.), *Not a stage! A critical re-conception of young adolescent education,* (pp. 11-38). New York:PeterLangPublishing.

Chapter 5

Reappraising "Juvenilia" as a Means of Re-Conceptualizing "Adolescence"

Zan Crowder

> *The second sister of Miss Alcott seems to think it was perfectly natural for children living in a Massachusetts hamlet in the first half of this century to write plays in fun that have all the bloodthirsty spirit and romantic symbolism of the old school melodrama, and to act the parts in them in those leisure hours when children might be better employed playing games of romp in the open air.* (Martin, 1994, p. iv)

The above quotation is a New York Times (11/5/1893) review of *Comic Tragedies* published in 1893 by Anna Alcott, five years after Louisa May Alcott's death. It references *Norna, or The Witch's Curse,* a play written by Louisa when she was fourteen years old and later adapted for a chapter in her novel *Little Women*. Reprinted in 1994 by the Juvenilia Press under the general editorship of Juliet McMaster, the play is indeed bloodthirsty and revolves around a young woman named Theresa who is forced to marry the evil Count Rodolpho and is subsequently imprisoned inside his castle. By the end of the first scene, Theresa has been stabbed to death onstage for refusing to reveal the whereabouts of her banished brother and a witch has appeared to curse the Count for his crime. The brother and the Count both resemble aspects of the Lord Byron persona, one, outcast and wandering, the other, dark and brooding.

It is a character trope that appears frequently in nineteenth-century *Juvenilia,* serving as a distinct literary marker for the times. The term juvenilia is a loose designation created by the publishing industry to indicate the writings of an author before reaching the full flower of artistic power. As a category, juvenilia is an arbitrary distinction established by authors and editors and treated by readers as a novelty that, if it has any value, is useful in tracing influences in a writer's artistic formation. In this respect, Byron is not unlike the pop culture figures of today who influence the dress, mannerisms and creative output of children. In the nineteenth century, Byron loomed large and young authors from Shelley to the Brontë children to the Tennyson brothers locate him within their work. His legendary personality is appropriated in many individual ways and is, I would argue, a terrific example of the dynamics between an overarching cultural force and the individual's response to such a phenomenon.[1] Because Alcott's reading of the Byron character is different from that of Shelley or Charlotte Brontë, he means different things to each of these young authors and his reference is personalized by each. Whatever influence he exerts, it is always fluid and contingent depending on authorial demands. In fact, the Byron character of Charlotte Brontë, the Duke of Zamorna, exhibits varying characteristics across the span of the Angrian Tales written throughout her teenage years. For Alcott in *Norna*, the character Rodolpho gets his just deserts and dies in agony at the final curtain.

The play *Norna* was written and enacted by the Alcott children for their personal amusement and the reading of it now is, on the one hand, quite entertaining due to its sheer audacity and verve. On the other hand, the glimpse it affords into the private lives of a soon to become illustrious family can seem disconcertingly voyeuristic, not unlike the feeling of watching behind-the-scenes reality shows which are so popular today. The tension between public and private is always present when one reads juvenilia and it is a central reason why the field is so rich for exploration. Quite often, an author's juvenilia was not written explicitly for publication and only appears, as Anna Alcott's collection does, after the author has achieved critical and commercial success. The juvenilia is then published and generally appraised critically through a particular lens that is necessarily backward looking. Through this lens, informed as it is by the author's "adult" work, the juvenilia is frequently found to be interesting solely because of its role in the author's coming to be.

This apprenticeship model depends entirely upon later, mature work that represents full artistic development and fits neatly into a linear, chronological timeline. This teleological progression coincides perfectly with the stages of life model that developmentalism has thrust upon us as educators. Both models emphasize the evolutionary trend toward perfectibility prevalent in so many modernist narratives. It is a harmonious view that presents progress as a straight path to completion or wholeness and which simultaneously seeks to universalize human experience without regard for how messy individual experience and its expression may actually be.[2] The view instantiates a permanent deficit model of childhood wherein youth and adolescents are necessarily incomplete because they must, according to the model, be lacking in something present in adults. What this something is appears mostly to be chronological/biological time on Earth without any reference to how such time has been spent.

In this essay I seek to align my argument for a reappraisal of juvenilia with Vagle's (this volume) plea for a contingently and recursively relational vision of young adolescents. His argument that educators should spend "more time seeing young adolescents in innumerable, lived (de-naturalized) contexts"(p. 20) coincides with my view that the category of juvenilia, a mirror image for the developmental definition of "adolescence", needs desperately to be troubled. The apprenticeship model, I argue, is just as much a cultural construction as adolescence, born, in fact, of the same circumstances and social forces and capable of blinding us to our own assumptions and power relations in the same ways. An interrogation of the literary apprenticeship model that stresses the situatedness—the present of the text—of a young writer is, as I see it, the same project presented in Vagle's plea for a contingent and recursive view of youth. At issue across these fields is the (re)definition of youth and a plea to reconsider the machinery that depersonalizes youthful voices and experiences.

It is my goal to challenge the linear model of juvenilia by proposing a view that takes the young writers at their word rather than binding them to their predetermined futures. Vagle (this volume) quotes Nancy Lesko who writes in *Act Your Age!: A Cultural Construction of Adolescence* that

> the evolutionary roots of adolescence impose a strong interest in the future over the present or the past; one eye is always on the ending, which spurs the documentation of movement or lack of it toward the desired characteristics. The temporal movement into the future is understood as linear, unidirectional, and able to be separated from the present and the past. (2001, p. 191)

Nowhere is this view so entrenched as in the traditional view of juvenilia. This view not only demands that the young writer be "this" so that he or she may become "that" but also ranks this and that in hierarchical order. It is the often troubling way in which policy makers and academics—and here I am implicated, as well—view the students with whom we work; as if they are merely practicing toward fulfillment rather than acting with autonomy and, dare I say, even skill.

In arguing for a contingent, relational view of juvenilia, I am suggesting that we explore the texts of young writers with an eye toward the personal negotiations of the authors, each struggling either independently or, as is often the case, collaboratively, to establish voices by which they might engage the outer world. These authors, as I will try to show, are not the innocents that developmentalists beginning with G. Stanley Hall would like to envision them. Often times their works are reflections of, resistances to, and negotiations with the dominant power structures that inform their lives. Although there is limited space here to explore the wide array of examples that such a topic deserves, it is my hope that the brief gloss given to a variety of authors will illustrate the kind of work that could be done.[3] A reconsideration of their works is a crucial undertaking, I believe, and can provide a tremendously useful analogy for the way that we (re)consider adolescents and, in the process, challenge the notions of standardized schooling as a one-size-fits-all industry, notions that arose and began to gain influence during the lives of these authors.[4]

Juvenilia and Adolescencen(TS)

A relevant question arises, then, as to how exactly those of us who are deeply committed to the education of our country's youth begin to reconstruct adolescence from the inside out? How do we approach these others, these shadows of ourselves, without bringing our (much more fully developed) assumptions and values into play? A reconsideration of juvenilia, based on contingency and the artistic expression of individual experience—albeit within the confines of cultural norms—might afford us the opportunity to re-imagine adolescence. Unlike social science research which seeks to report "student voices" as somehow empirically authentic, an investigation of juvenilia must necessarily acknowledge that it's subject is freighted with rhetorical posturing, normalizing stylistic conventions, contemporary fashion and diverse social relations. If we start from art, the calculus changes slightly. No longer are we concerned with truth but rather with exploration.

The texts of young writers are highly contextualized, dependent on class, status, race, gender, familial relationships, religiosity, political ethos, and numerous other factors within the "blizzard", as Lesko says, of socio-cultural influences swirling around the various authors. By investigating the ways in which these factors influence these authors, I insist that there is no standardized evolutionary formula that dictates their development and no predetermined stages through which each passes on his or her path to achievement. Rather, there are complex forces at work, coupled with individual action—here, the taking up of the pen—that allow these authors to become. While it is clear that the authors mentioned in this chapter all write from a position of relative privilege, most crucially with regard to educational opportunities, this fact should not negate the voices that they speak and the ways in which they interact with the world. While I am not attempting to downplay the critical role that privileged class and racial status play in the production of these writers' works, I also do not view it as a disqualifying factor. Quite simply we possess juvenilia today because these authors, even those whose families were not wealthy, came from social settings wherein their creative efforts were valued and supported, wherein they had the leisure time to produce artistic works and wherein a priority, however variable from writer to writer, was placed on the development of the intellect.[5]

The Contingency of Juvenilia

That said, it is be useful to present an overview of juvenilia in order to illustrate that the category, in and of itself, is as much a social construction as "adolescence". Although there is no consensus as to what constitutes such a category, the traditional definition in literary circles refers to some form of childhood writing and is applied to the writing that was executed by individuals who would later gain notoriety as adult writers. This second component is critical because juvenilia then suggests an immature level of development that evolves at some point into more sophisticated, polished and accomplished expression. In fact, the standard that applies when defining a piece as either "childhood" or "adult" writing is flexible; Charlotte

Brontë, born in 1816 was still writing her Angrian Tales in her early twenties and her first published work *Jane Eyre* was not produced until 1847 under the pseudonym of Currer Bell. The writings of Charlotte's brother, Branwell Brontë, are considered juvenilia up until age thirty-one whereas Percy Shelley had died by age thirty after publishing for twelve years, his first published work, *Zastrozzi*, appearing when he was eighteen (Alexander & McMaster, 2005). By fifteen, Samuel Clemens was writing newspaper articles that appeared in his brother's newspaper, in which he famously picked fights in print with competing newsmen while his brother was away on business (Twain, 1979). In one respect, this lack of definitional stability is encouraging. It allows a space for a reconsideration of youth and youthful expression without the strictures of chronological determinism. Indeed, the very term "juvenilia" might be seen as contingent. The real question is to the factors upon which its usage is contingent. In ways similar to the ideas explored by Lesko and Vagle regarding adolescence, the classification of juvenilia is often determined by those outside of the category. Still, its lack of an ossified determining structure suggests that there might be play within the field. Seen in another light, however, the very essence of juvenilia is over determined in that it serves wholly as an indicator of the heights to which the author would achieve...eventually.

In their seminal work on juvenilia, *The Child Writer from Austen to Woolf*, Christine Alexander and Juliet McMaster (2005) address this conundrum when they write, "We have chosen to consider works by writers up to twenty as our province, with some leeway beyond, though many of our writers are much younger" (p. 2). Further, Alexander and McMaster stress that although their consideration of juvenilia is generally dependent upon the greatness achieved by the authors at a later stage of life, they also acknowledge child writers such as Marjory Fleming (who died at age eight), Daisy Ashford (who penned a best-selling novel, *The Young Visitors*, at nine), and diarists Opal Whiteley and Iris Vaughan, all of whom produced only as children. Daisy Ashford's novel, published when the writer was thirty-six in 1919 and reprinted numerous times, includes a preface by J.M. Barrie who writes,

> The novelist will find the tale a model for his future work. How incomparably, for instance, the authoress dives into her story at once. How cunningly throughout she keeps us on the hooks of suspense, jumping to Mr. Salteena when we are in a quiver about Ethel, and turning to Ethel when we are quite uneasy about Mr. Salteena. This authoress of nine is flirting with her readers all the time. Her mind is such a rich pocket that as she digs in it (her head to the side and her tongue well out) she sends up showers of nuggets. There seldom probably was a novelist with such an uncanny knowledge of his characters as she has of Mr. Salteena. (1919, p. xiii)

While his praise smacks of condescension, Barrie is correct that the nine-year-old Ashford does demonstrate an awareness of sexual politics and social mannerisms that are uncomfortable to adult audiences accustomed to believe that their age gives them the exclusive privilege of adult knowledge.

The Young Visiters aside, the category of juvenilia has been the province of bibliophiles and ardent fans whose interest in the youthful writings of their favorite authors has appealed more to a collector's sense than anything else. Academically, the term "juvenilia" has been applied in a pejorative sense. The etiological relationship between juvenilia and juvenile is unfortunate. However, the two have historically been conflated much in the same way that adolescence has come to connote incompleteness or immaturity. William Michael Rossetti, in the preface to his 1900 edition of his sister Christina's poetry writes, "Section 4 (Juvenilia) is, of course, of less intrinsic worth than the other sections, but I am in hopes that it will count as not wholly uninteresting."(p. viii). His view sums up the general attitude toward writings by renowned authors while still in their youth. Like Alexander and McMasters he is also obliged to provide his own definition of juvenilia and the necessity of his doing so indicates one issue that is central to the problem of the genre as a whole. He writes, "I class among the Juvenilia all that the authoress wrote before attaining the full age of seventeen; all these things, and nothing else"(p. viii). Yet, his editorial decision is arbitrary. In general, the term "juvenilia" is simply meant to connote immaturity when compared with a writer's later works. This connotation, I argue, is highly subjective and relies much more on the literary marketplace and the writer's relation to it than to any particular age or stage of maturity. It doesn't seem over reaching to make the comparison between this literary phenomenon and the arbitrary, hierarchical definitions by which we circumscribe students through grade assignments, grade-level measures, and aptitude tests.

In a special edition of *Romantic Circles* centered on Percy Bysshe Shelley, Donald H. Reiman writes that "most biographers either laughed or frowned at his youthful enthusiasms, and several editors chose to exile his early poetry—including even "Queen Mab"—to the backs of their editions under the damning heading of 'Juvenilia'" (1997, p. 1). It is easy to hear in the words of Rossetti and of Reiman the echoes of a long-established developmental discourse whose hierarchical structures invalidate the words, thoughts and actions of those within particular biological and chronological boundaries. Again there is an emphasis on the arbitrary nature of literary taste as well as the constructedness of the entire category of juvenilia.

An argument could be made that juvenilia should be defined by publication date. Such a definition would imply a gatekeeper but while subjective and still arbitrary, is at least reasonably justified. This is not the case, however. Juvenilia is not determined by publication: Christina Rossetti was published by fifteen, Shelley by eighteen, Tennyson by seventeen and Jane Austen had finished drafts of what would become *Sense and Sensibility* and *Pride and Prejudice* by twenty-one. Juvenilia, instead, is determined in hindsight. Just as adults have consistently redesigned the liminal borders between childhood and adulthood to align with given cultural norms, critics, publishers and the authors themselves have determined when the transition from youthful writing to adult writing is complete. It is a fluid border, depending upon the author but it is hierarchical nonetheless.

Towards a Reappraisal

There is an indication, however, that this might change. In a previous note I have pointed to scholars who are trying to make the case for a reconsideration of young writers. Reiman, in the same article, reports that while collaborating on a new collected edition of Shelley, the editors discovered that: "Shelley's earliest, least sophisticated poems, which every critic who has dealt with them has, at some time or other, laughed at as puerile nonsense—have gained credibility from this editorial process. They turn out to be much more interesting psychologically, intellectually, and aesthetically than we would have thought possible when we began" (p. 8). This last statement is cause for celebration.

Vagle's (this volume) plea, that we recognize the contingency of youthful experience, should be answered by a similar statement. Imagine what our educational institutions might look like should, Arne Duncan, current U.S. Secretary of Education, suggest that adolescents are much more psychologically, intellectually and aesthetically interesting than our social norms had led him to believe. The question is whether we, the gatekeepers in academia, and we, the audience, can move past preconceived notions of adolescence and the productive output of its inhabitants. Any author briefly considered here is certainly not the same writer as their adult selves but a writer they are nonetheless, worthy of being read and yes, even evaluated—but, without the baggage of their futures and, indeed, our pasts.

And our relationship to the past is of extreme importance. I have already alluded to this but it bears restating here. Young writers from Byron to Shelley to Austen and through the nineteenth century poets such as Tennyson, Rossetti and Barrett belong not only to a specific cultural milieu but also to a specific era that is extraordinarily influential in creating our current conceptions of childhood and adulthood. The great irony of this is that these writers do not fit into the template that was so informed by their contemporary intellectual and juridical movements.

The Romantics, with their use of the child as a standard of innocence and purity as well as with their emphasis on nature as the ultimate guiding hand seem to have led to the reform movements stressing developmental stages as espoused by G. Stanley Hall and his predecessors. In an incredible twist of fate, it appears that the industrialized, depersonalizing efficiency movement in education was born out of Romantic ideals, which in England and the U.S. actively criticized the mechanized drive of progress. Lesko (2001) has argued that the influence of German Romanticism on Hall's theories led to the particular version of adolescence still prevalent today. In Hall's own words,

> As for years, an almost passionate lover of childhood and a teacher of youth, the adolescent stage of life has long seemed to me one of the most fascinat-

> ing of all themes, more worthy, perhaps, than anything else in the world of reverence, most inviting study, and in most crying need of a service we do not yet know how to render aright. (1905, p. xviii)

His missionary zeal is still echoed today in the rhetoric of educational reformers whose banner is accountability. Lesko is convincing in pointing out that whiteness and maleness are really what Hall has in mind for his reverence much as, I would argue, the arguments of free market advocates are really about keeping social divisions intact much more than they are about lessening the achievement gap. Just as the voices of marginalized students and parents do not fit so easily into the discourse presented by Hall, nor do the voices of the young authors I include here reflect Hall's developmental doctrine. This fact makes particularly relevant an investigation of writings by "adolescents" whose output flourished during the age when these ideas were gaining prominence. How, for instance, did these writers situate themselves within the arguments concerning their own status as human beings?

Interestingly enough, G. Stanley Hall ends his opus *Adolescence: Its Psychology* with an exhortation that deserves to be quoted at length within the context of juvenilia as it appears to be a call that is in ways similar to the very one that I am making.

> It is, I believe, high time that ephebic literature should be recognized as a class by itself, and have a place of its own in the history of letters and in criticism. Much of it should be individually prescribed for the reading of the young, for whom it has a singular zest and is a true stimulus and corrective. This stage of life now has what might almost be called a school of its own. Here the young adults appeal to and listen to each other as they do not to adults, and in a way the latter have failed to appreciate. Again, no biography, and especially no autobiography, should henceforth be complete if it does not describe this period of transformation so all-determining for future life to which it alone can often give us the key. To rightly draw the lessons of this age not only saves us from waste ineffable of this rich but crude area of experience, but makes maturity saner and more complete. (1905, p. 589)

It is this "rich but crude area of experience" that Mark Twain ruefully comments upon in *My First Literary Venture* when, as an adult of forty, he tells the following story of his own adolescence concerning a feud he conducted in print with the editor of the rival paper. The origination of the feud was an editorial written by his brother Orion Clemens complaining of barking dogs:

> He had lately been jilted, and one night a friend found an open note on the poor fellow's bed, in which he stated that he could not longer endure life and had drowned himself in Bear Creek. The friend ran down there and discovered Higgins wading back to the shore. He had concluded he wouldn't...I thought this a fine opportunity. (1922, p. 95)

The opportunity, enhanced by Orion's absence from town, was fulfilled when the sixteen-year-old Clemens designed several illustrations of Higgins (J.T. Hinton, in actuality) accompanied by the following typeset under the headline *'Local' Resolves to Commit Suicide*:

> 'Local,' disconsolate from receiving no further notice from 'A Dog-Be-Deviled Citizen,' contemplates Suicide. His 'pocket-pistol' (i.e. the bottle,) failing in the patriotic work of ridding the country of a nuisance, he resolves to 'extinguish his chunk' by feeding his carcass to the fishes of Bear Creek, while friend and foe are wrapt in sleep. Fearing, however, that he may get out of his depth, he sounds the stream with his walking stick. (Twain, 1979, p. 75)

Rich and crude, indeed. Another question that begs asking, however, is whether Twain benefited from the experience and enjoyed a saner and more complete maturity as a result. By taking a recursive view, I would argue that Twain is simply courageous, subversive and defiant over and over throughout his long career. The question of increased maturity and improved sanity is ridiculous.

There is a sense of pugilistic kinship between the work of Twain cited above and the young Shelley whose eight-year-old poem, *Verses on a Cat* ends with this stanza:

> But this poor little cat
>
> Only wanted a rat,
>
> To stuff out its own little maw:
>
> And it were as good
>
> Some people had such food,

To make them hold their jaw! (1800)

Not all juvenilia is so explicitly combative because each author responds to the exigencies of the outer world in individualized ways. The preceding stanza's of Shelley's early poem present no warning to the final, grand "Shut up!" and appear to otherwise be a calm meditation on worldly desires written in perfect meter. One could suggest that Shelley is experimenting with poetic form and its relation to content; the juxtaposition of the ending to the previous verses serving as a release from conventional strictures. Or, one could suggest that the writer is reflecting on the very uses of poetry as a weapon. Perhaps the poet is making a larger statement about the relationship of humans to their appetites. Howsoever one looks at it, these possible interpretations are much more interesting than the dismissive and reductive "He's just being juvenile" reading.

A Degree of Truth in All These Opinions

Jane Austen, about whose juvenilia a relatively large amount of criticism has been written, responded to the novelistic conventions of her day by crafting razor sharp satires of them. Her early work displays all of the wit of her published novels but are a treasure trove in and of themselves for her pointed comments on the popular sentimental novels of her day as well as the engrained and, in her eyes, ridiculous, social norms of the day[6] (Austen, 2000). Again, this could be read as youthful rebellion but we don't read her that way once she has become an adult. In her "mature" writings we read her as subversive and pointedly satiric. To be sure, she softens her prose, arguably out of commercial interests, just as Louisa May Alcott does, both authors adaptable not in the face of development achieved, but in the real world dilemma of financial necessity and literary gatekeeping strictures.

Not only do these writers engage with conventions of their day, they are also overtly political and extremely aware of contemporary events. Percy Shelley is expelled from Oxford at age nineteen for publishing a pamphlet entitled *The Necessity of Atheism* (Keach, 1997). At age eleven, Elizabeth Barrett wrote a poetic eulogy for England's Princess Charlotte, daughter of George IV and at age fourteen a dramatization of an imagined conversation between Charlotte and her mother Queen Caroline whose relationship with the King was stormy, at best. The Brontë children's fantasy lands of Angria and Gondol are populated by characters based on contemporary personages. Christina Rossetti, in 1850, at age twenty, wrote a short prose piece entitled *Maude,* which is often read as autobiographical. It is the story of a fifteen-year-old who,

> ...also knew that people thought her clever, and that her little copies of verses were handed about and admired. Touching these same verses, it was the amazement of every one what could make her poetry so broken-hearted as was mostly the case. Some pronounced that she wrote very foolishly about things she could not possibly understand; some wondered if she really had any secret source of uneasiness; while some simply set her down as affected. Perhaps there was a degree of truth in all these opinions. (1993, p. 5)

The final line is eloquent in its simplicity and it again underscores the importance of maintaining a contingent view of childhood and adolescence. Rossetti seems to be sighing for the lack of her own agency. She is also admitting that there are more ways than one of defining an adolescent. A developmental stage can simply not account for the myriad forces at play in the lives of individual youth.

Writing Who I Am Now

I end this essay with the concluding lines of Elizabeth Barrett's autobiography written when she was fourteen years old. Her life in the *Manor of Hope End* is worlds away from the financial difficulties that often plagued the Rossetti family. Throughout the piece, she has offered the reader (whom she disavows in the following lines) an opportunity to wonder at her erudition, to be overwhelmed by her religious fervor and her poetic zealotry, to be swept away by her authorial preeminence and to understand her complex relationship to words. Finally, she writes:

> Perhaps these pages may never meet a human eye--and therefore no EXCESSIVE vanity can dictate them tho a feeling akin to it SELF LOVE may have prompted my not unwilling pen.--In writing my own life[,] to be impartial is a difficult task and being so can only excuse such an attempt from

> one so young and inexperienced! Elizabeth Barrett Browning Glimpses into My Own Life and Literary Character (1820/1984)[7]

The rhetorical move of disowning responsibility based upon youth is a conventional one for writers of the nineteenth century. Byron and the Tennysons both employ the same caveat in their writing. There is a sense that even now, in the early nineteenth century, youth is something to be apologized for, connoting as it does such a lack of development, a lack of sophistication. The thing is, though, there doesn't seem to be a chance in the world that the fourteen-year-old Elizabeth Barrett believes her own insufficiency for a moment. In fact, in reading her autobiographical essay, one gets the feeling that she is entirely aware that each time she takes up the pen, she is creating herself anew and that this persona is every bit as viable as those preceding or those to come. The plea for a contingent, recursive view of adolescence recognizes this phenomenon. Anyone who ever endeavors to write seriously must also recognize this relational aspect between self, expression and society, an aspect that is always fluid. What seems incredible is the number of stakeholders in the educational complex who have either never learned this lesson or are unwilling to admit that they once knew it. Because such an admission would, of course, mean that their claims to authority are built on air. It would mean that they would have to work towards ongoing dialogue rather than resorting to dogmatic decree.

References

Alcott, L.M. (1994). *Norna or, the witch's curse.* J. McMaster (Ed.). Edmonton, Alberta: Juvenilia Press. (Original work published 1893).

Alexander, C. (2005). Play and apprenticeship: The culture of family magazines. In C. Alexander and J. McMaster (Eds.), *The child writer from Austen to Woolf* (31-50). Cambridge, UK: Cambridge University Press.

Alexander, C. & McMaster, J. (2005). Introduction. In C. Alexander & J. McMaster (Eds.), *The child writer from Austen to Woolf* (1-10). New York: Cambridge University Press.

Ashford, D. (1919). *The young visiters or, Mr. Salteena's plan.* New York: George D. Doran Co.

Austen, J. (2000). *The minor works.* Cambridge, UK: Chadwyk-Healey.

Barrett, E. (1984). Glimpses into my own life and literary character. In P. Kelley & R. Hudson (Eds.), *The Brownings' correspondence, vol 1.* (348-356). Winfield, KS: Wedgestone Press.

Barrie, J. M., (1919). Preface. In D. Ashford. *The young visiters or, Mr. Salteena's plan* (7-18). New York: George D. Doran Co.

Barton, A. (2008). *Tennyson's name: Identity and responsibility in the poetry of Alfred Lord Tennyson.* Aldershot, England: Ashgate.

Butler, M. (1975). *Jane Austen and the war of ideas.* Oxford, UK: Oxford University Press.

Castle, T. (2002). Boss ladies watch out! *Essays on women, sex, and writing.* New York: Routledge.

Donzelot, J. (1979). *The policing of families* (R. Hurley, Trans.). New York: Pantheon Books.

Doody, M.A. (2005). Jane Austen, that disconcerting child. In C. Alexander and J. McMaster (Eds.), *The child writer from Austen to Woolf* (101-121). Cambridge, UK: Cambridge University Press.

Gilbert, S.M. & Gubar, S. (1979). *The madwoman in the attic: The woman writer and the nineteenth century literary imagination.* New Haven, CT: Yale University Press.

Grumet, M.R. (1988). *Bitter milk.* Amherst, MA: The University of Massachusetts Press.

Hall, G.S. (1905). *Adolescence: Its psychology and its relation to physiology, anthropology, sociology, sex, crime, religion and education.* New York: D. Appleton and Co.

Keach, W. (1997). Early Shelley: Vulgarisms, politics and fractals—Young Shelley. *Romantic Circles.* Retrieved September 9, 2011 from http://www.rc.umd.edu/praxis/earlyshelley/keach/keach.html

Lesko, N. (2001). *Act your age!: A cultural construction of adolescence.* New York: RoutledgeFalmer.

Martin, C. (1994). Review of 'comic tragedies'. In J. McMaster (Ed.). *Norna, or the witch's curse* (p. iv). Edmonton, Alberta: Juvenilia Press. (Original work published 11/5/1893).

Nissenbaum, S. (1996). *The battle for Christmas.* New York: Random House.

Reiman, D. (1997). Early Shelley: Vulgarisms, politics, and fractals--Shelley comes of age: His early poems as an editorial experience. *Romantic Circles.* Retrieved September 9, 2011 from http://www.rc.umd.edu/praxis/earlyshelley/reiman/reiman.html

Robertson, L. (1998). Changing models of juvenilia: Apprenticeship or play? *English Studies in Canada,* 24(3), 291-298.

Rossetti, W.M. (Ed.). (1900). *New poems by Christina Rossetti: Hitherto unpublished or uncollected*. London: Macmillan and Co.

Showalter, E., & Mahon, P. (Eds.). (1993). *Maude by Christina Rossetti, "on sisterhoods" and a woman's thoughts about women by Dinah Mulock Craik*. New York: New York University Press.

Taylor, B., (2005). Childhood writings of Elizabeth Barrett Browning: 'At four I first mounted Pegasus, In C. Alexander and J. McMaster (Eds.) *The child writer from Austen to Woolf* (138-153). Cambridge, UK: Cambridge University Press.

Twain, M. (1922). *The writings of Mark Twain, definitive edition* (Vol. 7). New York: Gabriel Wells.

———. (1979). *Early tales and sketches: 1851-1864, Volume 1*. E.M. Branch and R.H. Hirst (Eds.). Berkeley, CA: University of California Press.

Vagle, M. D. (this volume). Trying to poke holes in Teflon: Developmentalism; young adolescence; and contingent, recursive growth and change. In M. D. Vagle (Ed.), *Not a stage! A critical re-conception of young adolescent education* (pp. 11-38). New York: Peter Lang Publishing

Waldron, M. (1999). *Jane Austen and the fiction of her time*. Cambridge, UK: Cambridge University Press.

Section 3

Making a Reoriented Conception of Growth and Change "Actionable"

Mark D. Vagle

The work of re-orientation must take place on multiple levels, simultaneously. This simultaneity makes me think of numerous conversations I took part in as a public school administrator. We routinely would discuss (debate, argue) how to make systemic change in our school. How do we create concrete, observable actions in the here-and-now, while simultaneously keeping our eye on large, overarching philosophical commitments that were often much more abstract?

This same question holds here as well. How does a theoretical change—in this case, a re-oriented conception of growth and change—take hold in the practice of educating young adolescents? The work of Brown, Bishop, Burns & Hall, and Conklin, collectively, help us consider this question. They thoughtfully and directly engage with one or more of the re-orienting pleas by wondering what any of this might mean in the day-to-day living and schooling of young adolescents. They do imaginative work—not as in "make believe"—but as in the careful, creative work that artists do.

This section begins with Enora Brown's chapter, *Both/And/All of the Above: Addressing Individual, Social, and Contextual Dimensions of Educating Middle School Youth*. In it, Brown embraces my pleas to push beyond constrictive stage-bound perspectives and instead embrace the particulars of young adolescent's lived experiences. However, she cautions us to not tip the scale too far away from broad social factors. She suggests that we must imagine a *Both/And Approach* in our efforts to rethink constructions of adolescence and middle school education. Such an approach, for Brown, must at once address the moment-to-moment and the broader social and historical contexts (e.g., hierarchical societal relationships, institutional structures, policies, and practices, and historical and current realities), which shape those moments. Brown's advocacy for a conception that resists either-or logic (i.e., a focus on moments or a focus on social contexts) not only broadens and deepens the theoretical conception, but also reminds us that the particular lived realities of classrooms must resist either-or thinking. For example, when considering my plea for a difference curriculum, Brown argues that we must pay careful attention to what ends sameness and difference curricula might serve. She suggests that instead of assuming difference or sameness curricula are either, at face value, good or bad, educators consider when one or the other (or both) might promote disparate, discriminatory practices or promote socially just and fair educative practices with youth. In this way, Brown asserts, difference and sameness curricula might be interpreted as interdependent and both having the potential to serve both damaging and hopeful ends. Brown's point is an important one as it requires educators to actively inquire about curricular practices—as opposed to blindly assuming that a developmentally responsive curriculum automatically takes cares of such matters.

Penny Bishop in *Multiple Discourses and Missing Voices* wants to make sure that young adolescent voices are present in any meaningful conversation about what their schooling should entail. Bishop draws on some of her experiences working with teachers, principals, and students in a week-long institute designed to improve the practices in their middle schools—the outcome of such institutes demonstrate how insightful young adolescents are about what should take place in schools. This sort of practical particularization (from those who are being "schooled") provides a nice bridge between contingent, recursive theoretical conceptions and the day-to-day realities of living in schools. In fact, Bishop suggests that one of the best outcomes of a contingent, recursive conception might just be that it can help us see young adolescents as active participants in the world right now—not later. That including young adolescents in decisions regarding the curriculum, school policies, and classroom practices is a most humane way to treat young people—and in this humanity we can be reminded of important matters such as trust, freedom, and recognition.

In a similar way, Les Burns & Leigh Hall in *Using Students' Funds of Knowledge to Enhance Middle Grades Education: Responding to Adolescen(TS)* also ask us to turn to young adolescents—in this case by drawing on young adolescent's funds of knowledge outside of school in order to influence student motivation and engagement. Burns and Hall argue that any successful (difference-based) curriculum must be responsive, not necessarily to the developmental stage, but to young adolescent's identities, capacities, knowledges, and experiences. By making "plural" concepts such as identity, Burns and Hall draw out the complexities and multiplicities at play. They argue that a normalized conception of identity (singular), cognitive capacity, and the like have been over-generalized and institutionalized in ways that are *administratively expedient rather than pedagogically justifiable.* The power of this phrase cannot be overstated. To make a contingent, recursive conception actionable would demand that we question whether our policies and practices are, indeed pedagogically justifiable.

In the final chapter in this section, *What's Interbeing Got to Do with It? Shared Experiences, Public Problems, and the Unique Individual,* Hilary Conklin stresses how important it is for us not to lose the public in the particularizing. Throughout her chapter, Conklin carefully and thoughtfully works back and forth along—what might be perceived as—a characterizing-particularizing binary. Concerned that over-particularizing might cause other problems (e.g., distracting educators from the public-ness and interdependence of the young people who share an educational space), Conklin uses Buddhist monk Thich Nhat Hanh's (1988) concepts of inter-being and mutuality to demonstrate how as individuals, young adolescents' experiences are inevitably infused in the experience of others. In other words, Conklin helps us think about the fact that there really is no "pure" individual experience. This extends and complicates my plea for a move away from characterizing and toward particularizing. For one, it means that particularizing does not happen in a vacuum. It also means that day-to-day contingent, recursive living is not neutral and can be just as dangerous as the developmental—as Conklin asks us to be sure not to underestimate young adolescents' connectedness to one another.

References

Hanh, T. N. (1988). *The heart of understanding.* Berkeley, CA: Parallax Press.

Chapter 6

Both/And/All of the Above: Addressing Individual, Social, and Contextual Dimensions of Educating Middle School Youth

Enora Brown

Introduction

Educators have faced the pressing, and long-standing question: What is best for the education of middle school youth? Seemingly straightforward, this question is complicated. It entails consideration of our *traditional and critical* views about youth and the concept of developmentalism, our perspectives on the purpose and goals of education, and our philosophies on the educator's role in teaching-learning processes. Initiated by G. S. Hall in 1904, the *traditional perspective* is grounded in a biologically driven discourse, which pervades 21st-century views of adolescents—as inherently "at risk"—and of middle school education—as a means to control their way-ward tendencies. In the context of pathologizing views of youth, limited educational practices, and new reform policies, Vagle (this volume) invites us as educators to engage multiple critical perspectives that may forge new constructions of youth and new possibilities for middle-level education. He extends three pleas for us: to move *from* a developmental view that makes generalizations about youth and promotes one-size-fits-all curricula for students *to* a multifaceted, contextualized view of adolescents, as individuals in educative relations, which promotes differential and invigorating curricular experiences.

In this chapter, I wholeheartedly embrace Vagle's call to challenge the "facts," and to rethink adolescence and middle school education, from a *critical perspective*, by addressing each of the pleas that he extends. I will present three arguments to consider in our collective efforts to determine what is best for the education of early adolescents. The arguments grew out of and extend views presented in earlier critical writings on human development and middle school (Brown & Saltman, 2005; Brown, 2010a). First, through a *critical social constructiv-*

ist lens, I argue that we should approach our inquiry from a *Both/And perspective.* This view addresses *both* the individual *and* the sociostructural dynamics at the local and national level, as they shape adolescents and their educative relations with others (Elliott, 2001; Brown, 2011). Next, I argue that *structures of social inequality* and *relations of power* in school and society generate important common, generalizing experiences for youth based on their own and others' dimensions of social difference (e.g., gender, race, social class), which converge with and uniquely define *individuals'* identities and particular learning experiences and interactions (Holland & Lave, 2001). *Both* generalizing *and* particularizing experiences are important. Third, I argue that it is important to *problematize "difference" and "sameness" models,* in order to address the ways in which *both* may offer curricular limitations *and* possibilities, in the context of relations of power and social inequality (Hall, 2005). A central thread that runs throughout each of the arguments is that it is essential for us to address *social inequalities* and *relations of power* that infuse the lives of adolescents and educators, *both* intersubjectively *and* materially—that is, how we think and how we live. Despite the discomfort for all of us to confront these issues within and around us, my belief is that the future constructions of early adolescents and the educational processes through which *both* youth and educators grow *and* change may benefit in profound ways.

This chapter begins with an analysis of *the continuities* of *traditional* thought on adolescence and middle level education, which exist in three official documents, spanning 100 years from 1904 to 2004. My analysis of the conceptual continuities in *Adolescence* (Hall, 1904), *Turning Points* (Carnegie, 1989; Jackson & Davis, 2000), and *Focus on the Wonder Years* (Rand, 2004), include a discussion of the current implications of these discursive threads for youth and educators in middle schools, and provide a springboard from which we may consider critical alternative views. Next, I present each argument in relation to Vagle's three pleas for a critical perspective on adolescence and middle level education, with a discussion of conceptual assumptions that undergird my advocacy for a *Both/And Approach.* Finally, I introduce an analysis of small group and classroom dialogue from a middle school ethnography to illustrate the dynamics operating in educative interactions, and to highlight the value of a *Both/And*

Approach that may expand the boundaries of our thinking and practice. The theory-based arguments and attendant discourse analyses may enhance our future constructions of youth and the educative experiences that we foster in middle schools.

Continuity of Traditional Thought and Critical Possibilities

From G. S. Hall's two-volume publication of *Adolescence* in 1904 to the Carnegie Foundation's publication of *Focus on the Wonder Years* in 2004, the traditional perspective has established and normalized a biologically-driven developmental discourse, which posits explicit and implicit gender-, race-, and class-coded hierarchical categories of youth. For example, Hall states, "Femininity…excels in persuasion, sympathetic insight, storytelling…", "…Certain races of men are ascendant, and others, like the Bushmen and Australians, are decadent stocks…," and "Onaism…has its octopus-grasp in nearly all institutions for the defective classes" (Hall, pp. xiii, 337, 434; Bederman, 1995). Initially, Hall conceptualized adolescence as a period, marked by "primal hereditary impulsions" and "fundamental traits of savagery" (p. x). He reasoned that as white boys (not females or people of color), relived their evolutionary past during adolescence, they needed a regimented educational process to sublimate and redirect their pubertal proclivities towards "arrest…perversion… hoodlumism, juvenile crime, and secret vice" (p. xiv). Thus, "inculcation," "drill and discipline," and "mechanical, repetitive, authoritative" teaching methods, were required to insure that white male youth moved towards full humanity (i.e., adulthood), to fulfill their destined role to advance civilization (pp. xii). Once Hall's work established the "nature of adolescence," the purpose of middle-level education and requisite pedagogy, the first junior high school was opened in 1910, to fulfill the proscribed mission for adolescent development and for the Americanization of the populace in a new industrialized republic. His construction of early adolescence laid the foundation for early/mid-20th-century child development research, followed by William Alexander's conceptualization of *the middle school* in 1968, designed to meet the unique development needs of youth (Alexander, 1968).

Present-day official corporate-sector documents and national policies have preserved conceptual threads from Hall's *traditional* views. These continuities are important to unearth and examine in current academic, policy, and civic discourse, in order to understand their function in constructing past and present meanings about adolescents, which position youth in the social order, and justify the emergence of related educational goals and practices. Their transparency in pivotal documents is an essential element in identifying and supporting genuine conceptual "openings" or connections for dialogue on the middle school, and for determining whether and to what degree the recommended visions are, in fact, intentionally directed towards implementing a rigorous, quality education, and developing a critical thinking, democratic-minded citizenry, or are veiled or inadvertent efforts to serve corporate or other economic and political interests. Continuities of thought in key corporate-sector position papers on middle school reform, *Turning Points 1989 and 2000* and *Focus on the Wonder Years* (2004), and U.S. Department of Education reform policies, *No Child Left Behind (NCLB)* (2001) and *Race to the Top (RTTT)* (2009), provide insight into this question.

Turning Points: Preparing American Youth for the 21st Century, by the Carnegie Council (1989), is a pivotal publication, which marks an embryonic shift in middle-level education. It describes adolescents as "youth adrift" who are "extremely vulnerable to high-risk behaviors," e.g., "sexual promiscuity," "poor decisions," "permanent addiction," "school failure," and are "at risk of reaching adulthood…[or] participatin[g] in a democratic society" (p. 8). The 1989 Report warns that the turbulent and perilous *nature of adolescence* is a harbinger of social and economic decline "for young adolescents' future and the future of the nation." It issues a clarion call to "transform middle grade schools," to insure the future participation of youth in a "skillful, adaptable workforce" within a "technically-based and interdependent world economy" (pp. 10, 11). This cataclysmic race- and class-coded view of youth, which is reminiscent of Hall, provided the rationale in the 21st century, for restructuring public education and for stringent educational reform at the middle level. *Turning Points 2000* (Jackson & Davis, 2000) began to chart the path, by *removing* crucial terms from recommendations that were present in *Turning Points 1989*, i.e., "cooperative learning," "critical thinking," "the elimination of tracking" (p. 9), and *establishing* standardized curricula, direct instruction, and test–based assessment as regulatory pedagogy for teachers to attain the new educational goal—academic achievement for each adolescent. Carnegie solicited the Center for Collaborative Education to create Turning Points, a national network of schools to implement comprehensive education reform model targeting student learning. In tandem, the Rand Corporation's *Focus on the Wonder Years* (2004), challenged the validity of the middle school concept, that is, separate middle level education, "core middle school practices" (p. xvii), in "setting the trajectories for subsequent life success" (p. iii), questioned the value of privileging "developmental responsiveness" to students' social-emotional needs over "cognitive capabilities," and "academic rigor," and disputed the existence of evidence-based "effectiveness of middle schools," in fulfilling the national policy mandates of *No Child Left Behind*.

These corporate-sector promulgations on adolescent education have been reified in academia, professional organizations, and popular media, through a plethora of biological-determinist research, drawing causal links between adolescent brain development and risk-taking behaviors, violence, teen pregnancy, poor decision-making, and other "social aberrations." *Newsweek's* article, "Getting Inside a Teenage Brain" (2000), states:

> You probably recognize the species: it's known for making stupid decisions...barely able to plan beyond the next minute...clueless when it comes to reading parents' facial expressions...exhibits poor self-control...seems to think with its hormones more than its brain...all thumbs when juggling several tasks. Such is Homo teenageris. (Begley, 2/28/2000)

Such widespread pejorative discourse becomes official knowledge, through accessibly-written brain science books for the public, *The Primal Teen* (Strauch, 2003) and *Why Do They Act that Way?* (Walsh, 2004), television, and other venues. Strauch's use of research on rats and chimps to analogize the evolution of human adolescence in her chapters (e.g., The Adolescent Animal) is eerily reminiscent of G.S. Hall. Sercombe (2010) stringently critiques this essentialist view, which disregards/omits the bidirectional relationship between brain development/structure and experience/agency, the interdependence of biology/brain science and social constructionism, the recklessness and social aberrance of adults, and which fails to document early adolescents' risk proneness or address their ability to be as responsible, thoughtful, and disciplined as adults. The pervasive discourse of deviance from brain science mobilizes the public and provides rationale for professional educational practice. Pejoratively referring to middle schoolers as "hormone-fueled, socially-charged, technology-obsessed," the National Forum to Accelerate Middle-Grades Reform uses "new brain research" to rethink adolescent engagement in learning ("Rethinking Middle School Education", 2011). Their goals—academic excellence, developmental responsiveness, social equity—and commitment to greater internal/external accountability, straddle middle grades and standards-based reform, and are indirectly aimed at attenuating so-called "adolescent problems"—teen pregnancy, drug abuse, school violence (Aymes, 2008). Males brilliantly exposes systematic adolescent "scapegoating," documenting poverty/adults as predictor/source of these problems (Males, 1994, 2009).

Unexamined assumptions from brain science instantiate notions of the "sexual adolescent" and certain developmental "truths" in myriad early adolescent texts, guide "developmentally responsive" program practices (Moran, 2000). Their recursive production-consumption throughout the *circuit of culture* "builds consensus—naturalizing the adolescent construct, regulating young adolescents' social identities, and normalizing schools' "developmentally appropriate" practices (Gramsci, 1971; Hall, 2005).

Vestiges of Hall's views prevailed from the early 20th to 21st century, indicating their sustained strength, despite vastly different social, economic and political contexts. Emergent capitalist industrialization, Victorian era cultural norms, and the newly established universal public education to Americanize the nation's burgeoning workforce, contextualized Hall's views in the 20th century. These conditions structurally presaged, but differed from those in the 21st century. A microelectronic, global capitalist economy, neoliberal agenda, and privatization of public education for an increasingly unemployed workforce, contextualize current iterations of Hall's conceptions of youth, which continue to anchor the goals of middle level education and pedagogical practices in classrooms. As neoliberal policies, *No Child Left Behind* and *Race to the Top,* utilize *technicist forms of power* to substantively reform—standardize and privatize—education, erode the academic preparation, quality, and protective rights of teachers, institutionalize rote learning vs. higher order thinking and push students out of school—they are institutionalizing / naturalizing particular views of youth, and further stratifying schools, along racial, social class, and ethnic lines (Hursh, 2008; Kozol, 2005).

The link between public policy and constructions of youth is exemplified in Adequate Yearly Progress (AYP) mandates and criteria for States' competition for RTTT funds. AYP requirements generate rewards for *so-called Reward Schools, achieving students, and "good" teachers,* which predominate in wealthy, academic-oriented, white school communities, and levies sanctions against *so-called Challenge Schools, failing students, and "bad" teachers,* which predominate in poor, vocational-oriented school communities of color. These AYP-generated policies are grounded in and inscribe views of youth, achievement-based social identities and situated, hierarchical positionalities to adolescents. In accord with trends in students' proscribed life options and trajectories—"push-outs" vs. high school graduates have a future in the military or jail vs. college or business—there are comparable ascriptions and rankings for their schools and their teachers. Additionally, States' competition for RTTT charter school funds require them to legislatively enforce achievement test-based AYP merits and sanctions, teachers' merit pay based on student achievement, and the removal of teachers' union protection (Blueprint, 2009; Brown, 2010b; Lipman, 2003).

Despite the verbiage and lofty promises, the documents and policies belie an agenda, whose deleterious effects on teachers and students have reduced the overall quality of education, especially for poor middle school youth of color. Surveillant monitoring and "blacklisting" of teachers through *TeacherFit,* which probes teachers' "soft skills," and the demonization, deranking, and deintellectualization of educators, through alternative certification programs and other means, is reducing the stability of school personnel and drastically changing the educational climate for youth (Rossi, 2011; Compton & Weiner, 2008). Students are subjected to direct instruction scripts, narrow, fact-based curricula, rote test preparation, and decreasing material/human resources. All are demotivating factors for students' engaged, exploratory inquiry. These mandated policies and structural shifts ignore the sources of long-standing *social inequalities,* such as disparate funding patterns and historically segregated; rich vs. poor resourced schools; and conveniently blame *individuals* for their success or failure, by holding students, teachers and parents accountable for their effort or choices relative to academic achievement. One must question how these market-driven policies, their attendant views of youth, and *discourse of individual vs. social responsibility,* which targets individual performance outside of the context of structural inequality, can serve the best interests of youth, especially the poor and students of color.

Under these conditions, there is an ever-increasing need for us to examine and critique both *traditional and critical perspectives to discern and protect* what is best for the education of *all* middle school youth, across multiple lines of difference. Towards this end, Vagle (this volume) invites us to participate in conversant critiques to decenter developmentalism, to challenge naturalized, decontextualized generalizations of early adolescence, and to create new educative possibilities for middle school youth. Drawing on Nancy Lesko's sociohistorical work (2001), he carefully considers both discursive limitations and possibilities in three *traditional* texts, *Research Summary on Young Adolescents Development Characteristics,* from the academic community, *This We Believe,* from the premier professional middle school organization, and *Turning Points 2000,* a joint corporate-sector/government-sponsored reform, and extends three pleas to facilitate our theoretical and practical efforts to create the best schools for early adolescents. He calls for a move—from a developmentally responsive to a contingently and recursive relational vision, from characterizing young adolescen*ce* to particularizing young adolescen*ts,* and from a "sameness" to a "difference" curriculum. He invites us to consider multiple critical perspectives, which embrace more individual-focused, context- and relationship-driven, "difference" approaches to teaching and learning, and encourages us to seek convergent conceptual "openings," which promote dialogue with *traditional*, foundational middle school documents and policies, and allow teachers and students to "take hold of the standards" instituted by NCLB, sans the imposition of external authority. In the next section, I present three arguments to address each plea, and to advocate a *Both/And Approach* grounded in *critical social constructivism*.

Both/And Approach: Three Pleas and Critical Arguments

This chapter embraces Vagle's important pleas to push beyond constrictive stage-bound perspectives, by recognizing: the significance of adolescents' **individual characteristics** and differing experiences within and across multiple contexts, the participation of youth in **interactive relationships**, which scaffold continual, **moment-to-moment growth** in the present, amongst peers and teachers, and the imposed **limitations of developmentalism**, which naturalize constructed age-defined qualities of and curricular goals for early adolescents. My overarching premise is that we must utilize a *Both/And Approach* in our efforts to rethink constructions of adolescence and middle school education. This means that as we consider, or rather, **in order to consider** the limits of developmentalism and related curricular format and goals, the significance of adolescents' individual characteristics and particularities, their interactive relationships and moment-to-moment experiences in local classrooms, we must simultaneously address the **broader social and historical context**. It is crucial for us to address the pivotal, often veiled role of dynamics within the social order that are integral to processes of youth development and education in middle school. We must consider the hierarchical societal relationships institutional structures, policies, and practices, and historical and current realities, which shape our notions of youth, frame the individual and collective learning experiences of young adolescents, and infuse curricular aims and pedagogical practices of educators in classrooms. We must consider the relations of power, which frame our material and intersubjective realities.

From this perspective, I argue that *both* micro *and* macro level processes, *both* individual *and social* dynamics, *both* past *and* present-day

day realities mutually define each other in dynamic ways, and operate in young adolescents' growth and learning. Middle school students are engaged at *micro levels,* in interpersonal relations in school, community and family, and at *macro levels,* as interactive members of various, intersecting social groupings/institutions within society, wealthy-poor, urban-rural, U.S. citizen-undocumented resident. In addition, middle school youth have their *individual*/personal perceptions, cognitive patterns, intrapsychic orientation, qualities and characteristics, which are shaped through their active engagement and exploration in micro-macro level social relationships (Rogoff, 1990). Youth are also products and inheritors of their *individual/personal and familial history,* their *social histories* of relative privilege or discrimination, as member-participants within various national, ethnic, racial and other stratified groupings (David, 1992; Elder, 1974; Kenny, 2000; Lee, 2009; Reed, 1997; Rodis, Garrod, & Boscardin, 2000). Thus, the micro and macro, individual and social, personal/social histories and present processes, not only shape adolescent development, but also inform our conceptualizations of adolescence, views of and educative relationships with early adolescents, and our middle school educational goals and curricula.

This view is grounded in a central tenet of *critical social constructivist theory,* which asserts the interdependent nature of both poles in each process (e.g., internal-external, psychological-social) and honors the dialectical, mutually constitutive relationship that exists between these analytic dimensions. Both dynamic dimensions of each process are invaluable in our analyses of early adolescence and curricular experiences of youth in middle school classrooms. Through these multiply-embedded contexts, bidirectional individual-social, past-present processes at micro-macro levels, students are continually self-authoring and co-constructing their immediate and cumulative learning experiences with others. Our participation in and understanding of how these interwoven lived realities eventually become the historical backdrop for future possibilities for youth may provide nuanced insights for our theoretical and practical work (Elliott, 2001).

My first argument addresses Vagle's plea to move from a *developmentally responsive to a contingently and recursive relational vision.* I concur with Vagle that it is crucial for us to acknowledge, interrogate, and denaturalize constructed meanings ascribed to physiological changes during early adolescence, in order to create openings for new, equitable constructions and possibilities for youth. Thus, I raise three issues to consider: 1) ascriptions of "normal" vs. "abnormal" development across social difference and material inequalities; 2) the impact of policies on moment-to-moment classroom interactions; and 3) the significance of personal/social and institutional/societal history for learning processes.

To disrupt the discourse on adolescence, we must counter Hall, by warding against making/reproducing tacit and explicit differential attributions of "normative" and "deficient" development to youth based on race, class, and gender. Characteristic representations of adolescents are often imbued with intersecting racialized, gendered, and social class meanings. Pranks, considered "normal" behavior for white male adolescents (e.g., Operation TP—toilet papering buildings), may be considered criminal activity, reflecting "delinquent tendencies" of Black and Latino boys; boys' naturalized outspoken, animated classroom behavior is encouraged, but frowned upon or chastised as inappropriate gendered behavior for girls; consumer-driven desires for/ownership of the latest technology or fashions by wealthy youth, who can afford them, are normalized as deserved entitlements, while these desires/possessions amongst poor youth, who cannot afford them, are considered aberrant, undeserved entitlements, indicative of their misplaced values/priorities (Gans, 1989; Katz, 1995).

Rigorous scholarship incisively deconstructs these trends in the canon. Spencer's (Spencer & Tinsley, 2008) Phenomenological Variant of Ecological System Theory (PVEST) and research illustrates the convergence of adolescents' psychological processes and protective/risk contributors across intersecting contexts, shaping adolescent growth and identity. Her research counters dominant academic discourse, marginalizing African American adolescents relative to normal human developmental processes, by decontextualizing their experiences, pathologizing their behaviors, and disregarding inhibiting social factors. Spencer highlights the empowering effects of disrupting demonizing, stereotypic, deficit model assumptions about youth of color, and of supporting their efforts to cope with adverse conditions and stigmatizing experiences.

Ferguson's book, *Bad Boys: Public Schools in the Making of Black Masculinity* (2001), highlights racial/gendered assumptions about African American boys, which are manifest and institutionalized in schools' disciplinary practices. Her work provides a poignant example of school personnel, who, failing to view Black boys as children traversing normal adolescent development, "adultified" them as incorrigible, hypersexual troublemakers, needing control, surveillance and moral rectification in the "Punishing Room." White boys are often perceived and responded to as "naughty-by-nature," a benign quality that they will eventually outgrow (Sheets & Gay, 1996). As we move within/from a "developmentally responsive" orientation, it is incumbent upon us to do so in ways that affirm the humanity of all youth. We must keep a vigilant eye on stigmatizing social inequalities—racism, sexism, classism, ableism, homophobia—which skew our views of development across social difference, jeopardizing growth potential for so-called "disposable" adolescents (Giroux, 2009).

Next, I agree with Vagle's first plea, about the importance of attending to the unique changing micro/macro social contexts through which students learn, question, explore, and construct knowledge recursively, on a moment-to-moment basis. This understanding may move educators away from regimented "developmentally responsive" teaching modes or biased views of students, thereby, honoring and fostering students' varied individual/collective, immediate/cumulative growth processes, as they occur through contextualized learning experiences, within and outside of classrooms.

However, I argue that relational dynamics, occurring in *present, moment-to-moment interactions* amongst youth and teachers are complex. They are shaped by current national policy mandates. Thus, our understanding of present processes is a necessary move, but not sufficient. More is required. McNeil's ethnography, *Contradictions of School Reform (2000)*, documents the moment-to-moment classroom effects of standardization: teachers' *defensive teaching* altered course content, students' lost opportunities for independent thinking, "standardization undermine[d] academic standards" (p. 506), and illustrates macro level policies impacting micro-level teaching-learning practices in local schools' daily teacher-student interactions.

Finally, I argue that *moment-to-moment interactions* amongst youth and teachers are intricately laced with and shaped by *historical* dynamics and discourses within immediate interpersonal and broader societal relationships. Holland and Lave's (2001) concept, *history-in-person*, asserts that histories of social inequality operate fully in the present, via individuals' daily engagements in cultural practices. Thus, "the energy of enduring struggles...[are] realized in local practice" (p. 13) and enacted and negotiated locally through students'/teachers' interpersonal, educative relationships. Thus, the personal and social histories of students and educators interface, are invoked in and frame current interactions in schools. These tacit or explicit features of classroom exchanges (i.e., feelings, thoughts, practices around social difference) may influence moment-to-moment learning. One might expect students' learning experiences and teacher-student relationships to vary in classrooms where teachers, on the one hand, consciously or unconsciously display gender or class bias; criminalize Black or Muslim youth; overrepresent Mexican youth in special education, or, on the other hand, actively encourage rigorous, equitable learning experiences for girls and the poor; interrogate their own and others' racialized/gendered disciplinary practices; and affirm linguistic and religious diversity in classrooms (Artiles, 2006; Brantlinger, 1993; Sadker, Sadker, & Zittleman, 2009; Sirin & Fine, 2008; Valenzuela, 1999). As students and teachers bring their own personal and social histories, expectations, and interpretive lenses into classroom interactions, they co-construct meanings, make sense of each other and teaching-learning experiences in present-time, and construct aspirations for probable futures (Brown, 2007; MacLeod, 1995; Saltzberger-Wittenberg, 1999).

Simultaneously, I argue that *the history of "enduring struggles"* operating in local school districts and classrooms, also operate and are influenced by enduring struggles at the institutional and national level. Histories of inequality and bias, embedded in established policies, normalized behaviors and expectations, and so-called objective achievement standards and disciplinary practices, are naturalized and rendered "invisible," through avowed color- gender- class-blind discourses of sameness. Often muted, these enduring struggles are reciprocally enacted and negotiated through discursive practices and struggles within/between divergent school communities and state and national Departments of Education, which provide mandated guidelines for curriculum and instruction, teacher-student classroom relations, and official norms for school governance and culture.

Philanthropic and government-funded STEM programs, targeting the math-science "girl problem," embody elements of historical struggles against gender discrimination and for women's rights; local student marches, opposing NCLB-driven middle school closings/K-8 mergings in poor Latino and African American communities, embody enduring struggles against segregated schools and for racial equality. These historical struggles and power relations at *both* the interpersonal *and* institutional level have present-day implications—for educators' differential perspectives about youth, for variations in students' educational experiences in classroom interactions, and for entire communities' differential resource allocation and disparate effects of local, state, and national policy. *Both* past *and* present interpersonal *and* structural relationships that infuse daily individual and collective learning experiences deserve educators' careful and reflective inquiry. Our recognition of these dynamics and our willingness to *be self-reflective* in addressing them in our day-to-day work and civic participation, are central contributing factors to the quality of moment-to-moment educational experiences of youth (Westheimer, 2009).

Next, Vagle's second plea is to move *from characterizing young adolescence to particularizing young adolescent*s. I argue that *particularized* unique, *personal* qualities and interpretive experiences of youth are interwoven with ostensibly *common, generalizable* features, forged through youths' similar positionalities and layered experiences in ordered social hierarchies in schools and communities (Elliott, 2001). I argue that *structures of inequality* and *relations of power* are instrumental in creating both the generalized and particularized experiences of youth. Middle school students vary along intersecting dimensions of social difference (e.g., ableness, gender, sexuality, race, class), which situate them within hierarchies that shape their material lives and intersubjectivities. Social differences mediate and give meaning to each adolescent's educative experiences and to teachers' and peers' perceptions about and reciprocal interactions with them. Youth may experience/participate in interactive patterns, which structure the types of individual, particularized learning experiences they have in the classroom. Based on social differences, collective members of marginalized societal groups (e.g., disabled youth, Muslim girls, transgendered youth, Black boys) may have experienced past and present forms/patterns of discrimination/restricted options (i.e., racism, sexism, ableism), and members of dominant social groups (e.g., white American youth, wealthy adolescents, or male students), may have experienced varying degrees of historic patterns of privilege/expanded opportunities, which shape their expectations, others' views of them, and available resources and power. These patterns of differential, but shared, experiences amongst social groupings may be reproduced with consistency within structures of inequality, and impact the rigor of students' educational experience, quality of their moment-to-moment learning, and tenor of their peer and teacher-student relations.

Sustained experiences of privilege/discrimination, which students from varying locale have in common, may overlay individuals' unique classroom experiences. Hence, under certain conditions, there is a place for *both* carefully articulated generalizable *and* important particularizing experiences for each middle school child. As we attend to dimensions of social difference, it is important for a *critical perspective* to attend to *structures of inequality* and *power relations*, which instantiate/naturalize internalized meanings, privilege dominant Discourses, justify ideologically driven educational reform, and structure social experiences—thereby marginalizing/privileging some youth and affirming inequality in classroom practices and school policies.

Vagle's third plea is for us to move *from a "sameness" to a "difference" curriculum*. I argue that it is crucial for us to problematize our view of *"difference" and "sameness,"* to determine whether and what "difference" models promote or sustain inequality and whether or what "sameness" models promote fair and just practice. Within structures of inequality, social interactions and discourses amongst individuals and groups in school and society create meanings and employing practices, which equate "difference" with being "unequal," "deficient," or "abnormal." Thus, "difference" curricula based on deficit views of certain youth (e.g., Native American, Puerto Rican) are detrimental and further track students, while contextually-grounded "sameness" models, based on equitable views of the human competence of all youth can be rigorous and empowering. It is important to examine "difference" models in curricula and peer or teacher-student interactions, which may inadvertently, promote disparate, discriminatory practices, while "sameness" models may promote socially equitable educative practices for middle schoolers. "Difference" and "sameness" models are not inherently "good" or "bad", but interdependent contributors to equitable, thought-provoking, and engaging curricular experiences.

I am suggesting that each pole of Vagle's three pleas has merit. Under conditions of structural inequality, each has relative value to the degree that it validates the humanity and broad-based capabilities of young adolescents, and ensures equal, rigorous educational experiences for all. We should examine *both* the limitations *and* possibilities on each side of the ledger, or along the continuum, *from* a developmentally responsive *to* a contingently and recursive relational vision, *from* characterizing young adolescen*ce* *to* particularizing young adolescen*ts*, and *from* a "sameness" *to* a "difference" curriculum. In the final section, I present middle school classroom dialogue relative to Vagle's pleas, from this Both/And perspective.

Discursive Analysis in Middle School Classrooms: Possibilities and Limitations

I analyze excerpts from small group and classroom discourse, from a 2-year ethnography on youth identity in a progressive, independent middle school, committed to economic and cultural diversity. Analyses of middle class to wealthy students' experiential views and teachers' pedagogical practices illuminate the arguments of my *Both/And Approach* to Vagle's pleas, and their implications in *real time* for a *critical* view of adolescence and middle level education. In *Group Dialogue*, boys of color discuss their differential treatment by teachers, their identities and educational experience.

1. Ned: [Smarts] always raising their hand in class...making other people feel stupid.

2. Alan: [S]ometimes...[teachers] say the world is divided between nerds and stupid people...
3. Van: [Smarts]...never get in trouble. [Teachers] just leave them be.
4. Alan: I think teachers like them... don't like anyone that's...cool..."
5. Van: Smart[s] get the work done...
6. Alan: [Teachers] don't like you for who you are. [They] like you for your work.
7. Ned: [T]eachers treat them better and talk to them more. They have more conversations with them.
8. Alan: Like actually have a real conversation with them about school. Like they'll start off the conversation with them a lot, like have a conversation about like school and then end up having a normal conversation....
9. Me: [W]hat group would you say [teachers] like?
10. Ned: The White kids. (All laugh; surprised)

The boys' dialogue illustrates my argument regarding Vagle's first plea: *teachers' tacit/explicit racialized attributions of deficient vs. normative development differentially shape recursive, moment-to-moment interactions, which embody students'/teachers' personal/social histories*. The boys describe teachers' views of "stupid people" vs. "nerds," and feeling "stupid" relative to Smarts "always raising their hand" (Lines 1, 2). They address implications of teachers' unspoken racial ascriptions to students they dislike/"like" (i.e., "cool" vs. "white kids") (Lines 4, 9-10). They experience patterns of teachers' disparate practice, of having "more," "normal," "real" conversations with white students (Lines 7, 8), and recognize that teachers "like you for your work," not "for who you are" (Lines 5, 6). Ivan, a white, self-identified "nerd," concurs, "I think teachers like nerds... because... generally... their intention in school is to grow intellectually." This intersubjective dynamic reaffirms dominant societal discourses on race and fosters conferred power at the local level, through particular types of teacher-student alignments.

Their dialogue indicates that teachers' differential views of students, based on race, *disrupt equal "developmental responsiveness"* to all adolescents across social difference, and create *unwelcome particularizing learning experiences, recursively, in real-time*. Teachers' biases are linked to disparate quality and tone of teacher-student educative conversations, which impact student emotions and emergent social identities in the classroom. Mirroring Hall's/society's eugenics discourse, these constructs of race-"intellect"-likability-learning are conjoined, contributing to classroom hierarchies of power, as teachers'/students' divergent and convergent personal/social histories of racism/ privilege interface in the classroom, shaping their interpretive self-other lens and interactive dynamics.

The boys of color and other students' dialogue also illustrate my argument regarding Vagle's second plea: *students' generalized experiences of discrimination/ privilege, within social hierarchies, both shape teacher-student classroom interaction patterns and converge with unique, particularizing experiences.* The boys' observation of teachers' racially coded discipline treatment, "[Smarts]...never get in trouble," converges with Ivan's, a white boy, and a group of Black girls' generalizable experiential views of differential disciplinary practice and its effects. Ivan, defines/disputes essential racialized identities, "White-smart," "Black-popular," as shared, recursive experiences. He says, "[N]ot everyone says..."'you're Black, you can't be smart,' [or] 'you're White, you can't be popular' but still these trends keep going," and locates them hierarchically into "top group"/white (implicit) bottom/black groups.

Disciplinarily, Ivan candidly states that teachers "treat a white...and a Black student differently...believe the white...assume it's the Black student," making racialized ascriptive "assumptions" about who's culpable, innocent, and guilty. A group of Black girls' discuss a teacher's reaction to bathroom requests, "She acts like I'm going to set a bomb off or something," revealing the painful effects of these "unfair" moment-to-moment disciplinary experiences on their emotional lives, "I feel bad...get an attitude"; on their academic engagement, "that makes me want to leave...zone out...forget everything;" and on their so-called resistant interactive relations with teachers, "I'll...get on her nerves on purpose," " I retaliate." Girls' and boys' dialogue reveal incisive *generalized discriminatory/privileged* experiences, that frame their *particularized, individual* learning and disciplinary episodes, their compatible/discordant relationships and emotional/academic dynamics with teachers, and mirror society's racialized zero tolerance and criminalization policies (Brown, 2011). Students' perceptive interpretive lens, grounded in their personal/social histories, forged common understandings, across racial/gender groups.

These shared experiences reflect curricular issues, illustrating my argument regarding Vagle's third plea: *problematized "sameness" and "difference" curricula may interdependently contribute to both restrictive, discriminatory curricular practice and equitable, thought-provoking learning experiences.* Adolescents' dialogue indicates how teachers' normative vs. deficit views, racialized assumptions, preferences and recursive actions, inform immediate interactive dynamics with students, and differentiate their learning opportunities and racialized experience of intended "sameness"/equivalent curriculum. Students' descriptions of social inequalities and disparate teacher-student educative relationships shaped their socially positioned identities and emotional experiences in the classroom, indicating that this type of "difference" curriculum is problematic. Common experiences of bias overlay and derail students' feelings of self-worth, and jeopardize the quality and rigor of unique, individualized, exploratory engagement in the classroom. "Sameness"/equal curricula can attend to students' varying interests, needs, and growth patterns, on the continuum towards just and fair "difference" curricula.

These conversations indicate that middle school students' material and intersubjective classroom experiences at the *micro* level, reflect dynamic power relations, structural hierarchies, and access to human resources *in the present, local classroom*, which also mirror *society's* race/class structures of inequality, and embody *historical enduring struggles* around racial discrimination and equality, at the *macro* level. These *social* dynamics and common experiences around race, which influenced the tenor and affective/intellectual dimensions of *individual* students' relational learning experiences, serve as an exemplar for classroom dynamics that may surface around ethnic, social class, language, sexuality, and ability differences in the middle school classroom.

My *Both/And Approach* posits that if educators attend to the multiple individual and social relational factors occurring in minute-to-minute classroom time, their own and students' personal/social histories and biases, and the sociohistorical realities and structures of inequality operating in the present, then a "routine" educational experience may be transformed into variegated, rigorous, engaging, humanizing inquiry for one and all. *Classroom Discussion* describes an

Accountable Talk reading class, based on a newspaper article, *NBA Makeover*.

Students discussed probable rationale for the NBA's proposed dress code. Race became a central issue. The teacher allowed for an open discussion, despite her vocalized reservation, "I think this is really provocative. It may not have been the best thing to read." She dealt with her immediate discomfort, conveying the pedagogical message: "In this classroom, the issue of race is discussable, manageable, and integral to this learning experience. Students are capable of wrestling with their own and others' viewpoints, within/across race/class lines, and can understand themselves and others."

The teacher was not restrained by notions of limited intellectual/emotional capabilities during early adolescence, the pressures of test-directed learning, or the suppression of adolescents' socially aberrant poor decision-making in conversation. Her "move" in the moment towards an equitable *"sameness-difference" curriculum,* allowed *individual students,* who inititated conceptual connections to race, to be engaged in an area of interest, and *all students* to develop and debate their arguments, draw connections both to *personal/social history* and *current dynamics* at *micro/school* and *macro/society levels,* and animatedly deconstruct the article's implicit/explicit messages. The rich disciplinarily integrative discussion, embodying *technical-practical-emancipatory knowledge,* culminated with students querying their own social practice and relations around social difference (Beane, 1997; McLaren, 2006). Judith's attuned pedagogical practice enabled a space for fluid, honest dialogue, students' keen observations, thoughtful analysis, and engaged consideration of new ideas with peers. Her decisions in this educational moment embodied her implicit views of youth; her concept of adolescent development and goals for middle school education; and her philosophy of her role as educator in teaching-learning processes. This classroom moment resists current efforts to reaffirm traditional adolescent views and educational practices, and embraces *critical Both/And* moves towards what is best for middle school youth.

Conclusion

My arguments and discursive analyses, relative to Vagle's pleas, highlight *both* the dynamic, historically imbued complexity of moment-to-moment classroom interactions *and* unfettered early adolescent developmental discourses; the interdependent generalized *and* particularized collective/individual experiences of youth, characterizing peer and teacher-student educational dynamics and relationships; and the value of problematizing "sameness" *and* "difference" curricula, in the context of social inequality. My arguments encourage *critical* theoretical analyses of and self-reflective attention to adolescent discourse, educational purposes and practices, from national reform policy to local classrooms—to ensure that we nurture vs. inhibit learning and enhance future personal and academic possibilities and goals for youth. In attending to social difference, *critical perspectives* must examine *structures of inequality* and *power relations* that privilege dominant Discourses, normalize meanings, and reaffirm inequality amongst early adolescents. My arguments are integral to promoting each adolescent's human potential across lines of difference, fostering just, fair school climates and societal contexts, and facing the challenge of promoting "openings" that *both* enable scholarly conversational debate *and* maintain a long-term commitment to attain enriching, *democratic education* for all early adolescent youth.

References

Alexander, W. (1968). *The emergent middle school.* New York: Holt, Rinehart, and Winston.

Ames, N. (2008). *National forum to accelerate middle-grades reform: History of key events and accomplishments.* Retrieved October 1, 2011 from http://www.mgforum.org/LinkClick.aspx?fileticket=fOYQTT0aTBs%3d&tabid=99&mid=451

Artiles, A., Klingner, J., & Tate, W. (Eds.). (2006). Representation of minority students in special education: Complicating traditional explanations. *Educational Researcher, 35*(6), 3 – 5.

Beane, J. (1997). *Curriculum integration: Designing the core of democratic education.* New York: Teachers College Press.

Bederman, G. (1995). *Manliness and civilization: A cultural history of gender and race in the Unites States, 1880-1917.* Chicago: University of Chicago Press.

Begley, S. (2/28/2000). Getting inside a teen brain. *Newsweek Magazine.* Retrieved July15, 2011 from http://www.thedailybeast.com/newsweek/2000/02/27/getting-inside-a-teen-brain.html

Brantlinger, E. A. (1993). *The politics of social class in secondary school: Views of affluent and impoverished youth.* New York: Teachers College Press.

Brown, E. (2007). The place of race in teacher identity: Self-narratives and curricular intervention as a practice of freedom. Kaleidescope Feature in Special Issue: Teacher Recognition and the Struggle for Identity, *Teacher Education and Practice, 19*(2), 257-279.

———. (2010a). A critical perspective on human development: Implications for adolescence, classroom practice, and middle school policy. In K. Lee & M. Vagle (Eds.) *Developmentalism in early childhood and middle grades education: Critical conversations on readiness and responsiveness* (183-208). New York: Palgrave Macmillan.

———. (2010b). *"For your own good" or "less is more": The mythical depiction of educational reform as social equality and investment in the future of all youth.* Paper presented at the 2010 Annual Meeting of the American Anthropological Association, New Orleans, LA.

——— .(2011). Freedom for some, discipline for "others": The structure of inequity in education. In K. Saltman & D. Gabbard (Eds.), *Education as enforcement: The militarization and corporatization of schools* (2nd ed.) (pp. 130-164). New York: Routledge.

Brown, E. & Saltman, K. (Eds.). (2005). *The critical middle school reader.* New York: Routledge.

Carnegie Corporation of New York. (1989). *Turning points: Preparing American youth for the 21st century.* New York: Carnegie Corporation of New York.

Compton, M., & Weiner, L. (Eds.) (2008). *The global assault on teaching, teachers, and their unions: Stories for resistance.* New York: Palgrave Macmillan.

David, J. (1992). *Growing up Black: From slave days to the present—Twenty-five African Americans reveal the trials and triumphs of their childhoods.* New York: Harper Perennial.

Elder, G. (1974). *Children of the Great Depression: Study in social structure and personality.* Chicago: University of Chicago Press.

Elliott, A. (2001). *Concepts of the self.* Cambridge, UK: Polity Press.
Ferguson, A. (2001). *Bad boys: Public schools in the making of black masculinity.* Ann Arbor, MI: University of Michigan Press.
Gans, H. (1995). *The war against the poor: The underclass and antipoverty policy.* New York: BasicBooks.
Giroux, H. (2009). *Youth in a suspect society: Democracy or disposability?* New York: Palgrave Macmillan.
Gramsci, A. (1971). *Selections from the prison notebooks.* New York: International Publishers Company.
Hall, G. S. (1904/2005). *Adolescence.* New York: Routledge.
Hall, S. (2005). From representation: Cultural representations and signifying practices. In E. Brown & K. Saltman, (Eds.), *Critical middle school reader,* (pp. 295-310). New York: Routledge.
Holland, D., & Lave, J. (Eds.). (2001). *History in person: Enduring struggles, contentious practice, and intimate identities.* Santa Fe, NM: School of American Research Press.
Hursh, D. (2008). *High stakes testing and the decline of teaching and learning: The real crisis in education.* Lanham, MD: Rowman & Littlefield Publishers.
Jackson, A., & Davis, G. (2000). *Turning points 2000: Educating adolescents in the 21st century.* New York: Teachers College Press.
Juvonen, J., Le, V., Kaganoff, T., Augustine, C., & Constant, L. (2004). *Focus on the wonder years: Challenges facing the American middle school.* Santa Monica, CA: Rand Corporation.
Katz, M. (1989). *The undeserving poor: From the war on poverty to the war on welfare.* New York: Pantheon Books.
Kenny, L. (2000). *Daughters of suburbia; growing up white, middle class, and female.* New Brunswick, NJ: Rutgers University Press.
Kozol, J. (2005). *The shame of the nation: The restoration of apartheid schooling in America.* New York: Crown Publishers.
Lee, S. (2009). *Unraveling the "model minority" stereotype: Listening to Asian American youth* (2nd ed.). New York: Teachers College Press.
Lipman, P. (2003). *High stakes education: Inequality, globalization, and urban educational reform.* New York: Routledge/Falmer.
MacLeod, J. (1995). *Ain't no makin' it: Aspirations in a low-income neighborhood.* Boulder, CO: Westview Press.
Males, M. (March/April, 1994). *Bashing youth, media myths about teenagers, Extra!* Retrieved September 17, 2011, at http://www.fair.org/index.php?page=1224
———. (2009). Does the adolescent brain make risk taking inevitable?: A skeptical appraisal. *Journal of Adolescent Research,* 24(1), 3-20.
McLaren, P. (2006). *Life in schools: Introduction to critical pedagogy in the foundations of education* (5th ed.). Upper Saddle River, NJ: Allyn & Bacon.
McNeil, L. (2000). *Contradictions of school reform: Educational costs of standardized testing.* New York: Routledge.
Moran, J. (2000). *Teaching sex: The shaping of adolescence in the 20th century.* Cambridge, MA: Harvard University Press.
Reed, R. (1997). *Growing up gay: The sorrows and joys of gay and lesbian adolescence.* New York: W. W. Norton & Co.

"Rethinking Middle School Education" (n.d.). *National Forum to Accelerate Middle Grades Reform*. Retrieved July 15, 2011 from http://www.mgforum.org/Home/tabid/36/Default.aspx

Rodis, P., Garrod, A., & Boscardin, M. (2000). *Learning disabilities and life stories*. Upper Saddle River, NJ: Allyn & Bacon.

Rogoff, B. (1990). *Apprenticeship in thinking: Cognitive development in social context*. New York: Oxford University Press.

Rossi, R. (7/22/11). CPS flips, drops teacher test.' *Chicago Sun-Times*, 4.

Sadker, D., Sadker, M., & Zittleman, K. (2009). *Still failing at fairness: How gender bias cheats girls and boys in school and what we can do about it*. New York: Scribner.

Saltzberger-Wittenberg, I. (1999). *The emotional experience of learning and teaching*. New York: Routledge.

Sercombe, H. (2010). The gift and the trap: Working the "teen brain" into our concept of adolescence. *Journal of Adolescent Research, 25*(1), 31-47.

Sheets, R.H., & Gay, G. (1996). Student perceptions of disciplinary conflict in ethnically diverse classrooms. *NASSP Bulletin, 80*(580), 84-94.

Sirin, S., & Fine, M. (2008). *Muslim American youth: Understanding hyphenated identities through multiple methods*. New York: New York University Press.

Spencer, M.B., & Tinsley, B. (2008). Identity as coping: Youths' diverse strategies for successful adaptation. *Prevention Researcher, 15*(4), 17-21.

Strauch, B. (2003). *The primal teen: What the new discoveries about the teenage brain tell us about our kids*. New York: Anchor Books.

U. S. Department of Education. (2001). *No Child Left Behind Act*. Washington, DC: U. S. Department of Education.

U.S. Department of Education. (2009). *Race to the Top program executive summary*. Washington, DC: U. S. Department of Education. Retrieved October 1, 2011 from http://www2.ed.gov/programs/racetothetop/executive-summary.pdf

U. S. Department of Education. (2010). *A Blueprint for reform: The reauthorization of the Elementary and Secondary Education Act*. Washington, DC: U. S. Department of Education. Retrieved October 1, 2011 from http://www2.ed.gov/policy/elsec/leg/blueprint/blueprint.pdf

Vagle, M. D. (this volume). Trying to poke holes in Teflon: Developmentalism; young adolescence; and contingent, recursive growth and change. In M. D. Vagle (Ed.) *Not a stage! A critical re-conception of young adolescent education* (pp. 11-38). New York: Peter Lang Publishing.

Valenzuela, A. (1999). *Subtractive schooling; U.S. Mexican youth and the politics of caring*. Albany: State University of New York Press.

Walsh, D. (2004). *Why do they act that way? A survival guide to the adolescent brain for you and your teen*. New York: Free Press.

Westheimer, J. (2009). No child left thinking: Democracy at-risk in American schools and what we need to do about it. In H. Shapiro (Ed.), *Education and hope for troubled times: Visions of change for our children's world* (pp. 259–271). New York: Routledge.

Chapter 7

Multiple Discourses and Missing Voices

Penny A. Bishop

The Call for Critical Perspectives

When I began my first teaching job in the early 1990s I was, like many new teachers I presume, eager and idealistic. The middle-level concept, something I had not studied explicitly in my teacher preparation, drew me in immediately. I found satisfying coherence in its attention to the whole child and the particular emphasis on relationships, yet I was perplexed by a largely missing discourse on gender. My undergraduate thesis had focused on girls' identity development, informed by the then growing body of literature on the inequitable education of girls in the U.S. As a result, I was equipped (biased? armed? blindsided? fortified?) with a decidedly gendered perspective when I joined the middle school teaching ranks. I recall wondering why the intersections between the middle-level concept and girls' development seemed to be more or less absent in the influential texts of the era (e.g., *This We Believe, Turning Points*) given what I viewed as obvious overlap. Were my tired teachers' eyes just overlooking these connections?

In retrospect, of course, I see greater complexity. A quick ERIC search of *Middle School Journal*, the most widely disseminated publication aimed at middle school educators, provides an interesting entry point for consideration today. The journal is archived electronically on the Education Resources Information Center (ERIC) database back to 1975. Out of a total of 869 journal articles, only 14 come up under a search for the keyword "girls"; 7 under "boys"; and 26 under "gender." Interestingly, not one of these articles appears prior to 1993. Although obviously not empirical, my cursory exploration of the database provides a sense of the field of middle grades education, of what is deemed worthy to disseminate and therefore what 'counts.' From it, we can see relatively little attention paid to gender within the middle school movement prior to the 1990s and how it has, at least in this one venue, grown surprisingly little since then.

My point here is not to advocate for heightened attention to gender (although in another venue I might very well do so). In fact, in his anchor essay, Vagle (this volume) makes a strong case for shedding such classification or characterization in favor of particularizing. Rather, I include this anecdote to provide one illustration of the relative lack of critical stances within our field historically.

Vagle's point that the concept of development stems from a white, male, middle-class, heterosexual perspective is well grounded. Although we see a more diverse group of influential thinkers and leaders in the field today, the middle school movement was shaped largely by white men. The five individuals "widely recognized as the founders of the middle school movement" (Smith & McEwin, 2011, p. xix) are white and male. Of the total group of eighteen identified by Smith and McEwin as "substantive" contributors to middle-level education only four are women and none are people of color.

While this situation is not unique to our field, it raises questions about the diversity of perspectives informing our collective work. It clearly calls for more air to be let through what Vagle terms the "lid of developmentalism" (p. 17) and the many other lids that are perhaps too tight. Multiple critical discourses are essential to the growth and ongoing improvement of middle grades education. Vagle's call for the "amplification of….muted perspectives" (p. 12) is long overdue.

In this chapter I build upon Vagle's plea for a contingently and recursively relational perspective by examining the concept of contradictory identities in light of James (1974) work on polarities. I then explore societal perspectives on adolescents as *being* vs. *becoming* and on our accompanying expectations of and for youth. The upside of characterizing is considered next, exploring the pragmatic side of generalities and questioning the potential oversimplification of developmentalism's 'frozen in time' status. Finally, I propose we include the missing student voices in our discourses and move from academic rhetoric to action at the policy and practice levels

Multiple and Opposing Identities

In his anchor essay, Vagle invited us to poke holes in the teflon lid of developmentalism to provide air and space for other perspectives. He asserted that treating early adolescence as "a distinct developmental stage [is] an assumption that in effect 'freezes' students in time and space without agency, context, politics, or power" (p. 17). Indeed, the contingent and recursive perspective he proposed appears to allow for the myriad contexts in which humans *are*. It provides a place to consider "seeing young adolescents in innumerable, lived (denaturalized) contexts" (Vagle, p. 20). One of the greatest merits of Vagle's position, in fact, is his use of this quote from Lesko (2001),

> to consider the simultaneity of what may appear to be contradictory identities such as adolescents being mature and immature and learning and learned at the same moments in time, as opposed to being immature and learning at one point in time and necessarily moving toward a state of maturity and learnedness in adulthood. (p. 15)

Although largely lacking in contemporary discourse, entertaining multiple and opposing identities simultaneously has long been linked to young adolescents. Almost 40 years ago, British educator Charity James described the educational needs of young adolescents as polarities that exist simultaneously:

> The need to need/the need to be needed, the need to move inwards/the need to affect the outer world, the need for routine/the need for intensity, the need for myth and legend/the need for fact, the need for stillness/the need for activity, the need for separateness/the need for belonging. (1974, p. 18)

This perspective, admittedly characterizing more than particularizing, enables us to consider these multiple and concurrent identities as fluid, rather than frozen in time.

One primary critique of the developmental discourse is that it describes "young adolescents as developing creatures who, if different, are viewed as variations of the norm—as if the norm itself is somehow not a construction..." (Vagle, p. 25). It is not without irony that the stimulus for a developmental perspective appears to have stemmed from a remarkably similar desire to make room for difference—for the particulars, if you will. Eichhorn, for example, encouraged the field to adopt the medical concept of developmental age, precisely because it was "much more consistent than the graded concept, which does not allow for the great variation in student attributes" (p. 25, in Smith & McEwin, 2011). Our contemporary challenge is both to embrace this variation in attributes and to honor students' simultaneous and multiple identities. Vagle's call for considering the young adolescent as a whole person is an important start to tackling this challenge.

Young AdolescenTS as Whole People

Perhaps the best possible outcome of Vagle's argument for a contingent and recursive perspective on young adolescents would be viewing each student as a person who *is* in the here and now, rather than a person who *is becoming*—that we move to a "social construction of adolescence that views young adolescents as "whole" people" (p. 17). This stance calls for considerable belief in young adolescents; in their power and knowledge; and in the notion that they already possess what they need to participate meaningfully as citizens of our world.

These beliefs contrast starkly with the view many societies hold—including my own in the U.S.—about the value and worth of middle school aged youth. As a teacher educator, I routinely introduce teachers to the concept of negotiated curriculum (e.g., Beane, 1997) or other teaching approaches that place student concerns and interests at the center. Many are quick to say, "Yes, but *my* students could never do this...." This lack of faith is further embodied by the pervasive use of derogatory terms to describe the age group. I have taught with teachers who referred to middle grades students as "hormones with legs" and with others who claimed sixth graders were "sub-human." These degrading comments do little to foster societal faith in the age group and do much to erode the great potential of young adolescents.

Sadly, this demeaning attitude toward youth is not limited to this time or place, as James revealed,

> Can twelve to sixteen be isolated as an age range with identifiable problems of its own...? If aunts count as evidence, I have a formidable one to offer on behalf of this particular brief. When I was 14, mine looked at me and said, 'People of your age ought to be put away for four years where none of us would have to see you'. (p. 6)

Given the increasing trend toward earlier puberty over the decades, James' aunt very well could have been speaking about ten to fourteen-year-olds in the U.S. in the 21st century, rather than in mid-20th-century Britain. 'Seen and not heard' comments echo still today in various ways. In contrast, "a contingent recursive curriculum assumes that young adolescents already have what it takes to live, learn, and theorize their world" (p. 33), and therefore holds the potential to shift conditions of long-standing power dynamics.

The Upside of Characterizing

Whether negative or positive, perhaps characterizing has been relied on so heavily by the field because of a need to define and classify, both as humans uncomfortable with liminal status and as educators needing to teach each day in real classrooms with real students. It is typical for those defining liminality, historically an anthropological term, to use adolescence as an example of such status. Kahane, for example, asserted, "Teenagers, being neither children nor adults, are liminal people: indeed, for young people, liminality of this kind has become a permanent phenomenon....Postmodern liminality" (1997, p. 31). In the absence of established structures, people are tempted to impose their own, to bring meaning to the liminal state (Horvath, Thomassen, & Wydra, 2009).

For all of its limitations, characterizing has offered a pragmatic side to the world of theory and research. Teachers face daily demands of classroom life and complex, ever changing students. The best middle grades teachers know that education is about relationship and that to do their job effectively they must know each student well, in his or her myriad contexts and relationships. Identifying general traits of the age group does not require the exclusion of particulars. As the mother of boys ages 11 and 13, I do not have to look far to see the complexity of their lives and how that complexity intertwines with their myriad relationships. Concomitantly, understanding some common characteristics of young adolescents—of my sons and their many friends who traipse regularly through our home—provides a helpful orientation to my parenting, just as it did to my middle school teaching. I am not prevented from particularizing. Knowing that these young adolescents are often experimenting with various identities or that they increasingly value peer relationships helps mediate my approach and interactions with them. Not all the time, of course. But it does not freeze them in time. Nor does it freeze my perceptions of them in time. On the contrary, in fact, it reminds me of the continual changes they are experiencing, often simultaneously.

Characterizing and generalizing can be dangerous, however, as Vagle reminded us that categories are built with particular aims in mind and are not neutral acts (p. 20). Indeed, "to claim to be neutral is both foolhardy and disingenuous because it flies in the face of what our work is about, that is, using research for the improvement of the human condition through education" (Nieto, 2011, p. 1). Who gets to define what constitutes the improvement of the human condition through education is, of course, deeply political. Both the developmental and the contingent, recursive perspectives become dangerous when they omit crucial stakeholder voices.

Eliciting the Missing Voices: From Discourse to Action

The shortcoming of most discourses in education is that all too often students remain outside of them. Students' perspectives, self-reported attributes, contexts, and identities have played a meager role in the dominant discourse of developmentalism over the decades. In contrast, the student perspective has the potential to be an integral part of a contingent and recursive conception of growth and change. Vagle advocates that the agency for curriculum and standards "be displaced from outside authority and (re)placed into the hands of young adolescents and their teachers" (p. 29). Similarly, he proposed that the term 'young adolescent education' replace 'middle grades education' as a means to keep the student at the center of our field. Finally, Vagle offered, "if all educators dedicated to young adolescent learners are not collectively challenging themselves to bring *all* [emphasis mine] possible perspectives to bear, in the end, the young adolescents will suffer" (p. 15).

How might we use this alternate theorizing as a means to reorient our beliefs about who gets to participate in the discourse? And how do we ensure all really means all? Too often, all ultimately means adult, thus reinforcing existing power dynamics. Advancing a new discourse is an opportune time for our field to include missing voices. How might a contingent, recursive perspective be further shaped by students' identification of their views and lived experiences?

While useful in informing theory, bringing students' perspectives into conversations with teachers provides the added benefit of contributing to school improvement efforts, moving from discourse to action. We risk much when we underestimate the power of student involvement when young adolescents participate in shaping the culture of school and of learning. What happens when we acknowledge that young adolescents are experts about themselves and their education? Consulting those most likely to be knowledgeable about their learning needs—and those historically least likely to be asked—has the potential to provide educators with a critical glimpse into the minds of the individual and collective students in their classrooms. These new perspectives can inform pedagogy in powerful ways.

Various models of student agency can invite these perspectives. Consider one, a weeklong middle grades institute, wherein teachers, principals and students gather to improve the practices in their middle grades schools. Common to all experiences is the intentional and careful positioning of student as expert. Students serve as consultants, panelists, and initiators involved in and informing the adult learning of the week. They sit in on classes, offering their opinions and advice. They convene panels on life as a middle schooler; on what it's like to be 13; on what's great—or not so great—about their schooling experience.

After working closely with middle school student consultants for a week, one participating teacher offered these thoughts:

> This institute, especially the close work with students, moved my perceptions of teacher from authority figure to partner. I saw successful demonstrations of how middle school students can control and direct their own education if teachers first let them and then provide support. (Middle Grades Teacher, 2011)

Notably, this teacher's emphasis was not on what he learned about young adolescents in general, but rather how he came to understand the powerful role students can take in advancing their own understanding. As Vagle noted, these particulars cannot be generalized, but "such a project opens up the particular so that we, instead, see a realm of possibilities that can be constantly pursued" (p. 26).

While this teacher's words are hopeful in considering a movement from discourse to action, Cook-Sather (2002) identified twin challenges associated with advancing student perspective in the dialogue about youth and school reform: 1) a change in mind-set; and 2) a change in the structures in educational relationships and institutions. While giving "more air" (Vagle, p. 35) to alternative theorizing enables us to attend to Cook-Sather's first challenge, only action will attend to the second. Listening to students requires considerable courage. If we have faith in students' *being* rather than *becoming*—in young adolescents as whole people—then we have a responsibility to act. Yet, what if such actions run counter to the accountability era in which we find ourselves?

Action in an Era of Accountability

Advocating that students play a greater role in the discourses that inform their school experience provokes inevitable questions: "If students help develop curriculum, how do you meet the standards? How are your test scores?" Rarely, however, does the conversation move from concern about standardized tests scores to discussions of disrupting the status quo or advocating for alternatives. Rather, we see educators often paralyzed and powerless by the increasing fear that accompanies the wide publishing of test scores by school and by teacher; the firing of entire faculties and principals; and the closing of schools. Nieto noted that

> Much of what we know about education runs counter to current reform efforts in US education and, as is often the case, the most powerless and marginalized, both students and teachers, are the greatest victims. Numerous policies and practices come to mind: the stubborn insistence that there are some mythical "best practices" that work for all students in all situations; ... the policy of testing students to death, in the process taking the joy and creativity out of teaching and learning; the indiscriminate bashing of teachers as if they alone, and not the ills of society, were the cause of student failure.... (2011, p. 1)

At a recent visit to a wealthy district on the west coast of the U.S., I was struck by the traditional methods that remained pervasive in each building. The school board, superintendent and principals alike expressed their concerns to me that they were not moving effectively into the 21st century, particularly with regard to technology integration. Their test scores were adequate; there was no sense of urgency, they explained, which is why little innovation had occurred over the past decade. As I talked with the teachers, they widely agreed that the most effective learning stems from curriculum that holds relevance for the students themselves. They often identified interdisciplinary and project-based work as times when students were most engaged and eager in their classrooms, referring to it as "the old middle school concept, remember that?" They were quick to add, however, that "We don't do that type of teaching anymore." As one veteran teacher summarized, "If it's not on the test, then we don't teach it."

A contingent, recursive perspective reinforces Nieto's point that there are no "best practices" that work for all students in all situations; as such, the perspective calls for significant disruption in the status quo. It supports practices that students—in their own contexts and particulars—participate in and lead, including curriculum development and assessment. Vagle asserted,

> We have set up a system that is designed primarily to test, measure, and control young people. It is difficult to keep the young adolescent and their learning at the forefront of policy and practice when their test score becomes the primary way they are talked about and educated. (p. 33)

A shift to a contingent, recursive perspective has the *potential* to redefine how we think about teaching and learning, what constitutes curriculum, and how we define and measure student outcomes. If it has the *power* to disrupt deeply rooted practices and policies, we will only learn through action.

A Call to Action

While in academia we have the luxury to debate such perspectives, improving the daily lives and education of young adolescents demands more than rhetoric. Willinsky (2011) invited us to consider this question:

> there are many ways of doing something valuable with the knowledge that we acquire in our study of education. We draw on such knowledge in our teaching, as well as in our work with teachers, schools, administrators, and policymakers. We share our work with other scholars by presenting it at conferences and publishing it in scholarly journals and books. Does that mean that we are already doing enough with what we know? (p. 1)

We are not, in fact, doing enough with what we know. I add to Vagle's pleas my own plea for action and for academics to consider how to translate the best of the developmental vs. contingent, recursive debate into policies and practices that meet real students' needs in real classrooms. The re-orientation and adoption of multiple perspectives may be a helpful paradigm shift within our field, but it alone is insufficient for real change.

As we consider how to take action at the policy level, young adolescents from the institute I described earlier had these practice level recommendations for their teachers:

Treat our ideas like they're important
Let us be ourselves
Sometimes we need to be alone
Don't talk down to us
Make our work more fun
Recognize my activities out of the classroom
Spend more time together (sometimes we actually want to be with you!)
Listen to what I have to say
Be yourself
Help us when we need it
Please give us some time and space
Trust us sometimes
Let us come to you for help
We are human beings too, so treat us like it
Don't plan my future without me

Table 1: Practice level recommendations

The contingent and recursive perspective reminds us to strive continually to understand our young adolescents, a view that aligns with the long-held middle grades emphasis on community and relationship. At the end of the day, developmental, contingent, recursive or otherwise, isn't the field of middle grades education really about humanity? It is about creating a humane and just education for the students in our shared schools.

References

Beane, J. A. (1997). *Curriculum integration: Designing the core of democratic education.* New York: Teachers College Press.

Cook-Sather, A. (2002). Authorizing students' perspectives: Toward trust, dialogue, and change in education. *Educational Researcher, 31*(4), 3-14.

Horvath, A., Thomassen, B., & Wydra, H. (2009). IPA3 Introduction: Liminality and cultures of change. *International Political Anthropology, 2*(1), 3-4.

James, C. (1974). *Beyond customs: An educator's journey*. London: Agathon Press.

Kahane, R. (1997). *The origins of postmodern youth: Informal youth movements in a comparative perspective.* New York: Walter de Gruyter.

Lesko, N. (2001). *Act your age: A cultural construction of adolescence.* New York: Routledge/Falmer.

Nieto, S. (2011). *Speaking truth to power in educational research.* Retrieved June 26, 2011 from http://aera.net/uploadedFiles/Meetings_and_Events/2012_Annual_Meeting/Nieto%20AERA%202012%20essay.pdf

Smith, T. W., & McEwin, C. K. (Eds.). (2011). *Legacy of middle level leaders: In their own words.* Charlotte, NC: Information Age Publishing.

Vagle, M. D. (this volume). Trying to poke holes in Teflon: Developmentalism; young adolescence; and contingent, recursive growth and change. In M. D. Vagle (Ed.), *Not a stage! A critical re-conception of young adolescent education* (pp. 11-38). New York: Peter Lang Publishing.

Willinsky, J. (2011) *Increasing education research's standing as a public good.* Retrieved June 26, 2011 from http://aera.net/uploadedFiles/Meetings_and_Events/2012_Annual_Meeting/Willinsky_AERA%20Statement1b.pdf

Chapter 8

Using Students' Funds of Knowledge to Enhance Middle Grades Education: Responding to Adolescen(TS)

Leslie David Burns & Leigh A. Hall

Introduction

This chapter discusses how responding to adolescents' self-reported identities can generate contingent, recursive curriculum designs that enhance motivation, engagement, and therefore cognition and learning in middle grades classrooms. Though our referents for this discussion come from the fields of literacy and English education in which we work, we respond to all three of Vagle's pleas (this volume) in ways that apply across all content areas. First, we call for a movement away from characterizing "adolescence" as a universally predictable stage of human development. Instead, we argue for particularized treatment of adolescenTS as individuals—even as they engage in communities, groups, and cultures that (sometimes) involve adoption of predictable discursive practices, and even as their cognitive abilities mature. Second, we argue for movement away from curriculum and instruction based on *developmentally* responsive pedagogies currently institutionalized as the norm in middle grades classrooms. Instead, we argue for a particularized mode of responsive curriculum and instruction based on recursive and relational assessments of adolescents' identities and the multiple funds of knowledge they bring to school with them. Data from these assessments can be used to generate classroom environments that motivate and engage youth in ways correlated with increased academic achievement. In conclusion, we call for movement from a "sameness" curriculum to a "difference" curriculum in which schools and teachers use data about their students' identities to select resources and instructional strategies, design literacy activities for classroom practice, and create assessments that are equitable and relevant to young adolescents' application of knowledge and skills in their ongoing educations, careers, and daily lives.

Beyond Development: From Adolescence to AdolescenTS

In research on secondary English education conducted over the last fifty years, studies using the principles of developmental psychology have been both prominent and productive. Such work has used theories of human development to study, describe, and even quantify general characteristics of individuals as classified by age groups and grade levels. The notion of cognitive development (e.g., Piaget) has been useful in understanding broad phases of maturation that humans go through as they age. As Vagle notes in this volume, the precepts of stage developmentalism have helped us address some needs of young adolescents, but they have done so at a cost. Vagle points out that curricular applications of developmentalism have not been careful enough. They have failed to account for important nuances and critiques from critical theory related to issues of power and identity.

Although developmentalist research in secondary English education has helped guide educators to understand, for example, what a normalized group of 7th grade-level early adolescents may be capable of in cognitive terms compared to younger and older students (Brass & Burns, 2011)—that research has been over-generalized and institutionalized in ways that are administratively expedient rather than pedagogically justifiable. For example, while numerous studies (e.g., Combs, 1976; Crowhurst, 1980; Pope, 1978) of complexity in student writing at different grade levels have repeatedly shown that students' use of complex sentences increases as they age, such studies have been used to argue that all students develop syntactic maturity at a developmentally predictable rate. Such conclusions have led standardized reading programs that prescribe possible reading resources according to Lexile measurements per grade level. Lexile measures are used to determine the readability of a text for students at a particular grade level and are determined by averaging word frequency and sentence length, with the assumption that these measures can help educators "match" certain texts with a particular grade level based on what students at that developmental level are (supposedly) able to comprehend (or not). Such a move makes selecting instructional resources efficient while ignoring the fact that many students at a given grade level might not and should not be expected to read at a certain level of text complexity. The wholesale application of developmental stages as universal and predictable constructs in the design and implementation of middle grades education ignores developmental psychology's own principles regarding the profoundly variable nature (and normal distribution) of actual human development. Youths' cognitive development is extremely relative, and it depends on multiple variables including race, social class, culture, gender, and many other factors that are not explicitly considered in developmentalist perspectives.

While stage developmentalism has been used by middle grades educators (NMSA, 2010) to argue that schools should be responsive to the needs of young adolescents, its principles are problematic specifically due to over-generalization about what it means to be a young adolescent. Erikson's (1968) model of ego identity development suggests that adolescence is a time when individuals are examining who they are and trying out many new identities that shift constantly. However, those identities do not necessarily adhere to traditional conceptions of human development (e.g., Caskey & Anfara, 2007; Jackson & Davis, 2000). Rather, young adolescents' identities—and therefore their needs and capacities as learners—are ever-changing and varied regardless of broader notions of the "stages" that all students supposedly enter at particular times in life. In any given classroom, some students will function exactly as developmental psychologists would predict; others will be more advanced in their cognitive and identity development; and others still will be at earlier stages of any developmental continuum.

When educators design curriculum and implement instruction on the assumption that all youth are (or ought to be) "on level", they fundamentally ignore the diversity of human populations and their variance in any social context and position any student who does not fit the institutional definition of that grade level's "stage" to fail. Alternately, educators who operate primarily on the basis of developmental stages are likely to marginalize students who are capable of going beyond grade-level expectations, and they are extremely likely to respond negatively toward students whose racial, cultural, socioeconomic, and gendered identities do not conform to a given stage's assumptions. The very notion of adolescence as a stage of human growth is less than 100 years old, and its principles are in fact socially constructed rather than physiologically or cognitively inherent. They are bound by certain cultural (Western, White, and Modernist) assumptions about social roles, childhood, and what it means to behave as an adult. Curricula based on stage developmentalism are more oriented to models of social efficiency than they are to actual responsive teaching designed to educate critical thinkers and citizens.

Responsive teaching and curriculum ought to account for broad principles of human development. Such principles can even be used as baselines for selecting resources, designing assessments, and framing tasks for youth to engage in during academic learning. However, truly responsive curriculum and instruction involves assessing the identities of particular students in particular classrooms at particular times. It involves using the data gathered during these recurring assessments to tailor education so that it is strategically relevant to the learners a school serves. Responsive teaching is about collaboration between educators and learners—collaboration that positions youth as "primary knowers" (Aukerman, 2007)—learners who are treated as knowledgeable, fully engaged participants in their own learning rather than passive receptacles for direct transmission of content knowledge. This alternate brand of responsive teaching focuses on empowering students rather than controlling subjectivities. It enables teachers to work with diverse students and respond to their identities and needs, and it has measurable cognitive results in terms of increased performance (Steele, 2010). Following Lesko's arguments (2001), approaches that assume growth and change are contingent means that educators must pay close attention to the microcontexts of the classrooms and communities in which they collaborate with youth. Moreover, assessment of data in these microcontexts must be recursive in order to ensure both curriculum and teaching change and develop along with the youth they are intended to support. As Lesko asserts, "a recursive view of growth and change directs us to look at local contexts and specific actions of young people, without the inherent evaluation of steps, stages, and socialization" (p. 196).

Adolescents do develop—sometimes in predictable ways and at predictable times. Global study of adolescent development can be useful. But it is dangerous to use such research to standardize adolescence in public education contexts (e.g., using Lexile measurements of texts to determine what books are acceptable for students to read at a particular grade level), or to institutionalize curricula intended to address the needs of adolescenTS that are inherently variable. Development depends on identities, which depend on experiences. Relevance, as the key element in motivating youth to learn, is the key to engagement. And if engagement is the key to successful academic performance in school, then responsive teaching based on assessing the identities, capacities, knowledges, and experiences of youth in specific classrooms must be the heart of any successful curriculum.

In order to understand why teaching based on youths' identities is crucial to enhanced learning in middle grades contexts, it is necessary to discuss the constructs of self-efficacy, motivation, and engagement in learning.

Motivation, Engagement, and Responsive Teaching

Fundamentally, a student's motivation to learn is related to his/her sense of self-efficacy—his or her confidence that s/he can participate, understand, and succeed (Wigfield, 1997). For example, when learners feel confident that they can understand and participate in classroom literacy practices, they become more willing to persist even when challenged by new texts or problems. When young adolescents experience early and ongoing success with academic reading and other classroom work, they develop a continuing impulse to learn and thereby engage more purposefully (Thomas & Oldfather, 1997). They become more motivated because of the positive feelings and beliefs that success generates in their minds.

Beyond its relation to self-efficacy, motivation to learn in classrooms results from a blend of internal and external reasons for participating in school. These reasons may be intrinsic (due purely to personal enjoyment and/or interest), extrinsic (due to external inducements), or a combination of the two (Otis, Grouzet, & Pelletier, 2005). Interest and attitude play a role (Guthrie & Alao, 1997), as does freedom to choose both the texts to be used and the purposes for learning (Schraw, Flowerday, & Reisetter, 1998). Support from teachers is significant as is positive social interaction (Wentzel, 1997).

When students decide academic work will consistently benefit them they begin to consciously regulate their behaviors in ways that generate intrinsic motivation and result in increased engagement (Otis et al., 2005).

Engagement can be defined as willing, focused, active participation, and is characterized by purposeful use of strategies to achieve goals (Guthrie & Wigfield, 2000). Numerous studies in literacy demonstrate that when youth are enabled via curriculum design and responsive teaching to engage in learning using resources relevant to their daily lives and experiences, their academic achievement increases (Alvermann et al., 1996; Guthrie & Davis, 2003; Moje & Hinchman, 2004). Simply put, engaged learners have stronger learning outcomes than disengaged learners (Guthrie et al., 2006). The question, then, is: How can teachers of young adolescenTS generate positive motivations that lead to increased classroom engagement?

Guthrie and Wigfield (2000) outline an *engagement perspective* teachers can use to guide their work toward these ends. Generating motivation and engagement involves establishing six inter-related conditions (Guthrie et al., 2006). First, establishing explicitly stated knowledge goals related to content area learning provides students with clear purposes for every single classroom activity. Second, to complement the establishment of explicit knowledge goals teachers should introduce, model, and assign students to practice learning and thinking strategies such as predicting, summarizing, and questioning content in a text or a performance situation. These first two conditions alone—knowledge goals and strategy instruction—often have positive effects on students' learning (Grolnick & Ryan, 1987). Third and fourth, providing a variety of interesting texts and allowing students choice in both what they learn and how they demonstrate understanding increases engagement. When students can choose at least some of the texts they read, the tasks they complete, or the peers they interact with while learning, their motivations increase and they become more purposefully engaged (Guthrie et al., 2006). Fifth, teachers can generate real-world interactions to increase engaged learning. A real-world experience with text in an English class, for example, might be taking the opportunity to listen to and interview a Holocaust survivor while reading Anne Frank's (1993) *The Diary of a*

Young Girl. Finally, real-world interactions require students to work toward shared goals and to collaborate on a regular basis, which increases motivation and engagement (Guthrie & Davis, 2003).

The six conditions described above constitute a perspective teachers can use to design instruction and increase students' self-efficacy, which in turn opens the way to generating positive motivations that lead to engaged learning. As a result of increased engagement, students tend to participate more, understand more, and feel motivated to continue working over time. At its heart, focusing on the conditions for engagement is about supporting learners' ability to act on their own and participate in their own educations (Reeve & Jang, 2006). Contrary to the ways in which research on motivation is sometimes translated, these conditions are not simplistically intended to make learning more fun for young adolescents or to merely boost their self-esteem. They systematically lighten students' cognitive loads and literally make it easier for them to learn the intended and assessed curricula of middle grades classrooms. Perhaps most importantly, the engagement perspective underscores the utility of going beyond pre-packaged and/or developmental programs schools often use to remediate learners who do not conform to institutionalized expectations. Rather, the engagement perspective requires teachers to assess adolescents' identities and use that data to contextualize instruction so that it is relevant not only for the purposes of the school, but also, and especially, to the youth that school is supposed to serve.

In the next section, we describe how using students' funds of knowledge from outside of school can help educators respond to a broader array of diverse learners, escape the constraints of stage developmentalism without sacrificing its utility, and move beyond institutionalized notions of adolescence to truly meet the needs of adolescenTS.

Using Students' Funds of Knowledge to Make a "Difference"

In their research about the nature of students' knowledge outside of school, Moll, Amanti, Neff, and Gonzalez (1992) and Moje et al. (2004) generated categories for different types of knowledge ("funds") that children bring with them to school. The goal of their research is to consider how educators can use such knowledge to design curriculum and instruction that responds to students' needs in local communities, while also helping them succeed in the present U.S. system of educational accountability.

Students' funds of knowledge come from many sources, and knowledge may cross categories or overlap contexts. Funds of knowledge are sources of experience, information, and understanding that people bring to any learning process (Moje et al., 2004). For example, young adolescents bring knowledge with them to school that has its roots in their family and community lives such as the work their parents do at home and in their jobs, or their religious and cultural practices in their local communities. People also understand the world based on funds from popular culture such as television, film, music, art, and other forms of mass media they consume. By collecting data about students' family structures, relationships, working lives, domestic activities, and household routines or traditions, teachers gain insight into students' existing areas of skill and interest, vocabularies, and norms for social interaction that may vary by culture, gender, social class, and other variables that cannot be accounted for via the application of a universal stage developmentalism on its own. Teachers can then use that data to select resources more strategically, adapt instructional techniques, and teach disciplinary content using scenarios students are more likely to understand and participate in.

Data collected by assessing students' identities and funds of knowledge doesn't replace the need to teach content or academic literacies. It supplements, complements, and contextualizes classroom work. A teacher, for example, who uses students' knowledge of video games is not teaching video games as an end in itself. Rather, that teacher is using systematically collected assessment data to identify and use the topics, models, content, and structures of video games to help students understand, talk about, and practice disciplinary knowledge and skills they need in order to perceive academic content as relevant to their everyday lives. Consequently, assessing and using students' funds of knowledge leads to the treatment of adolescenTS as individuals rather than members of a homogenized mass. That individualized treatment increases engagement, which strongly correlates with increased learning.

A caution: According to Friese et al. (2008), it is not acceptable to select resources for teaching and learning solely on the basis of students' interests and knowledge outside school. Just because the majority of students in a particular classroom enjoy a television program, book, film, or musical genre does not mean it is appropriate or useful for academic instruction. We do not subscribe to the clichéd notion that TV "rots the brain," for example, but we absolutely acknowledge sometimes a text is considered by some education interest groups to be inappropriate for use in teaching young adolescents even though they might consume and produce those texts on a regular basis. A potential resource may involve content that some would perceive as profane or otherwise exclusively for adult audiences, or because they believe it simply lacks quality in terms of structure, content, and production. While these judgments about appropriateness and quality are always socially constructed (and often highly contestable), they are often real issues that educators must consider when designing and implementing curricula for young adults in different contexts.

Many teachers may feel that using pop culture texts such as movies, music, and television programs involves "dumbing down" the curriculum compared to using traditionally defined "classic" texts and primary sources in school. However, texts that fail to interest students—as many novels and poems deemed "classic" do—results in decreased motivation, frustration for youth who struggle to comprehend those texts, and decreased engagement. Moje et al. (2004) found that popular culture was not only an important fund of knowledge unto itself, but also perhaps the most important fund of knowledge available for teaching student's disciplinary knowledge in schools. They found that using popular culture texts helped students feel more able to engage with their peers in ways that supported their most valued identities, increased their sense of efficacy as learners, and supported higher levels of achievement.

Assessing students' funds of knowledge is not only useful in terms of helping teachers select texts and topics students find interesting. Doing so also provides information about what students value most, how they interact with authority figures in their daily lives, how they are accustomed to using language, how they understand their own roles and responsibilities in communication with adults and peers, and more. So, for example, it is certainly plausible that a teacher might learn a majority of students in a classroom have parents who work in factories, or in managerial jobs, or in service industries that suggest particular topics and themes that would be familiar and therefore useful in selecting texts and designing activities for a class. But in addition, the teacher might find the majority of students are used to communicating with adults and peers outside of school in ways that are highly interactive and in which people are not only expected to seek attention but to compete for it based on cultural or local values. In such a case, the teacher can use that data to understand why certain students appear to speak out of turn during classroom interactions and recognize when and how to teach such children the expectations and modes of participation required in traditional academic contexts. At the same time, the teacher can use assessments of students' family and community funds to realize their needs for collaborative learning techniques, explicit instruction, and relevant content that affirm their identities while still teaching them the content and practices required in any formal curriculum.

There can be little doubt that teachers can better support young adolescents when they systematically assess funds of knowledge beyond school. However, such data can be used wisely or poorly. Moll et al. (1992) warn that educators must avoid stereotyping students based on findings about funds of knowledge. For example, assessment data showing a group of students overall enjoys hip-hop or country music does not mean that all students are the same, or that any hip-hop or country music will therefore be useful during instruction. Before applying such assessments wholesale, teachers must ask their students what particular texts and scenarios mean for them, how they use them, why they communicate in particular ways in particular situations, and so forth. Based on the refinement of funds of knowledge data, teachers can decide what students need for success in school and how to structure classroom interactions to the greatest advantage. Without that refinement, teachers risk alienating students even more, stereotyping them, or failing to connect their funds of knowledge to disciplinary content in ways that are clearly relevant and productive.

Similarly, the funds of knowledge data useful for teaching reading in one classroom is not always the same data that will be useful for teaching in another classroom—sometimes even within the same school (Moje et al., 2004). What students know, do, and value in one neighborhood or household or geographic location may vary compared with students in another group. Teachers must take care to keep up with students' ever-changing and expanding knowledges and experiences in order to be responsive. As is true with any form of assessment in education, teachers must contingently and recursively collect, review, and analyze data to make adjustments over time.

Conclusion: From Teaching Adolescence to Teaching AdolescenTS

Even as we strongly encourage teachers of young adolescents to work with youth via systematic assessment of students' funds of knowledge, we realize current demands for accountability and testing in public schools make it difficult to implement that approach. Developmental models dominate the construction of assessments used in high-stakes accountability, and as a result they dominate the ways in which middle grades classrooms are often structured. However, as Marsh (2006) concludes, "If we do not ensure...teachers are aware of the realities of children's out-of-school literacy lives, shaped as these are by popular culture, media, and new technologies, then we are likely to continue to have literacy curricula...that are anachronistic and inadequate..." (p. 173). If teachers allow themselves to simply implement the curriculum and tests required by schools and states without regard for students' existing funds, they will perpetuate the current status quo in which so many students struggle because they aren't given the time, resources, reasons, or opportunities they need to be successful (Scherff & Piazza, 2008).

Still, it is hard to bypass the workplace conditions and political realities of public schools that get in the way of using funds of knowledge data for responsive teaching. Current state/federal accountability systems in the U.S. constrain curriculum to an extreme degree, making it difficult and even risky for teachers to attempt instruction that integrates students' funds. Lee (1998) notes that students (as well as parents, administrators, and teachers) may resist curricula that don't look like traditional schooling because they violate assumptions about what should happen in school (teachers lecturing students who sit quietly in rows completing worksheets, read "classics," etc.). Most teachers will probably have to compromise their attempts to respond to students' funds and integrate that work into existing traditional structures.

However, just as teaching and learning are social practices, so are assessment and policy making. It may be necessary for teachers and schools to ensure students meet standards for high-stakes assessments, but that necessity must be understood for what it is—a political need for efficiency, not a pedagogically justifiable practice that helps adolescents learn. As Johnston and Costello (2005) note, "high stakes accountability testing has consistently been demonstrated to *undermine* teaching and learning" (p. 258) by forcing teachers to shortchange, drop, or simply ignore practices, texts, and knowledge about students that they would otherwise use to enhance instruction, motivation, and the learning environment. While we acknowledge political issues and the realities of standardized testing may impede teachers from using students' funds of knowledge as fully as possible, finding ways to blend our approach with existing practices is not only useful but essential to the well-being of schools in contemporary society. Our job is to use assessment to ensure that curriculum and instruction meet the needs of our students—not the other way around.

Systematically and continuously collecting, assessing, and revising data about students' identities and knowledge from their everyday lives to contextualize academic content as an extension of students' particular experiences supplants traditional curricula based on developmental discourses of adolescence and learning. Teachers who move away from developmental curricula dependent on "sameness" and move instead toward particular curricula oriented to individual *adolescenTS* have the potential to reduce, mitigate, alleviate, and even eliminate institutional barriers to student success. Using adolescents' funds of knowledge as baseline assessment data, teachers can scaffold curricula, select resources, and identify strategies for instruction and assessment. Such scaffolding places adolescents' identities at the center of the curriculum and particularizes their learning in terms they can use more fully than they can when schooling is generalized based on broad developmental models of who they are and what they can do.

Engineering a "difference" curriculum oriented to individual students' identities takes education beyond the accountability discourse of "gaps" that has resulted from traditional assumptions about what students should know and be able to do at a given age or grade level. These gaps are defined based on racialized and classist psychological notions of who young adolescents ought to be, and they are false specifically because they are over-generalized and misapplied as ways to (arguably) make education efficient. They are not efficient. They are also neither ethical nor pedagogically justifiable. The result of gap discourses based on stage developmentalism is that any adolescents whose identities fall outside the norms of traditional schooling renders those students as "struggling" and in need of remediation so that they conform to supposedly universal expectations. Those expectations are largely false and over-stated, and therefore damaging to youth and the schools. Utilizing a *funds of knowledge* approach for a "difference" curricula enables the implementation of existing high standards (even common state-level standards designed for bureaucratic efficiency). At the same time, it orients educators to respond to the real needs of adolescenTS. It empowers them to participate in their own educations, makes content and learning relevant to their lives, and prepares them for the very futures we claim it is our mission to secure.

References

Alvermann, D., Young, J., Weaver, D., Hinchman, K., Moore, D., Phelps, S., Thrash, E., & Zalewski, P. (1996). Middle and high school students' perceptions of how they experience text-based discussions: A multicase study. *Reading Research Quarterly, 31*(3), 244-267.

Aukerman, M. S. (2007). When reading it wrong is getting it right: Shared evaluation pedagogy among struggling fifth grade readers. *Research in the Teaching of English, 42*(1), 56-103.

Brass, J. J., & Burns, L. D. (2011). Research in secondary English, 1912-2011: Historical continuities and discontinuities in the NCTE imprint. *Research in the Teaching of English, 46*(2).

Caskey, M. M., & Anfara, V. A., Jr. (2007). *NMSA research summary: Young adolescents' developmental characteristics*. Retrieved July 4, 2011, from http://www.nmsa.org/Research/ResearchSummaries/DevelopmentalCharacteristics/tabid/1414/Default.aspx

Combs, W. E. (1976). Further effects of sentence-combining practice on writing ability. *Research in the Teaching of English, 10*(2), 137-149.

Crowhurst, M. (1980). Syntactic complexity and teachers' quality ratings of narrations and arguments. *Research in the Teaching of English, 14*(3), 223-231.

Erikson, E. H. (1968). *Identity: Youth and crises*. New York: W.W. Norton & Company.

Frank, A. (1993). *The diary of a young girl*. New York: Bantam Books.

Friese, E., Alvermann, D., Parkes, A., & Rezak, A. (2008). Selecting texts for English language arts classrooms: When assessment is not enough. *English Teaching: Practice and Critique, 7*(3), 74-99.

Grolnick, W. S., & Ryan, R. M. (1987). Autonomy in children's learning: An experimental and individual difference investigation. *Journal of Personality and Social Psychology, 52*(5), 890–898.

Guthrie, J., & Alao, S. (1997). Designing contexts to increase motivation for reading. *Educational Psychologist, 32*, 95-105.

Guthrie, J., & Davis, M. (2003). Motivating struggling readers in middle school through an engagement model of classroom practice. *Reading Research Quarterly, 19*, 59-85.

Guthrie, J., Perencevich, K., Wigfield, A., Taboada, A., Humenick, N., & Barbosa, P. (2006). Influences of stimulating tasks on reading motivation and comprehension. *The Journal of Educational Research, 99*(4), 232-245.

Guthrie, J. T., & Wigfield, A. (2000). Engagement and motivation in reading. In M. L. Kamil et al., (Eds.), *Handbook of reading research, volume 3* (pp. 403-422). Mahwah, NJ: Lawrence Erlbaum Associates.

Jackson, A. W., & Davis, G. A. (2000). *Turning points 2000: Educating adolescents in the 21st century*. New York: Teachers College Press.

Johnston, P., & Costello, P. (2005). Principles for literacy assessment. *Reading Research Quarterly, 40*(2), 256-267.

Lee, C. (1998). Culturally responsive teaching and performance-based assessment. *The Journal of Negro Education, 67*(3), 268-279.

Lesko, N. (2001). *Act your age: A cultural construction of adolescence*. New York: Routledge/Falmer.

Marsh, J. (2006). Popular culture in the literacy curriculum: A Bourdieuan analysis. *Reading Research Quarterly, 41*(2), 160-174.

Moje, E., Ciechanowski, K.M., Kramer, L., Ellis, L., Carrillo, R., & Collazo, T. (2004). Working toward third space in content area literacy: An examination of everyday funds of knowledge and discourse. *Reading Research Quarterly, 39*(1), 38-70.

Moje, E., & Hinchman, K. (2004). Culturally responsive practices for youth literacy learning. In T. Jetton & J. Dole (Eds.), *Adolescent literacy research and practice* (pp. 321-350). New York: The Guilford Press.

Moll, L., Amanti, C., Neff, D., & Gonzalez, N. (1992). Funds of knowledge for teaching: A qualitative approach to connect homes and classrooms. *Theory into Practice, 31*(2), 132-141.

National Middle School Association (NMSA). (2010). *This we believe: Keys to educating young adolescents.* Westerville, OH: National Middle School Association.

Otis, N., Grouzet, F., & Pelletier, L. (2005). Latent motivational change in an academic setting: A 3-year longitudinal study. *Journal of Educational Psychology, 97*(2), 170-183.

Pope, M. (1978). Syntactic maturity of students' oral paraphrases. *Research in the Teaching of English, 12*(1), 29-36.

Reeve, J., & Jang, H. (2006). What teachers say and do to support students' autonomy during a learning activity. *Journal of Educational Psychology, 98*(1), 209–218.

Scherff, L., & Piazza, C. L. (2008). Why now, more than ever, we need to talk about opportunity to learn. *Journal of Adolescent & Adult Literacy, 52*(4), 343-352.

Schraw, G., Flowerday, T., & Reisetter, M. F. (1998). The role of choice in reader engagement. *Journal of Educational Psychology, 90*(4), 705-714.

Steele, C. M. (2010). *Whistling Vivaldi: And other clues to how stereotypes affect us.* New York: W.W. Norton & Company.

Thomas, S., & Oldfather, P. (1997). Intrinsic motivations, literacy, and assessment practices: "That's my grade. That's me." *Educational Psychologist, 32*(2), 107-123.

Vagle, M. D. (this volume). Trying to poke holes in Teflon: Developmentalism; young adolescence; and contingent, recursive growth and change. In M. D. Vagle (Ed.), *Not a stage! A critical re-conception of young adolescent education* (pp. 11-38). New York: Peter Lang Publishing.

Wentzel, K. (1997). Student motivation in middle school: The role of perceived pedagogical caring. *Journal of Educational Psychology, 89*(3), 411-419.

Wigfield, A. (1997). Reading motivation: A domain-specific approach to motivation. *Educational Psychologist, 32*(2), 59-68.

Chapter 9

What's Interbeing Got to Do with It? Shared Experiences, Public Problems, and the Unique Individual

Hilary G. Conklin

As a new parent to a now 18-month-old toddler, I have recently become rather obsessed with growth charts. At my daughter's two-month and four-month weigh-ins, the pediatrician proclaimed she was thriving—her infant poundage placed her perfectly in the 50th percentile on the doctors' growth charts. What a relief to first-time, anxious, exhausted parents! Our baby was happy and healthy.

Only a few months later, this picture of contented normalcy suddenly took a turn. By her nine-month visit, the growth charts showed she had plummeted to the tenth percentile in weight, signaling that, in pediatric terms, she had "fallen off her growth curve." At 12 months, the alarm bells sounded further: she was nearing the fifth percentile, and we left the pediatrician's office with advice for fattening her up. My motherly guilt set in, particularly given that, as a breastfeeding mother, I had been her primary source of nutrition for these last 12 months.

Yet as we began our doctor-prescribed regimen of extra snacks, avocados, nutrient-absorbing vitamins, and supplementary oils, something didn't feel right. Our daughter appeared happy, healthy, and active. She ate well and seemed to do all the other things that healthy babies do. How could these growth charts be suggesting that she was no longer thriving, when that determination so clearly defied the evidence in front of us? Who were these other babies, anyway, who formed the foundation of the growth charts?

Some investigation led to an interesting discovery. In 2006, the World Health Organization (WHO) released a new set of child growth standards and accompanying growth charts. These new standards were based on 8,440 children from Brazil, Ghana, India, Norway, Oman, and the United States who were raised under optimal health conditions, including having mothers who "followed health practices such as breastfeeding their children and not smoking during and after pregnancy" (World Health Organization, 2011). The new standards made breastfed infants the new target "norm" for growth, while the previous standards were based on the growth of infants who were almost all formula-fed. The new growth charts, then, provide different growth curves and different growth patterns than those featured in the commonly used Centers for Disease Control and Prevention (CDC) charts, and thus, different determinations of which babies are considered overweight, underweight, or "normal." A recent summary on the use of WHO and CDC growth charts advises:

> Clinicians should be aware that fewer U.S. children will be identified as underweight using the WHO charts, slower growth among breastfed infants during ages 3-18 months is normal, and gaining weight more rapidly than is indicated on the WHO charts might signal early signs of overweight. (Grummer-Strawn, Reinold, & Krebs, 2010, emphasis added)

Yet, while I had been adhering to the American Academy of Pediatrics' recommendation of breastfeeding for most infants (American Academy of Pediatrics, 2005), the growth charts on which our pediatricians in Georgia and Illinois recorded our daughter's weight were the CDC's—those based on formula-fed infants. After plotting my daughter's weights on the WHO charts, suddenly, our daughter appeared to be back to normal again.

This shift in the frame of reference for viewing my daughter's growth points to some of the complicated tensions inherent in the construction of norms of development and how we go about characterizing particular populations of young people. I use this personal example, then, as a starting point to both deepen and complicate Vagle's (this volume) plea that we "move from 'characterizing' young adolescenCE to 'particularizing' young adolescenTS." I respond to Vagle's plea by trying to think through questions such as: Where do individuals fit in among the broader population? In young adolescent education, how should educators think about individuals when they teach classrooms of students? In considering these questions, I draw upon a variety of personal and public examples to illustrate moments when the use of characterizations, norms, and percentages of particular populations can be both very productive and also problematic or even irrelevant. By drawing connections among babies, young adolescents, childhood vaccinations, the democratic notions of *pluribus* and *unum*, and the Buddhist notion of interbeing, I seek to raise questions about what it might mean to "move from 'characterizing' young adolescenCE to 'particularizing' young adolescenTS."

Tensions in Characterization(s)

On one hand, the example of my daughter's growth above serves as a vivid illustration of the ways in which norms are, indeed, socially constructed—and can lead to people (both a mother and a baby in this case), at times, being constructed as "not enough" (Hughes-Decatur, 2011). When we think about growth, development, change, or learning, so much depends on the valued end points and how those end points have come to be. Vagle comments that

> Capturing the contingent and recursive particulars could then move the construction of adolescence away from describing young adolescents as developing creatures who, if different, are viewed as variations of the norm—as if the norm itself is somehow not a construction—toward a social construction of adolescence that views young adolescents as "whole" people living in contexts, in time. Such time is marked by multiplicity rather than simplicity. These particulars cannot be generalized or characterized, and this perhaps is what makes Lesko's perspective scary. (pp. 25-26)

The case of growth charts illustrates how, using one norm or standard, a baby can be seen as unhealthy—a variation from the norm—while the new norm transforms the same baby into a healthy child (and simultaneously makes other babies suddenly less healthy). Yet Vagle wants more than just a re-norming or a recognition of this norming process. He wants us to think about "whole people living in contexts, in time...marked by multiplicity rather than simplicity." Does this mean that I should throw out my growth charts altogether and think about my daughter in her own time and context? Herein lies one of the tensions in what Vagle asks us to consider.

Although I have demonstrated some clear problems with norms like the growth charts I describe above, as a novice parent, I have also found it extremely helpful to have some general guidance about what I might expect to see my baby do or need. During my pregnancy, it was a comfort to know that most babies are born healthy and to know that there are lots of different signs along the way that typically signal a baby's healthy development. Having now discovered a new growth reference, I am comforted to have some affirmation that my daughter is growing in a healthy way. As she gets older, I find it helpful to be able to reference general guidelines on the amounts of sleep that are likely to be appropriate for her. Similarly, knowing when I might expect to see her crawl, stand, walk, and talk gives me a sense of what to anticipate from her, and the kinds of things that might make sense to have in her environment or not (i.e., board books with sturdy, rip-proof pages: YES; bookcases that can be tipped over with a bit of toddler tugging: NO).

In a similar way, as Vagle, too, suggests, novice teachers of young adolescents can gain useful guidance from learning "what to expect when working with young adolescents" (p. 25). Many teachers with limited classroom experience, for example, may find it useful to know that young adolescents' growth often appears out of sync with their cognitive development: a very tall young adolescent boy may cause teachers to expect more complex thinking from him than his much shorter classmate just because of his size. At the same time, my research with novice secondary teachers suggests that teachers can benefit from learning the general principle that young adolescents frequently have many profound questions about the world and can indeed think in sophisticated ways (Conklin, 2008; Conklin, Hawley, Powell, & Ritter, 2010). However, they should also know that young adolescents often need a great deal of very concrete instruction and scaffolding to help them take advantage of their sophisticated thinking abilities. Thus, should young adolescents be given challenging primary historical sources to read? Yes. Should they be given these texts to work on independently for 45 minutes with no reading supports or other guidance to facilitate their learning? If teachers want to maximize students' understanding of the texts, probably not.

Now, having written those last two questions and answers, it's time for the caveats. As Vagle notes, "While characterizations can make some rhetorical sense, they quickly become problematic when they lead to categorical thinking" (p. 27). Should young adolescents be given challenging primary historical sources to read? Well, yes—if they are texts that teachers can help the particular students in their classrooms find value and connection in. Yes, if the texts are ground-

grounded in an understanding of those students' particular lives and that facilitate learning toward meaningful goals established in that classroom context. Should all U.S. seventh graders read the Declaration of Independence? That depends. How is the teacher using the text? To what ends? How does it relate to other learning these seventh graders have engaged in? Could some seventh graders glean something useful from an independent reading of the Declaration of Independence with no support or guidance? Probably.

Vagle's caution that "any act of characterizing almost inevitably leads to generalization and oversimplification and is never neutral," (p. 27) is a critical point. In some cases, reliance on characterizations obscures other important—and sometimes devastating—realities. While the rates of healthy births were a source of solace to me, this characterization of normal pregnancy became meaningless to my sister-in-law, whose pregnancy ended with stillbirth. Statistics and trends often provide extremely helpful guideposts, yet they do not tell us about an individual experience or existence.

Just as nurses, midwives, and doctors need to be aware of the multiple circumstances of pregnancy and treat each situation with care, so, too, do educators of young adolescents need to work to understand and listen to each young person and her particular passions, ways of being, and lived context. The Chinese adoptee living with Caucasian parents in a working-class, rural Iowa town and attending an otherwise all white middle school will surely have different young adolescent experiences than the African American boy living with his biological parents in an affluent, predominantly African American Atlanta suburb. Neither child will benefit from teachers who see them only in terms of some general norms of young adolescence—nor will they benefit from being seen only in terms of the quick categories I have just named in order to highlight various potential social and cultural dimensions of a young adolescent experience. As Vagle wisely points out, educators need to be wary of how any of these categories confine our thinking about the young people in front of us or cause us to think that young adolescents can only be one particular way depending on the markers people use to describe them. Though they may share some experiences, all Chinese adoptees living in rural Iowa towns will not be the same young adolescents. As Vagle notes, they are "whole people living in contexts" in situations "marked by multiplicity rather than simplicity." (pp. 25-26)

The Interbeing of Young AdolescenTS

Having affirmed some of Vagle's assertions, let me now turn back again on this very point and muddy the waters. After discussing some of the tensions in looking both at trends in the broader population in relation to the individual experience, I now want to once again offer a caution on paying too much attention to the individual. Vagle explains:

> My sense is that by continuing to characterize young adolescence, we run the risk of losing the young adolescent in the process. I ask those interested in the education of young adolescents to take Caskey and Anfara's warnings a step further and actively resist characterizing in favor of particularizing so that the platform (i.e., Young adolescence) itself becomes individualized. (p. 29)

Vagle suggests then, that we focus on young adolescenTS rather than young adolescenCE. But here is where I want to trouble this proposal.

While "particularizing" a young adolescent brings well-warranted attention to each child and highlights her individuality and unique experience in particular situations, the act of individualizing also has the potential to distract educators from the public-ness and interdependence of the young people who share an educational space. Thich Nhat Hanh (1988), a Buddhist monk, explains the mutuality of our earthly existence:

> If you are a poet, you will see clearly that there is a cloud floating in this sheet of paper. Without a cloud, there will be no rain; without rain, the trees cannot grow; and without trees, we cannot make the paper. The cloud is essential for the paper to exist. If the cloud is not here, the sheet of paper cannot be here either. So we can say that the cloud and the paper inter-are. "Interbeing" is a word that is not in the dictionary yet, but if we combine the prefix "inter-" with the verb "to be," we have a new verb, so we can say that the cloud and the sheet of paper inter-are. (1988, p. 3)

Extending Hanh's ideas, perhaps we could say that my experience of a healthy pregnancy *inter-is* with the experience of my sister-in-law's stillbirth. While not essential to one another, the existence of each experience shapes and is shaped by the existence of the other; they are inescapably bound up together.

The notion of interbeing is one that Walter Parker (2003) discusses in his book *Teaching Democracy*, as he explains how living democratically as citizens involves an understanding of the interdependence of "both *pluribus* (the many) and *unum* (the one)" (p. 1). He argues that focusing too much on either one is problematic:

> Attending exclusively and defensively to the citizen identity while ignoring, denying, repressing, or trying to "melt" away cultural and racial identities avoids the fact that diversity is...essential to liberty...Doing the opposite has the same effect: By attending exclusively and defensively to our diverse individual, cultural, and racial identities, we ignore the shared political identity and its context—the commonwealth—on which we rely to secure and nurture our diversity. (p. 2)

In the sphere of public health, the issue of childhood vaccination illustrates the relationship between *pluribus* and *unum*. For a variety of reasons, including poverty, medical necessity, and parental beliefs, many children are increasingly entering school without vaccinations for common childhood illnesses such as measles, polio, and whooping cough (cf, Tsouderos, Shelton, & Germuska, 2011). However, when individual children are not vaccinated, the risk of epidemics goes up for everyone: both the unvaccinated children and anyone who interacts with the unvaccinated children. Keeping outbreaks at bay depends on high vaccination rates of individual children and families. The role of the individual citizen, then, is inextricably bound up with the common good. Understanding this relationship is an example of leading what Parker terms "the unavoidably connected and engaged life of the citizen, paying attention to and caring for the public household, the common good" (p. 11).

Now, how do these ideas of the public citizen and the common good relate to the distinction between young adolescenCE and young adolescenTS? I argue that there are good reasons to look at a larger population rather than only at the individual, particularized level not only because there is potentially important guidance to be gleaned from this broader view, but also because the broader perspective reminds us of our connectedness and relationship to one another in a classroom community. If we only help teachers look at the young adolescenTS in their classrooms, Vagle's suggestion to individualize the platform of young adolescence has the potential to point us down a path in which both teachers and young people lose sight of the potential learning and practice of democratic life that comes from understanding learners' interdependence and shared experience. Young adolescents are members of classroom spaces in which the whole can be greater than the sum of its parts: in public schools, everyone learns more if teachers and students work together to harness the collective energy, creativity, experience, and wisdom of the diverse young adolescents who share that learning space.

Just as it is dangerous to rely on categories and characterizations to describe and understand young people, it can be dangerous to underestimate young adolescents' connectedness to one another, their collective strength and commonality. Applying Hanh's (1988) ideas of interbeing to some of the examples Vagle uses, the young adolescent boy living in poverty and the pregnant young adolescent girl *inter-are* with a young adolescent girl who has never had sexual relations and who lives in affluence. The experience of each young adolescent is inevitably infused in the experience of the others.

Young adolescenCE, then, includes poverty, pregnancy, celibacy, and affluence—it includes the lived worlds of all the individual young adolescenTS. The social conditions that make it possible for a young adolescent to live in poverty also make it possible for another young adolescent to live in affluence.

While these diverse situations are interrelated, the notion of interbeing also reminds us of young adolescents' shared experiences. Viewing young adolescents in terms of their commonality has the potential to create a space in which these young people can share a sense of belonging. Having a sense that they are not alone in some of their experiences, in turn, can provide the validation that sets the stage for growth and learning. In the field of psychotherapy, for example, Yalom (2005) explains that one powerful aspect of having people take part in group counseling is the role of universality: clients who take part in group therapy feel relieved and validated to know that others have similar concerns, doubts, and feelings. As Yalom explains, "There is no human deed or thought that lies fully outside the experience of other people" (p. 6).

To be sure, teachers need to be cautious in identifying those young adolescent experiences and identities that may be shared—the equivalents of what Parker (2003) explains in civic terms as the "shared political identity and its context—the commonwealth—on which we rely to secure and nurture our diversity" (p. 2). Highlighting some students' experiences without taking into account political and social forces has the potential to give some young adolescents a strong sense of *not* belonging. For example, noting the commonality of young adolescents' developing sexuality may alienate gay youth if it is done in a way that does not recognize the political and social structures that marginalize these young people. Educators must thoughtfully consider how to bring young adolescents together around shared identities that help them as a class in "paying attention to and caring for the public household, the common good" (Parker, 2003, p. 11)—their learning community.

What might these shared identities or experiences include? One possibility is that young adolescents are linked by U.S. culture's portrayal of them as "under the control of hormones and unavailable for serious (i.e., critical) school tasks and responsibilities" (Lesko, 2005, p. 98). And, while they may not actually be under the "control" of hormones, young adolescents may be linked by experiences of unfamiliar growth and change in their bodies (some of which are indeed related to hormones). Further, many young adolescents are linked by their curiosity about the world and their efforts to make sense of what is going on around them. The Chinese adoptee living in rural Iowa and the African American young adolescent living in suburban Atlanta may well wonder about similar questions: Why is there prejudice? Why is there so much conflict? Or, like a group of culturally and economically diverse young adolescents in Madison, Wisconsin, they may ask questions like, "How did religions evolve?...Will there ever be a cure for AIDS? Why can't teenagers vote?" (Brodhagen, 1995, p. 88).

Toward Young Adolescen*s?

Where do these musings leave teachers of young adolescents? In the end, I may not be disagreeing with Vagle, then, but rather offering a caution for how others might take up his plea. My concern is that if educators are encouraged to "individualize" the platform of young adolescence, we may end up only focusing on the young adolescenT and lose sight of young adolescenTS as a group—a group that deserves and needs special recognition in part because of their historic marginalization (see Conklin & Lee, 2010).

To conclude, I want to return to infants one last time. The recent documentary *Babies*—a journey through four infants' first years of life in Japan, Mongolia, Namibia, and the United States—illustrates the simultaneous universality of infant development and its highly contextualized nature. While the urban American baby attends formal parenting and play classes with her parents, the rural Mongolian baby roams freely outside among the family cattle. Yet despite the clear cultural differences and childrearing practices, all four of these babies are curious about their environments, explore, and learn to stand and walk. The filmmaker Thomas Balmes explains of the documentary, "it's not just about babies. It's about being a human being in the world" (Rosenblum, 2010).

Educators of young adolescents, then, need to hold all of these tensions simultaneously. They must think about the young adolescenT, young adolescenTS, young adolescenCE, and young adolescenCES. They must think about universality and particular contexts, interbeing and individual experiences, *pluribus* and *unum*. So if we "actively resist characterizing in favor of particularizing" (Vagle, p. 29), we must also constantly be asking: What is lost if we only particularize?

References

American Academy of Pediatrics. (2005). *AAP policy on breastfeeding and use of human milk*. Retrieved June 16, 2011, from http://www.aap.org/breastfeeding/policy OnBreastfeedingAndUseOfHumanMilk.html.

Brodhagen, B. (1995). The situation made us special. In M. W. Apple & J. A. Beane, (Eds.), *Democratic Schools* (pp. 83-100). Alexandria, VA: Association for Supervision and Curriculum Development.

Conklin, H. G. (2008). Promise and problems in two divergent pathways: Preparing social studies teachers for the middle school level. *Theory and Research in Social Education, 36*(1), 591-620.

Conklin, H., Hawley, T., Powell, D., & Ritter, J. (2010). Learning from young adolescents: The use of structured teacher education coursework to help beginning teachers investigate middle school students' intellectual capabilities. *Journal of Teacher Education, 61*(4), 313–327.

Conklin, H., & Lee, K. (2010). Walking the borderland. In K. Lee & M. Vagle (Eds.), *Developmentalism in early childhood and middle grades education: Critical conversations on readiness and responsiveness* (pp. 233-254). New York: Palgrave Macmillan.

Grummer-Strawn, L. M., Reinold, C., & Krebs, N. F. (2010). Use of world health organization and CDC growth charts for children aged 0-59 months in the United States. *Morbidity and Mortality Weekly Report*. Centers for Disease Control and Prevention. Retrieved June 16, 2011, from http://www.cdc.gov/mmwr/preview/mmwrhtml/rr5909a1.htm

Hanh, T. N. (1988). *The heart of understanding*. Berkeley, CA: Parallax Press.

Hughes, H. E. (2011). *Phenomenal bodies, phenomenal girls: How young adolescent girls experience being enough in their bodies* (Doctoral dissertation). Available from ProQuest Digital Dissertations and Theses Database.

Lesko, N. (2005). Denaturalizing adolescence: The politics of contemporary representations. In E. R. Brown & K. J. Saltman (Eds.), *The critical middle school reader* (pp. 87-102). New York: Routledge.

Parker, W. (2003). *Teaching democracy: Unity and diversity in public life*. New York: Teachers College Press.

Rosenblum, C. (2010, May 6). All burbles and gurgles as life unfolds. *New York Times*. Retrieved June 27, 2011, from http://www.nytimes.com/2010/05/09/movies/09babies.html.

Tsouderos, T., Shelton, D. L., & Germuska, J. (2011, June 18). Low vaccination rates in some schools raise outbreak risks. *Chicago Tribune*. Retrieved June 28, 2011, at http://articles.chicagotribune.com/2011-06-18/health/ct-met-vaccination-rates-schools-20110618_1_measles-vaccinations-vaccination-rates-herd-immunity.

Vagle, M. D. (this volume). Trying to poke holes in Teflon: Developmentalism; young adolescence; and contingent, recursive growth and change. In M. D. Vagle (Ed.), *Not a stage! A critical re-conception of young adolescent education* (pp. 11-38). New York: Peter Lang Publishing.

World Health Organization. (2011). *Child growth standards: Frequently asked questions*. Retrieved June 16, 2011, from http://www.who.int/childgrowth/faqs/why/en/index.html.

Yalom, I. D. (2005). *The theory and practice of group psychotherapy*. New York: Basic Books.

Acknowledgements

I thank Scott Conklin for his helpful feedback on an earlier version of this chapter.

Section 4

Re-Conceptualizing Growth and Change "Outside" U.S. Contexts

Mark D. Vagle

Perhaps one of the greatest limitations of a developmental conception of growth and change is that it takes U.S. perspectives and elevates them to the status of *normal*. Moreover, at its origin developmentalism focuses, as Lesko reminds us, on making sure White, middle-class, heterosexual males are prepared to lead the nation. Although minoritizing discourses are more present and available today, they still reside on the periphery—they have not disrupted the assumed norm.

The chapters in this section do some of this important work. I use the term "outside" in the title of this final section in order to signal that the contexts are something other than U.S. I also use it to signal that sometimes the best disruptive move to make is to try to look outside a discourse—one needs to be forced to see other possibilities especially when the dominant discourse seems to have saturated the playing field. I use outside also to point at the hegemonic influence of U.S. perspectives and, hopefully (and perhaps idealistically), to provide some possible ways to push back against this hegemony. This is not to say, at a time of unheralded globalization, that it is actually possible to truly get outside of this hegemony. However, it does seem necessary to try. Finally, I use outside to signal a need for difference, for partiality, and for more contingencies.

Centering on Norwegian (Virtue), Indian (Sharma) and Australian (Pendergast & Bahr; Garrick, Keogh, Pendergast, & Dole) contexts, the authors in this section bring us into "particular" particularized contexts in concrete, lived ways. They lay out important contextualizations and then burrow into micro-contexts that can (if we are willing) help us shed U.S. developmentalism—even if only for fleeting moments.

Beginning with David Virtue's work, *Norwegian Perspectives on Educating Young Adolescen(TS)*, it is clear that socio-political contexts shape the way young adolescents are perceived and educated.

Although sociologists and anthropologists would suggest that this is a statement of the obvious, it is curious that stage developmentalism has continued to reign supreme (seemingly as apolitical) in spite of the obvious. As a *roving scholar* funded through the Fulbright foundation, Virtue spent time in a number of schools for young adolescents throughout Norway. One of the key perspectives Virtue gained from his experiences centered on the differences between U.S. and Norwegian prevailing discourses about young adolescen(TS). He suggests that the predominant U.S. conception paints a picture of a group of young people at-risk and in need of not only guidance, but also control—in effect a group of people who need to be protected from themselves. Conversely, Virtue perceived a different conception in Norway. In his closing, he describes a conception in which young adolescents are constructed as young *people* who possess certain inalienable rights; who are, to some degree, emancipated from adult constraints upon their thoughts, actions, and identities; and who, in an egalitarian school community, are able to participate in many aspects of daily school life as coequals with adults. This is precisely the sort of difference that contingent, recursive conceptions of growth and change can open up.

Traveling to the Southern hemisphere, Donna Pendergast and Nan Bahr provide another important glimpse into other possible conceptions of young adolescents. In their chapter, *What's Happening Down Under: Young Adolescent Education in Australia*, Pendergast and Bahr provide a historical tracing of young adolescent teacher education, locating places in which dominant discourses regarding characterizations rather than particularization dominate, much like they do in the U.S. However, they also offer some other more hopeful possibilities. Drawing on a chapter in their powerful book, *Teaching Middle Years: Rethinking Curriculum, Pedagogy and Assessment* (Pendergast & Bahr, 2010), they offer the assumption that young adolescents are *philosophy-makers rather than philosophy-takers* (Chadbourne & Pendergast, 2010, p. 23). This particularization of young adolescents is both intriguing and empowering. First, it situates young people as philosophers—as seekers of knowledge and understanding. Second, it situates them as the agents of such seeking—not the recipients. Taken seriously, this phrase would mean that *middle-level philosophy* should be re-cast based on what young adolescents say such a philosophy should entail. Although Pendergast and Bahr observe that middle years education in Australia still focuses on broad characterizations of young adolescence, their active push to particularize holds great promise.

Ajay Sharma, originally from India now in the U.S. academy, offers a unique perspective in his chapter, *'Particularizing' Young Adolescents in an Indian Context*. First, he describes what he sees as a grand narrative, which paints young adolescents as characters who are, for example, unable to cope with complex moral and ethical questions. Sharma's thoughts in this regard should be heeded as his concern does fall in line with commonsense assumptions about when is the "right" time in the developmental progression to allow young people to make important decisions about their lives. Typically, young adolescence would be the LAST choice. They aren't ready! They are not developed enough yet! They are too egocentric at that point in time! However, Sharma does not want us to stop here. Rather, he suggests that these sorts of characterizations of young adolescents is based predominantly on studies of middle-class U.S. students and contexts—which, of course, are incredibly limiting and damaging when elevated to a generalizable truth. As one way to counter this grand narrative, Sharma carefully describes aspects of his ethnographic research in a small, impoverished village in India. Here, he found particular young adolescents to be quite different—quite capable of posing important questions, making difficult decisions, and creatively responding to some ostensibly difficult conditions.

In the final chapter of this section, *Locked into Place through Teacher Education: The Discursive Construction of Young People in the Middle Years of Schooling*, we return to Australia in order to learn more about how preservice teacher education can be re-imagined. Garrick, Keogh, Pendergast, and Dole draw on Stevens et al. (2007) to suggest that young adolescent youth are routinely positioned discursively in pejorative ways—not making available other more fluid discursive spaces. Not only is this an important connection to the particularizing plea in the anchor essay, it is a most necessary reminder about how important it is to actively work to make available more discursive spaces. If the only available descriptions of young adolescents are hormonal, unfinished, and incomplete (Stevens et al., 2007) then, indeed, young adolescents will be seen as such. Moreover, future teachers of young adolescents will then be positioned as the ones who are to *finish* and *complete* their students. This is a tenuous scenario as it promotes a deficit-oriented pedagogy that firmly entrenches young adolescents in a linear developmental progression. The way out, according to Garrick et al. and Stevens et al., is to educate future teachers to see themselves and their students more fluidly. I would add that this fluidity might be marked by an assumption that teachers and students are finished-unfinished in a contingent, recursive manner. That is, one (no matter how old) is never fully finished or fully unfinished—the situation and context matters and being finished-unfinished happens over and over again in and over time. If future teachers could embrace and live this out in their pedagogy, then a new discursive space for young adolescents will have been made available.

References

Chadbourne, R. & Pendergast, D. (2010). The philosophy of middle schooling. In D. Pendergast & N. Bahr (Eds.), *Teaching middle years: Rethinking curriculum, pedagogy and assessment* (2nd ed.). Crows Nest: Allen & Unwin, 23-49.

Stevens, L.P., Hunter, L., Pendergast, D., Carrington, V., Bahr, N., Kapitzke, C., & Mitchell, J. (2007). Re-conceptualizing the possible narratives of adolescence. *The Australian Educational Researcher, 34*(2), 107–127.

Pendergast, D. & Bahr, N. (2010). *Teaching middle years: Rethinking curriculum, pedagogy and assessment* (2nd ed.). Sydney: Allen & Unwin.

Chapter 10

Norwegian Perspectives on Educating Young Adolescen(TS)

David C. Virtue

> *Cross-cultural study informs us through the juxtaposition of the familiar and the new, the known and the exotic. The best lessons lie in the differences.* (Wagner, 2006, p. 289)

In the anchor essay for this volume, Vagle issues a plea for a move from characterizing young adolescen(CE) to particularizing young adolescen(TS). He cautions that the characterizations of young adolescent(CE) so common in the mainstream middle level literature constitute, inevitably, an oversimplification that "suffocates the innumerable perspectives" (p. 25) of adolescent(TS), thus masking the situational realities of particular adolescents and the contexts in which they live. Moreover, these characterizations reinforce the firmly entrenched developmentalist perspective that limits the extent to which scholars can understand the intersection of the private and educational lives of young people. As Steinberg (2006) argues:

> Many times, scholarly observations of youth have been content to leave the definition of youth uncontested and separate from larger social forces. Thus, over the last few decades, youth has been viewed as 'non-social' or 'pre-social,' more the province of developmental psychologists with their universalizing descriptions of its 'normal' phase. Such academic approaches, although pursued with good intentions, have not served the interests of youth and those who seek to help them. By undermining an appreciation of the diversity and complexity of youth, such viewpoints have often equated difference with deficiency, and sociocultural construction with the natural. The complicated nature of youth, youth study, social work for youth, and adolescent and youth education demands more rigorous forms of analysis. (p. xiii)

Vagle (this volume, p. 25) concedes that "it would be impossible to describe all the possible contexts and microcontexts in which young adolescents find themselves" however, he urges middle-level educators "to open up these contexts" and engage in the kinds of "rigorous forms of analysis" Steinberg (2006) advocates. One way to move this work forward is to look more closely and critically at the diverse international contexts in which young adolescents live and young adolescence is constructed and given meaning.

As I have argued elsewhere, international scholarship and dialogue about young adolescent education can serve as a catalyst for critical self-reflection within the field of middle-level education (Virtue, 2009)[1]. In this chapter, I offer a comparative look at young adolescent education in Norway and the United States based on insights from my work as a Fulbright scholar[2] in Norwegian *ungdomsskoler* (lower secondary schools) from August 2010 to June 2011. I visited 43 schools primarily serving students in grades 8 through 10, with seven visits to *barneskole* (primary school) classes spanning grades one through seven. While I gave presentations and led workshops about many aspects of American culture, history, geography, and society, the most frequently requested presentation was "Life in U.S. Schools."

In the United States, young adolescents are typically schooled in middle schools or junior high schools—institutions separate from elementary and high schools—that house students in some configuration of grades 5 through 9. Junior high schools, and later middle schools, were born from a union of progressive education philosophy and developmental child psychology that imbued early adolescence, a stage of development marked by the onset of puberty, with certain meanings requiring curricula, teacher training programs and credentials, and, often, school buildings separate and distinct from other levels of schooling (Alexander, 1995). These components of the "middle school concept" are explicated in *Turning Points* (Carnegie Council on Adolescent Development, 1989), *Turning Points 2000* (Jackson & Davis, 2000), *This We Believe* (National Middle School Association [NMSA], 2010), and other seminal texts.

Young adolescent education, as it is practiced in Norway, exhibits many components of the middle school concept; but it is less clear whether stage developmentalism has underpinned the philosophies, practices, and programs in the Norwegian *ungdomsskoler* (lower secondary schools) in the same ways and to the same extent as it has the middle and junior high schools in the United States[3]. This has led me to wonder about the degree to which there is anything uniquely Norwegian about the way *early adolescence/ts* is/are understood as a factor/s for consideration in the structure, organization, and practice of schooling in Norway.

To what extent are Norwegian *ungdomsskoler* intentionally "developmentally responsive," as the term is understood in the American context, and how does this system position young adolescents in relation to their teachers and other adults in their schools? To what extent are these educators enacting a particular "middle school" (or, *ungdomsskole*?) philosophy?

The Norwegian *Ungdomsskole* and the Middle School Concept

According to NMSA (2010), education for young adolescents must be developmentally responsive, "using the distinctive nature of young adolescents as the foundation upon which all decisions about school organization, policies, curriculum, instruction, and assessment are made" (p. 13). Developmentally responsive structures and practices deemed particularly well suited to the needs of young adolescent learners include interdisciplinary teaming, heterogeneous grouping, flexible block scheduling, looping, and small school size. Using evidence of these structures and practices as measures of developmental responsiveness, Norwegian lower secondary schools would certainly be considered responsive to the developmental needs of young adolescents. During my time in Norway, I frequently observed these and other practices commonly associated with effective education for young adolescents in the United States. My comparative analysis focuses specifically on the organizational features of Norwegian lower secondary schools as they relate to recommendations in *This We Believe* (NMSA, 2010) and *Turning Points 2000* (Jackson & Davis, 2000).

Middle-Level Organizational Structures in the *Ungdomsskole*

This We Believe urges middle grades schools to have organizational structures that "foster purposeful learning and meaningful relationships" (NMSA, 2010, p. 31); to provide opportunities for teachers to "vary the use of time, space, staff, and grouping arrangements" (NMSA, 2010, p. 33); and to have democratic governance structures that include teachers, students, and other stakeholders in decision-making processes at all levels. The authors of *Turning Points 2000* specifically identify small schools, or schools-within-a-school; interdisciplinary teams; and advisory programs as "the structures commonly associated with a successful middle grades school" (Jackson & Davis, 2000, p. 144). Other structures frequently recommended for middle grades schools in the United States include common planning time for teachers (Warren & Muth, 1995), flexible block schedules (NMSA, 2007a), looping (Thompson, Franz, & Miller, 2009), and heterogeneous grouping arrangements (NMSA, 2007b).

Structures Supporting Meaningful Relationships

The middle level literature calls for schools to be organized in ways that allow for meaningful relationships among members of the school community to form and flourish. The authors of *Turning Points 2000* favor small schools with 600 or fewer students grouped into teams of 120 or fewer students. Within teams, students should be heterogeneously grouped for instruction and should "spend most of their school day with other students on the team" (Jackson & Davis, 2000, p. 133). Teams should be led by two to six teachers who have expertise in the four core content areas—English language arts, mathematics, science, and social studies—and who are located in close proximity to each other in an area of the school building that they jointly "own". To promote continuity and further strengthen relationships, schools can implement looping, an organizational arrangement in which teachers and/or administrators remain with the same group of students for multiple years.

Norwegian lower secondary schools are organized on a scale that allows for close personal relationships to form. Schools are small by U.S. standards—the largest school I visited had approximately 450 pupils in three grade levels (8 through 10) and the smallest had 14 pupils in seven grade levels (actually, five grade levels because there were no third or fourth graders that year). Students are grouped into classes of 20 to 30 pupils, with as many as five classes on a grade level.

These class groups remain together throughout their three years in lower secondary school, and their teachers often loop with them from grade to grade. This arrangement allows for students to form strong bonds with one another, so it is not surprising that Norway has a very high percentage of 15-year-olds reporting they have three or more close friends compared to other European countries, the United States, and Canada (Settertobulte & de Matos, 2004)[4]. In addition, Norway has taken a firm stance on anti-bullying, or mobbing, and two widely implemented interventions were developed there: the Olweus Program and the Zero Program (Stephens, 2011).

The meaningful relationships that form between students and adults in a school are fundamental to the middle school concept. *This We Believe* states: "Each student must have one adult in the school who assumes special responsibility for supporting that student's academic and personal development" (NMSA, 2010, p. 35), and many schools implement advisory programs as a way to formally allow for such mentoring relationships to form (Burkhardt, 1999). In Norwegian lower secondary schools, students are assigned a contact teacher who acts as a liaison between home and school and may remain in that role for the entire three years. In practice, the organizational features of the school (e.g., looping, teaming, small size) allow for many teachers to get to know students well and serve in an advisory capacity. As one teacher commented, "We get to know the pupils and their parents very well."

Democratic Governance Structures

Turning Points 2000 and *This We Believe* both encourage middle-level schools to implement democratic governance structures that include administrators, teachers, students, and other stakeholders in decision-making processes (Jackson & Davis, 2000; NMSA, 2010). Such structures should allow students to participate meaningfully in team governance and other areas of school decision-making (NMSA, 2010, p. 19). Moreover, teachers are urged to model democratic processes for students in their day-to-day work with colleagues and by using collaborative instructional strategies in the classroom.

Democratic values and civic engagement are highly valued in Norwegian schools (Hansen & Wold, 2007), and this is evident in the ways schools prepare students to be responsible, participating members of society (Bjerke, 2011; Milner, 2009) and in the ways the state prepares teachers to "stimulate an understanding of democracy, democratic participation and the ability for critical reflection" (Norwegian Ministry of Education and Research, 2010, p. 4). Schools emphasize democratic values and social and personal development within the formal curriculum, but also provide structured opportunities for students to participate in democratic processes in various ways. Hansen and Wold (2007) share one example:

> Norway is the only country in the world that has a student representation and council program included in the curriculum, giving nearly 50% of all students an opportunity to have been a representative either for the class advisory board or in the student council by the age of 14. (p. 704)

I witnessed teachers and students regularly enacting democratic processes, most visibly in the ways they negotiated, compromised, and arrived at consensus regarding certain decisions. I would sometimes arrive at a school prepared to work with a group of students for an hour or ninety minutes and the teacher would instruct me to "work out the arrangements for breaks with the students." I observed a social studies lesson in Østfold during which the teacher was introducing a two-week project on explorers and exploration. Teams of students were going to do research in the library and on the Internet to learn about a particular explorer, then prepare and deliver an oral presentation in front of the class. The teacher negotiated the terms of the assignment with the students, as evident in the following excerpt from my journal:

> Teacher: We are going to decide together on a date for presentation. Is this okay? (Students nod, some quietly say "yes" or "ja.")
>
> Do you have questions? (Teacher pauses.)
>
> I would like you to work in pairs, if that's okay with you?

There is a strong tradition of local control of schools in Norway, as in the United States, but in contrast to U.S. schools, Norwegian schools do not have top-heavy administrative structures. Each school has a principal or head, often a former teacher from the school, and some teachers with whom I worked had a certain percentage of their time allocated for administrative duties, such as leading a team or department. Decisions affecting the school are made by the head and various committees and councils composed of teachers, parents, and students.

Scheduling Structures

Turning Points 2000 and *This We Believe* recommend that middle-level schools implement flexible block schedules and give teachers a great degree of control over how the time is used (Jackson & Davis, 2000; NMSA, 2010). "Through flexible scheduling of blocks of time, teachers are able to vary the frequency and order of classes, and to lengthen or shorten class periods to reflect instructional goals and students' changing needs" (Jackson & Davis, 2000, p. 133). These ideas are very difficult to implement in the United States, as scheduling has increasingly become driven by accountability and testing policies. Administrators seek to maximize instructional time during the day, emphasizing those subjects that are tested (Musoleno & White, 2010).

Teachers in Norway exercise a great degree of control over the schedule, and in nearly every case I arranged my school visits with a classroom teacher or all members of a team. Rarely did I work directly with an administrator and when I did, he or she normally deferred decisions about my schedule to the teachers.

The school day in Norway lasts five-and-a-half to six hours, and lessons are 45 minutes to an hour long. The schedule at Oyslebø skole in Marnardal kommune was typical of the schedules at most schools I visited:

09.00–09:45	Lesson 1
09:45–10:30	Lesson 2
10:30–10:40	Break
10.40–11.20	Lesson 3
11:20–12:05	Lunch

12:05–12:50	Lesson 4
12:50–13:00	Break
13.00–13:45	Lesson 5
13:45–14:30	Lesson 6

A few features of this schedule are worth noting. My host teacher exercised control over the schedule and arranged, together with her colleagues, for me to meet with the students for double lessons (90 minutes). Students have 45 minutes for lunch, and because they bring their lunches to school, most of their lunch period is, in effect, free time. I learned early in the year that Norwegian students' lunch and recess breaks are sacred time, so I knew I would have to watch the clock carefully during my lesson 3 and 4 block to dismiss students at 11:20 for lunch, or they would probably dismiss themselves. Students spend most of the day in the same classroom, thus there is no structured time to change classes; but students do get recess breaks to play or socialize during the day. *This We Believe* recognizes the need for students to have ample opportunities for physical movement (NMSA, 2010), but too few schools in the United States schedule breaks or recess during the school day (Robert Wood Johnson Foundation, 2010). When I asked my 14 year-old niece if she had recess in her middle level school, she replied (as if I had asked a silly question): "No. Recess is for elementary school."

Each time I visited a class in Norway, I asked the students what they liked most about school.[5] Most often they said "friends" or, more specifically, "free time with friends." It was apparent that students valued their recess time. While a ten-minute break might not seem long, because Norwegian students spend most of the day in the same classroom—the teachers change classrooms each lesson, not the students—they are able to make the most of this down time. Students spend their free time with friends in their classrooms, in designated common areas of the school, or outside. Many students choose to go outside to kick a soccer ball or talk to their friends in small groups, while others find cozy places inside the school to socialize or just relax. Some schools have spaces intentionally designed for students to gather and interact, as recommended by Wolsey and Uline (2010).

Teachers enjoy the break times, too. During the short breaks between lessons, teachers sometimes need to hustle through the school to get to the next classroom, but during longer breaks teachers retreat to their cozy break rooms, which usually have fully equipped kitchens and fresh, hot coffee. The atmosphere in the break rooms is often enhanced by fresh-cut flowers or live plants, table cloths, and lit candles.

When I gave presentations in Norway about life in U.S. schools, students and teachers were often surprised to learn how little free time our students have during the day. As we reviewed some typical class schedules, I explained that the three to five minutes students have between classes is not break time but passing time; time to pass from one classroom to the next, with brief stops at a locker, a restroom, or a water fountain. Norwegians try to imagine what the corridors look like during these few minutes while hundreds or thousands of students try to get where they need to be before the next bell rings. It is not surprising that many students in the United States feel rushed during the school day (Booth, 2010). Students do not have designated time to relax, to play, or to socialize, even though the middle-level literature is clear about how important these activities are for their healthy development (Robert Wood Johnson Foundation, 2010).

Structuring Physical Spaces

According to *This We Believe*, a developmentally responsive middle-level school should have a physical structure that is "attractive, inviting, clean, and structurally sound" and should have walls decorated with student work to give them a sense of ownership (NMSA, 2010, p. 34). In most U.S. schools, teachers are assigned classrooms that they "own" and decorate according to their preferences, and in which they establish rules and procedures for behavior and non-instructional tasks. Teachers are instructed to control, manipulate, and manage numerous aspects of the physical environment of the school and to have their classrooms ready before the kids arrive as a way to regulate student behavior.

In contrast, each class of students in Norwegian lower secondary schools is assigned to a classroom where they spend most of the day together. They own these classroom spaces, and while I was a guest speaker in their classrooms, I sometimes got the impression that my host teachers felt like guests in these rooms, too. Teachers rotate from room to room, sometimes to four or five different rooms in a day. The students were often the experts regarding things like instructional technology in the room, the location of materials and resources, and other classroom-specific information.

Rarely did I see the rooms decorated elaborately; though before my second school visit, to a remote village north of the Arctic Circle, one student had hung a "Fuck George Bush" tee shirt on the bulletin board to welcome me. Teachers respect students' right to free speech and expression, and this particular expression was hardly acknowledged by the teacher, though it got some chuckles from the students (and I) when I arrived.

Some schools, like Ringstabekk Skole in Bærum Kommune, were organized according to the open classroom concept, with flexible floor plans and movable walls. Each team could adjust its space according to the instructional needs of the day, with large, open spaces for whole group instruction or small rooms for group work. In these schools, teachers still had their offices and staff rooms, but they seemed much more connected with the classroom spaces than in schools with more traditional arrangements in which teachers floated from room to room during the day. As one teacher in an open classroom school noted: "Teachers and students own the space together; jointly."

In many new and newly renovated schools in Norway, common areas have abundant natural light and nooks and areas where students can congregate in small groups with some degree of privacy. While students essentially "own" the classrooms, it is common for their schools or team teachers to require them to leave the classrooms during breaks and, in some schools, to leave the building and go outdoors. In Longyearbyen, Svalbard, a Norwegian territory near the North Pole, students told me they were required to go outdoors during break, "unless it is something like minus 40 degrees (Celsius)." In schools on the Norwegian mainland with similar policies, the threshold for cold is a more bearable minus 25 degrees Celsius.

The Humanist Imperative

The middle school concept explicated in *This We Believe, Turning Points 2000,* and other middle-level documents is driven by a developmentalist imperative: That "the distinctive nature of young adolescents [is] the foundation upon which all decisions about school organization, policies, curriculum, instruction, and assessment are made" (NMSA, 2010, p. 13). I frequently witnessed familiar middle school practices and structures in Norwegian lower secondary schools, but I never heard educators discuss them in terms of developmental responsiveness. While I occasionally heard some evidence of a developmentalist discourse in my conversations with Norwegian lower secondary school teachers, explanations of school characteristics were more often discussed in terms of *human rights; emancipatory principles* based on, for example, trusting relationships between adults and students; and *egalitarian values*—three elements that, together, constitute a humanist imperative that drives the program in the *ungdomsskole*. In many respects, the practices and organizational structures I observed in Norwegian lower secondary schools honor and nurture the personhood of young people. From this perspective, it is not the age or developmental stage of students that matter most, but their humanity. Norwegian educators might rephrase the developmentalist imperative stated in *This We Believe* in the following way: Schools must use "the [humanity] of young [people and their basic human rights] as the foundation[s] upon which all decisions about school organization, policies, curriculum, instruction, and assessment are made" (NMSA, 2010, p. 13).

Human Rights

A commitment to education as a right is at the core of the Norwegian principle of "education for all"; the idea that: "Children and young people must have an equal right to education, regardless of where they live, gender, social and cultural background or any special needs" (Norwegian Ministry of Education and Research, 2007, p. 5). The Norwegian commitment to human rights and, in particular, the rights of students contrast sharply with the treatment of rights in the middle level literature. Consider the discussion of democratic governance in middle-level schools in *Turning Points 2000.* Jackson and Davis (2000) state: "Democratic governance in middle grades schools may not be an 'inalienable right," but it is clearly the right way to engage an entire school community" (pp. 145-146), and later they stress the importance of allowing students "to become involved in meaningful democratic participation" because "middle grades students are mature enough to engage in thoughtful, sustained analysis and problem solving" (p. 149). The recommendations in the middle-level literature for democratic governance and dozens of other components of ideal schools are rationalized by appeals to what is developmentally appropriate, preferred, or needed; not by appeals to the rights of the student. To Norwegians, democratic governance in schools and, indeed, in most institutions in society *is* an unalienable right, and it is not a right delimited by one's age or maturity level.

Emancipation

Wagner (2006) defined the Nordic commitment to emancipation as "the notion that children should be free from excessive adult control and supervision" (p. 292). As I discussed above, students in Norwegian lower secondary schools are not so closely monitored, supervised, and regulated as students in U.S. schools. While schools in the United States often have dozens of rules and policies governing every aspect of student life, Norwegian schools have comparatively few written rules. It is common to see lists of rules in U.S. classrooms, but I saw posters with class rules or policies in fewer than five of the schools I visited in Norway. One student explained to me: "We don't need lots of rules written down. We know we should be nice to each other so that's what we do. We don't need someone to tell us that." As Hansen and Wold (2007) observed, Norwegian youth "have a good deal of freedom; however, along with this they are also given a great deal of responsibility for their own actions" (p. 703). A word that often came up during my discussions with teachers and students about the notion of emancipation is "trust." The practices and structures of the *ungdomsskole* foster trusting relationships between adults and young people in the school and, at the same time, require such relationships for the school to function as it does.

Egalitarianism

Scandinavian societies are characteristically egalitarian. Ferguson (2005) discussed how schools produce "ordered difference" among pupils (p. 311), but I found the opposite to be true in Norway. Norwegian schools, and to a larger extent Norwegian society, operate on egalitarian principles intended to produce ordered sameness among individuals, at least in terms of how the system treats individuals, distributes rewards and sanctions, and recognizes individual achievements. At the same time, the emancipatory aspects of Norwegian schools allow students to develop their particular identities and express their individuality. Students have ownership of school spaces, are given choice in their studies, enjoy freedom of expression (dress and speech are not censored as they are in the United States), and have ample free time during the school day. Norway is "a culture where egalitarian values are important, but at the same time leaves room for uniqueness" (Hansen & Wold, 2007, p. 700).

An Opening for a Creative Youth

The developmenatalist imperative that drives the middle school concept constructs young adolescen[CE] as a stage along a "normative linear trajectory toward the destination of adulthood" (Jones, 2009, p. 86). Consequently, when individual adolescen(TS) display characteristics that vary from the norm, they are constructed as deviant, exceptional, or pathological. The dominant discourse about young adolescen(TS) in the United States (and in other places) is that they are at-risk and their lives need to be controlled by us (adults) during the middle grades years because it is "our last best shot" to save them (Stepp, 2000). Middle-level practices and organizational structures—like teaming, flexible scheduling, and looping—are put in place "to harness, redirect, and control the vagaries of youth in transition" (Brown, 2005, p. 153).

Schools driven by a developmentalist imperative reinforce the view that the life course is divided into phases, "accentuating the differences between [childhood and adulthood] rather than the relationships between them" (Jones, 2009, pp. 88-89). This is problematic, because, as Skott-Myhre (2008) argues, childhood is not a space separate from the adulthood, "bounded in time and evolutionary development" (p. 8), but the creative expression of the life force that manifests itself in different ways and at different points in time for each individual.

Skott-Myhre (2008) contrasts the *subjectum*, an aspect of identity development associated with special people—usually artists, musicians, and children—who are "allowed a certain latitude to creatively produce themselves" (p. 4), with the *subjectus*, associated with people who are subjected to the authority of a sovereign power such as a teacher or coach in a middle-level school. In this view, the "child as a subjectivity never arrives but is constantly renewed as a unique expression of both location and time throughout the lifespan" (p. 8).

The humanist imperative constructs Norwegian lower secondary school students as young *people* who possess certain inalienable rights; who are, to some degree, emancipated from adult constraints upon their thoughts, actions, and identities; and who, in an egalitarian school community, are able to participate in many aspects of daily school life as coequals with adults. Constructing young adolescen(TS) in this way particularizes them and opens up space to consider how their individual, particular identities are created, renewed, and re-created within school settings. It allows us to explore the concept of *subjectum*, as Skott-Myhre (2008) recommends,

> [As] a position for rethinking youth-adult relations, one in which the social binary of youth-adult is collapsed into a relation that flees the social containment of both terms. ... Put another way, I am proposing that youth and adults within the postmodern world cannot easily be reduced to fixed social categories or psychological constructs but must be seen, instead, as both historically laden and prophetic in their production of whatever it is that will come next. (Skott-Myhre, 2008, p. 7)

My observations and my analysis, of course, have limitations. All of my conversations with students and teachers in Norway were in English, a second or, in some cases, third or fourth language for them. While commitments to emancipation and egalitarianism seem uniquely Nordic or Norwegian orientations to me, many Norwegians are concerned that globalization and Americanization are causing their society to become more individualistic and self-centered (Hansen & Wold, 2007). My American cultural frame of reference and the relatively brief period of my engagement with Norwegian society did not allow me to perceive such subtle cultural shifts that may have impacted my analysis had I been aware of them. Finally, while I sought to answer Vagle's plea to particularize young adolescen(TS), I necessarily made generalizations and broad characterizations as I described my experiences. These generalizations, though, allowed me to draw comparisons to the United States and highlight the key differences from which "the best lessons" were learned (Wagner, 2006, p. 289).

References

Alexander, W. M. (1995). The junior high school: A changing view. *Middle School Journal, 26*(3), 20-24.

Bjerke, H. (2011). Children as "differently equal" responsible beings: Norwegian children's views of responsibility. *Childhood: A Global Journal of Child Research, 18*(1), 67-80.

Booth, M.Z. (2011). This they believe: Young adolescents reveal their needs in school. *Middle School Journal, 42*(3), 16-23.

Brown, E. R. (2005). The middle school concept and the purpose of education. In E. R. Brown, & K. J. Saltman (Eds.), *The critical middle school reader* (pp. 151-157). New York: Routledge.

Burkhardt, R.M. (1999). Advisory: Advocacy for every student. This we believe and now we must act. *Middle School Journal, 30*(3), 51-54.

Carnegie Council on Adolescent Development. (1989). *Turning points: Preparing American youth for the 21st century*. Washington, DC: Carnegie Corporation of New York.

Ferguson, A. A. (2005 [2001]). From bad boys: Public schools in the making of black male masculinity. In E. R. Brown & K. J. Saltman (Eds.), *The critical middle school reader* (pp. 311-328). New York: Routledge.

Hansen, F., & Wold, B. (2007). Norway. In J. J. Arnett (Ed.), *International encyclopedia of adolescence, vol. 2* (pp. 699-712). New York: Routledge.

Jackson, A., & Davis, G. (2000). *Turning points 2000: Educating adolescents in the 21st century.* New York: Teachers College Press.

Jones, G. (2009). *Youth.* Malden, MA: Polity Press.

Milner, H. (2009). Youth electoral participation in Canada and Scandinavia. In J. Youniss & P. Levine (Eds.), *Engaging young people in civic life* (pp. 187-218). Nashville, TN: Vanderbilt University Press.

Musoleno, R.R., & White, G.P. (2010). Influences of high-stakes testing on middle school mission and practice. *Research in Middle Level Education Online, 34*(3), 1-10. Retrieved October 1, 2011 from http://www.amle.org/Publications/RMLE Online/Articles/Vol34No3/tabid/2306/Default.aspx

National Middle School Association. (2007a). *Research summary: Flexible scheduling.* Retrieved October 1, 2011 from http://www.amle.org/Research/Research Summaries/FlexibleScheduling/tabid/1140/Default.aspx

———. (2007b). *Research summary: Heterogeneous grouping*. Retrieved October 1, 2011 from http://www.amle.org/Research/ResearchSummaries/HeterogeneousGrouping/tabid/1264/Default.aspx

———. (2010). *This we believe: Keys to educating young adolescents.* Westerville, OH: Author.

Norwegian Ministry of Education and Research. (2007). *Education: from kindergarten to adult education.* Oslo, Norway: Author.

———. (2010). *National curriculum regulations for differentiated primary and lower secondary teacher education programmes for years 1 – 7 and years 5 – 10.* Oslo, Norway: Author.

Robert Wood Johnson Foundation. (2010). *The state of play: Gallup survey of principals on school recess.* Princeton, NJ: Author.

Settertobulte, W., & de Matos, M.G. (2004). Peers. In C. Currie, C. Roberts, & A. Morgan, R. Smith, W. Settertobulte, O. Samdal, & V. Rassmussen (Eds.), *Young people's health in context*. Results from the 2001/2002 survey in the Health Behavior in School-Aged Children Study. Health Policy for Children and Adolescents, No. 4. (pp. 34-41). Copenhagen: World Health Organization. Retrieved October 1, 2011 from http://www.euro.who.int/__data/assets/pdf_file/0008/110231/e82923.pdf

Skott-Myhre, H. A. (2008). *Youth and subculture as creative force: Creating new spaces for radical youth work*. Canada: University of Toronto Press.

Steinberg, S. R. (2006). Why study youth culture? In S. Steinberg, P. Parma, & B. Richard (Eds.), *Contemporary youth culture: An international encyclopedia (vol. 1)* (pp. xiii-xviii). Westport, CT: Greenwood Press.

Stephens, P. (2011). Preventing and confronting school bullying: A comparative study of two national programmes in Norway. *British Educational Research Journal, 37*(3), 381-404.

Stepp, L. S. (2000). *Our last best shot: Guiding our children through early adolescence*. New York: Riverhead Books.

Thompson, N. L., Franz, D. P., & Miller, N. (2009). *Research summary: Looping*. Retrieved January 6, 2012 from http://www.amle.org/portals/0/pdf/research/Research_Summaries/Looping.pdf

Vagle, M. D. (this volume). Trying to poke holes in Teflon: Developmentalism; young adolescence; and contingent, recursive growth and change. In M. D. Vagle (Ed.), *Not a stage! A critical re-conception of young adolescent education* (pp. 11-38). New York: Peter Lang Publishing.

Virtue, D. C. (2009). Comparative and international education and middle level education research: A world of possibilities. In S. B. Mertens, V. A. Anfara, & K. Roney (Eds.), *An international look at educating young adolescents* (pp. xiii-xxix). Charlotte, NC: Information Age.

———. (2011). Time to live, time to learn, time to grow. *Middle School Journal, 42*(3), 2.

Wagner, J.T. (2006). An outsider's perspective: Childhoods and early education in the Nordic countries. In J. Einarsdottir & J.T. Wagner (Eds.), *Nordic childhoods and early education: Philosophy, research, policy, and practice in Denmark, Finland, Iceland, Norway, and Sweden* (pp. 289-306). Greenwich, CT: Information Age.

Warren, L. L., & Muth, K. D. (1995). The impact of common planning time on middle grades students and teachers. *Research in Middle Level Education Quarterly, 18*(3), 41-58.

Wolsey, T.D, & Uline, C.L. (2010). Student perceptions of middle grades learning environments. *Middle School Journal, 42*(2), 40-47.

Chapter 11

What's Happening Down Under: Young Adolescent Education in Australia

Donna Pendergast & Nan Bahr

Introduction

Since 2007, there has been a flurry of activity in Australia to introduce significant changes to education policy for the nation. *The Melbourne Declaration on Educational Goals for Young Australians* (MCEETYA, 2008) identifies one of its eight inter-related action areas as 'enhancing middle years' development', which aligns with the 10-15 year age group of interest in this book. This places the spotlight firmly on education for young adolescents and young adolescent education practices. MCEETYA explains that:

> [T]he middle years are an important period of learning, in which knowledge of fundamental disciplines are developed, yet this is also a time when students are at the greatest risk of disengagement from learning. Student motivation and engagement in these years is critical, and can be influenced by tailoring approaches to teaching with learning activities and learning environments that specifically consider the needs of middle years' students. (p. 10)

The redevelopment of the National Curriculum is underpinned by questions as to the phases/stages of schooling which will support the curriculum, bringing into focus unresolved questions about inclusion of a middle phase/stage in what has historically been a two phase model. At the national level the Middle Years of Schooling Association (MYSA) has worked to connect the various definitions, explanations and ideas of middle schooling through the *Middle Schooling: People, Practices and Places Position Paper* (MYSA, 2008). Further, a proliferation of research projects, including a longitudinal study of a middle years' teacher training program in an Australian university has sought to understand the concepts of 'middle years' and 'the middle years of schooling' from the perspective of pre-service teachers about to become middle years' teacher specialists. This chapter explores the Australian education context for young adolescents, analysing selected policy documents and research in the field. We have structured the chapter around 3 P's— key publications; key policies; and key teacher education programs. The chapter engages strongly with each of the three pleas platform offered by Vagle, urging a move from: a developmentally responsive vision to a contingently and recursively relational vision; characterizing young adolescenCE to particularizing young adolescenTS; and a sameness curriculum to a difference curriculum.

The Australian Education Setting

Australia is located in the southern hemisphere and is the largest island nation in the world. Much of the land is uninhabitable with desert covering the centre of the continent. It is a highly urbanised country, increasingly so each year, with large urban centres in coastal regions, particularly on the eastern coastline. According to the Population Clock of the Australian Bureau of Statistics (ABS 2011), on 23rd July 2011 the resident population of Australia was 22,658,768, with an overall total population increase of one person every 1 minute, 37 seconds. Just under 20% of the population is 15 years or younger and the population is ageing as a result of reduced fertility and increased life expectancy (ABS, 2010a). In the last decade the number of schools in Australia decreased slightly to 9,468, with an on-balance slight decline in public (government) schools and an increase in non-government schools (ABS, 2010b). According to the ABS (2010b), there are just over 3.5 million students enrolled in Australian schools, 66% of whom attend government schools, 20% attend Catholic schools and 14% attend independent schools. There are roughly 280,000 teachers in Australian schools, just under one third of whom are male. Forty-two percent of secondary school (Year 7 or 8 to Year 12) teachers are male and less than 20% of primary school teachers are male.

For the young adolescent age group of interest in this book, the majority of students are in Year 4 or Year 5 when they are aged 10 and mostly are located in Primary Schools, which cater for up to Year 6 or 7, depending on the statutory requirements of the local region. For the majority of students, a transition to a secondary school will occur in Year 7 or Year 8. Students typically turn 15 in Year 10.

Alternative school structures exist, including single schools from Pre-school to Year 12 (P-12), though they are less common in number across Australia. Often, these single P-12 schools are organised around subschools that roughly align to primary, junior secondary and senior secondary divisions, with clear transition points between these subschooling stages for students.

Until relatively recently, those interested in undertaking study to become a teacher chose to become either a primary or a secondary school teacher. Hence young adolescents were taught by generalist primary teachers in the primary school setting, then by secondary school teachers with generally two subject teaching areas. In the last decade, middle years pre-service teacher education programs have become common place in Australian universities, with graduates highly sought after. According to the Australian and New Zealand Standard Classification of Occupations (ANZSCO, 2009, np), *middle school teachers* exist as a separate category of teacher who can:

> ...teach one or more subjects within a prescribed curriculum to middle school or intermediate school students and promote students' social, emotional, intellectual and physical development.
>
> Tasks of middle school teachers include:
>
> 1. presenting prescribed curriculum using a range of teaching techniques and materials;
> 2. developing students' interests, abilities and coordination by way of creative activities;
> 3. guiding discussions and supervising work in class;
> 4. preparing, administering and marking tests, projects and assignments to evaluate students' progress and recording the results;
> 5. discussing individual progress and problems with students and parents, and seeking advice from Student Counsellors and senior teachers;
> 6. maintaining discipline in classrooms and other school areas;
> 7. participating in staff meetings, educational conferences and workshops;
> 8. liaising with parent, community and business groups;
> 9. maintaining class and scholastic records;
> 10. performing extra-curricular tasks such as assisting with sport, school concerts, excursions and special interest programs; and
> 11. supervising student teachers on placement.

There are minor definitional differences compared to primary and secondary teachers, basically highlighting that primary teachers teach primary students; middle years teachers teach middle years students; and secondary school teachers teach secondary school students. The list of tasks varies only with respect to the number of subjects taught, with primary teachers responsible for a wide range compared to middle and secondary teachers, who teach 'one or more subjects'. Within this broad definitional approach, middle year's teachers are therefore defined by two factors: the number of subjects taught, and the year level of the students they teach.

Importantly, middle year's teacher education is not a requirement for teaching in the middle years, with the majority of teachers being either primary or secondary trained. This is an important factor as little or no special attention is paid to the preparation of teachers for young adolescents in the broader primary and secondary programs and hence it is common to reinforce the assumptions that Vagle (this volume) is urging us to contest. For example in Queensland, programs accredited with the Queensland College of Teachers to enable teacher registration require teacher education for the middle years to prepare graduates to teach in both primary and secondary contexts. Graduates are to have discipline, content and pedagogical knowledge across all the key learning areas of primary, *and* two specialist teaching areas aligned to secondary schooling (Queensland College of Teachers, 2011). This means that the graduates are not specialised at all, but rather have been prepared as both primary and secondary school qualified. This situation is a reinforcement of the view that a sameness curriculum is most appropriate for the middle years.

Middle Years Teacher Education Programs in Australia

In spite of this significant limitation, the first dedicated middle years teacher education program in Australia was developed and introduced by a team including the authors of this chapter. A degree structure, the program set out to fill what was characterised as a deficiency in the preparation of teachers to meet the unique needs of young adolescents. As such, this was the first program designed to particularize adolescenTS. This program set a national standard that has been replicated in many universities around the country.

Currently, there are 18 middle years teacher education specialist programs; 7 programs with a specialisation in middle years; and 8 that include middle years in some way. The program name, duration and institution are detailed in Table 1.

	Middle **in title**	**Middle years courses /major**	**Middle in program outline**	**Yrs.**	**Institution**
B Education (Middle Years)	✓			4	University of Queensland
B Arts/B Education (Middle Years)	✓			4	University of Queensland
Bachelor of Education (Middle and Secondary Schooling), Bachelor of Health Sciences	✓			4	Flinders University
Bachelor of Education (Middle and Secondary/Special Education) / Disability Studies	✓			4	Flinders University
Master of Teaching (Middle and Secondary)	✓			2	University of South Australia
Bachelor of Education (Primary and Middle)	✓			4	University of South Australia
Bachelor of Education (K-12 Middle Schooling)	✓			4	Charles Sturt University
Bachelor of Education (Primary and Middle Schooling)	✓			4	University of Southern Queensland

	Middle in title	Middle years courses /major	Middle in program outline	Yrs.	Institution
Bachelor of Education (Middle Years)	✓			4	Christian Heritage College
Bachelor of Education/Bachelor of Arts – Middle School	✓			4.5	James Cook University
Bachelor of Education (Middle and Secondary Schooling), Bachelor of Arts	✓			4	Flinders University
Bachelor of Education (Primary to Middle)	✓			4	Edith Cowan University
Bachelor of Education (Middle and Secondary Schooling)/Bachelor of Science	✓			4	Flinders University
Bachelor of Education (Middle School)	✓			4	James Cook University
Bachelor of Applied Science (Human Movement and Health Studies) & Bachelor of Education (middle & Secondary)	✓			4	University of South Australia
Bachelor of Arts (Australian Studies) & Bachelor of Education (Middle and Secondary)	✓			4	University of South Australia
Bachelor of Arts (Aboriginal Studies) & Bachelor of Education (Middle and Secondary)	✓			4	University of South Australia
Master of Teaching (Primary & Middle)	✓			1.5	University of South Australia
Bachelor of Education (Primary) *with specialisation in middle years*		✓		4	Royal Melbourne Institute of

	Middle in title	Middle years courses /major	Middle in program outline	Yrs.	Institution
					Technology
Bachelor of Education (Primary) *with Middle School Specialisation*		✓		4	Monash
Graduate Diploma in Education *Middle Years specialisation*		✓		1	Queensland University of Technology
Bachelor of Education (Primary) Graduate Course *Middle Phase of Learning specialisation*		✓		2	Queensland University of Technology
Bachelor of Education (Primary) *With Middle Years Ed programme available*		✓		4	Griffith University
Graduate Diploma of Education (Primary) *With Middle Years Ed programme available*		✓		1	Griffith University
Master of Teaching (Professional Practice) *With Middle Years Ed programme available*		✓		1.5	Griffith University
Bachelor of Teaching with Bachelor of Arts			✓	4	University of Adelaide
Bachelor of Teaching with Bachelor of Economics			✓	4	University of Adelaide
Bachelor of Teaching with Bachelor of Science			✓	4	University of Adelaide
Bachelor of Teaching with Bachelor of Mathematical and Computer Science			✓	4	University of Adelaide

	Middle in title	Middle years courses /major	Middle in program outline	Yrs.	Institution
Bachelor of Education			✓	4	University of Ballarat
Bachelor of Education			✓	4	University of Notre Dame
Bachelor of Education/Bachelor of Science			✓	4	University of Queensland
Bachelor of Education/Bachelor of Business			✓	4	University of Queensland

Table 1: Middle year teacher education names, type, duration and institution in Australia

What is noteworthy about the range and type of programs is that they intentionally seek to prepare teachers for teaching young adolescents, recognising this as a component that requires specialist knowledge and pedagogical capability. While each program brings with it a particular philosophical perspective regarding young adolescents, many of these programs use a textbook that was written specifically for the Australian middle year's teacher education setting. We will now turn to that book to determine the way in which young adolescents are characterised.

Middle Years Publications in Australia

Teaching Middle Years: Rethinking Curriculum, Pedagogy and Assessment (Pendergast & Bahr, 2010) is a book developed for use in university and school settings for the pre-service and professional development of teachers. Its title promises a 'rethink'. Taken-for-granted assumptions about teaching young adolescents form the lens through which the book has been conceptualized. Readers are led from an understanding of the limits of an undifferentiated sameness curriculum, of characterization of adolescenCE, and of developmental modeling for the production of middle years schooling that does not effectively target appropriate education for these young people. For example, readers are challenged to rethink the place of age and stage grand theories of development for curriculum design.

The book, now in its second edition, has twenty chapters built into five sections: The middle years as a site for educational reform; Curriculum practices for the middle years; Pedagogical practices for the middle years; Assessment practices for the middle years; and Middle schooling in action. The first section has a number of chapters that trace the rise of middle years education and then moves into philosophical challenges, which parallel the three pleas platform offered by Vagle, urging a move from: a developmentally responsive vision to a contingently and recursively relational vision; characterizing young adolescenCE to particularizing young adolescenTS; and a sameness curriculum to a difference curriculum. Those engaging with the book are led through a process of disrupting assumptions of young adolescents, and then facilitated to develop their own set of beliefs, particularly with respect to the development of a philosophy of teaching middle years students.

By way of example, chapter two entitled *The Philosophy of Middle Schooling*, is structured around key questions that middle years reformers often face. The authors commence the chapter by stating "throughout the chapter we identify our position on the issues but in a way that does not present readers with a prefabricated package. This approach reflects our assumption that middle schoolers are philosophy-makers rather than philosophy-takers" (Chadbourne & Pendergast, 2010, p. 23). The questions that form the basis of the chapter are:

1. Should middle schooling be adolescent-specific?
2. Should middle schooling prioritise the intellectual development of students?
3. Should young adolescents be made to fit the organisation of schools or should the organisation of schools be made to fit young adolescents?
4. What should the curriculum of middle schools consist of?
5. What concept of reality should the middle school curriculum be based on?
6. Should pedagogy in middle schools be teacher-centred or student-centred?

7. Should middle schooling aim to help build a better society and if so what would a better society look like?
8. Should middle schooling be an agent of social change?
9. Is there a 'one true' or 'pure' model of middle schooling?
10. Is it necessary to have a philosophy of middle schooling?

The chapter concludes with a structure for readers to develop a personal philosophy of young adolescent education. Moving on to the third chapter entitled *The Middle Years Learner* the reader's common-sense assumptions of young adolescents is again intentionally disrupted by the opening sentences:

> [A]dolescence is a problem notion, and any sense of an exact concept is undermined by the plethora of contested ideas and theories raging in contemporary literature and media. If adolescence is a murky term, then what of young adolescence? This chapter examines some of the stable and contested views of adolescence expounded in contemporary sources. Conceptions of young adolescence as a developmental stage are problematized and explored. (Bahr, 2010, p. 50)

The book follows this approach throughout, intending to open space for new ways of thinking about young adolescents and the education they experience.

Although designed predominantly as a resource for teacher education, both preservice and inservice, the book has also responded to, and subsequently influenced the development of Middle Years policy in Australia. The first edition of the book was extensively cited in all contemporaneous policy reform documents for Government, Federal and jurisdictional, and surprisingly also for our neighbours, the New Zealand Government. The second edition has formed the base for the literature review for the recent Queensland Review of Teacher Education (Caldwell & Sutton, 2010a), which will underscore the development of the next era of policy for the Middle Years in Queensland, and Australia more generally.

Middle Years Policy in Australia

Policy for Middle Years education in Australia has lacked a sense of cohesion. While there is shared acknowledgement that a seamless education from entry through to school graduation requires quality middle schooling, there is patchy agreement as to what this might mean. Recent policy documents have rationalised attention to middle schooling simply in terms of enabling smooth transition between earlier and later schooling. With regard to Vagle's pleas, the middle years are not considered relationally, adolescents are not particularized, and there has been active work against enabling a difference curriculum. The most recent Australian national policy framework is the Melbourne Declaration (2008).

Melbourne Declaration and National Curriculum

In 2008, the Australian State, Territory and Commonwealth Education Ministers published the Melbourne Declaration on Educational Goals for Young Australians. This has been the third Ministerial Declaration since the 1980s. The first was the 1989 Hobart Declaration. Next was the 1999 Adelaide Declaration. This Melbourne Declaration is unique in that it calls for a national curriculum and makes specific reference to middle years. This in itself would seem encouraging; however, the potential for positive impact in schooling has been skewed by the underpinning motives for considering middle years in this policy framework. The Ministers' were under national pressure to respond to disappointment with Organisation for Economic Co-operation and Development (OECD) benchmarking data on the relative ranking of Australian 15-year-olds in the 2006 OECD Programme for International Student Assessment. Australian 15 year olds ranked in the top 10, but there had been some decline in the Australian ranking and the Ministers' aspiration were set much higher. Attention on the middle years has been largely a function of this test preparation agenda. As a result, with an eye on the prize, performance of 15 year olds in standardised testing, there has been only notional attempt to distinguish middle years schooling. The umbrella stance on the middle years in the Declaration is that:

> Australian governments commit to working with all school sectors to ensure that schools provide programs that are responsive to students' developmental and learning needs in the middle years, and which are challenging, engaging and rewarding. (Melbourne Declaration, 2008, p. 12)

Although revolutionary in that the middle years has found specific mention in the Declaration, this policy has not brought a revolution. This statement situates the policy as developmentally responsive rather than contingently and recursively relational; characterizing young adolescenCE rather than particularizing young adolescenTS; and aligned to a sameness curriculum rather than a difference curriculum.

From this base vision of middle years as an intermediate phase in an undifferentiated schooling and curriculum landscape, the Australian Curriculum, Assessment and Reporting Authority (ACARA) has begun to shape the Australian Curriculum. This curriculum is still under development and will be rolled out across the nation in three stages. By the end of 2010, a framing paper had been produced, and the first of 14 curriculum areas were ready for trial in schools (English, Mathematics, Science and History). The entire suite of curriculum policy materials will have been completed and introduced to all schools in Australia by 2015. The shaping document (ACARA, 2010) outlines the intended overall structure of the Australian Curriculum. ACARA have elected to consider the curriculum in four stages: foundation to year 2; years 3 through to year 8; years 9 and 10; and, years 11 and 12. There is no mention of the middle years in the ACARA curriculum policy. There is no attempt to connect with an understanding of what learning in the middle years might bring for young adolescents. This is a function of the widespread debate regarding appropriate phases of schooling and elements to distinguish them. Each State and Territory, and often the educational systems within these states (for example, state versus independent sectors) have invested in schooling systems that draw on different views of middle schooling but they share developmentally responsive perspectives that attempt to characterize young adolescence as a stage. At greatest contention are the bounds of middle schooling. That is, they contest the year levels that should be considered relevant to the middle years. ACARA has attempted to avoid resolving these contentions by staying mute with regard to middle years. As such, the Melbourne Declaration has brought an empty revolution.

MYSA Position Paper

The Middle Years of Schooling Association (MYSA), the Australia-wide peak body organisation dedicated exclusively to the education, development and growth of young adolescents, in 2008, released the Position Paper *Middle Schooling: People, Practices and Places* which defines middle schooling as "an intentional approach to teaching and learning that is responsive and appropriate to the full range of needs, interests and achievements of middle years students in formal and informal schooling contexts" (MYSA, 2008, p.1). The middle years are described as from around age ten to fifteen, spanning the years from childhood to adolescence. The Position Paper also specifies three elements necessary for middle schooling:

1. Clear philosophy relevant to the context.
2. Comprehensive range of signature practices to engage young adolescents in relevant, meaningful and challenging learning, along with organisational initiatives to facilitate their implementation, such as:
    a. higher order thinking strategies
    b. integrated and disciplinary curricula that are negotiated, relevant and challenging
    c. heterogeneous and flexible student groupings
    d. cooperative learning and collaborative teaching
    e. small learning communities that provide students with sustained individual attention in a safe and healthy school environment
    f. emphasis on strong teacher–student relationships through extended contact with a small number of teachers and a consistent student cohort
    g. authentic and reflective assessment with high expectations
    h. democratic governance and shared leadership
    i. parental and community involvement in student learning.
3. Evidence-based approach with clearly articulated outcomes, such as:
    a. developing current and lifelong learning attributes
    b. enhanced academic outcomes
    c. creation of a love of learning.

The position paper has the following to say about young adolescents:

> Young adolescents in the middle years experience a range of significant physical, cognitive, emotional, social, and moral changes. During puberty, young adolescents experience more rapid and dramatic hormonal and structural changes than at any other period in their life. The sequence of physical change is generally similar from one person to another, although the onset, rate, and timing of these changes are highly individual, often creating stress and feelings of insecurity for the adolescent. Changes to brain and cognitive development peak during this period. Apart from the first five years of life, at no other time does the capacity and functioning of the brain undergo such an overhaul. This affects the learning ability of young adolescents and their success in managing the emotional, social and moral challenges of this stage. Disengagement, alienation and boredom in school often peak in the middle years and this may lead to a decline in achievement. Hence the middle years, particularly with respect to the productive engagement of young people in schooling and other contexts, is a priority for educators. (MYSA 2008, p. 1)

This statement provides a clear alignment with the notion that young adolescents should be regarded as individuals (adolescents) and not collectively defined (adolescence). However, it does point to the idea of young adolescence as being a 'stage' which features change, while still pointing to the individual experience of the changes. The connection to achievement and schooling does not reflect a developmentally responsive vision.

Flying Start Year 7 into Secondary

Some Australian States and Territories have been working through their own agendas of reform for education. The most prominent of these has been the *Flying Start* initiatives of the Queensland State Government. In its own response to the OECD benchmarking disappointments, and the Melbourne Declaration, the Queensland State Government commissioned a report by Masters evaluating the quality of education and providing recommendations for action. The Masters Report (2009) identified three objectives; improving children's development, wellbeing and school readiness (focus on the early years); improving transitions from primary to secondary school and supporting adolescent development (year 7 to high school initiative); improving school discipline and the quality of teaching (teacher education regulation and registration initiatives).

For advocates of specialised middle years education, it seemed that attention on the transition point between primary and secondary schooling in Queensland would resurface the debate and development of effective schooling for young adolescents. It was hoped that the traditional two-stage organisation of education might be challenged and that consideration of a different kind of approach to education in the middle years might be aired. The Queensland Government maintained momentum from the Masters report by commissioning a process of review to identify actions for implementation, and advocates for the middle years were heavily engaged with the review team.

Two reports from the review process have been released (Caldwell & Sutton, 2010a, 2010b). The first report provided an overview of middle years literature. The much awaited second report provided the recommendations for action. Unfortunately, the recommendations provide little central direction. The review team clearly was uncertain how to position the call for a revolution in middle years alongside the strident voices of the traditionalists. For example, the first recommendation from the second report is "that, in the interests of avoiding confusion or 'opt out', employing authorities should give a firm policy direction as to the place and future of middle schooling in their jurisdictions" (Caldwell & Sutton, 2010b). Instead of confirming a place for middle years advocates in the design of education for Queensland, the review team deferred a determination and actually cast doubt on validity of middle years consideration. There had been a steady development for middle years policy in Queensland since 2003 when the Queensland State Government released their *Middle Phase of Learning Action Plan* in response to Ministerial Advisory Committee for Educational Renewal (MACER) report, *The Middle Phase of Learning* (2003). However, the review of the Flying Start has caused a rupture. The result has been inattention to the philosophical and underpinning goals of middle years education even as the State has begun to invest in a fundamental change to primary secondary transitions with the move of grade 7 students to secondary school contexts from 2015.

The policy processes have pulled toward generalised views of learners devoid of contingently and recursively relational visions, with age and stage developmental containers for adolescence rather than a view to adolescents, and with commitment to undifferentiated curriculum. At the national, state/territory, and schooling sector level, the flights toward a simplistic view of education have disrupted the opportunities for middle years education.

Conclusion

In this chapter we have journeyed through three perspectives on advocacy for Australian Educational reform for the middle years: key publications, key teacher education programs, and key policies. The impact of reform for middle years will continue to be disrupted unless the shifts proposed by Vagle take hold. In Australia, we have seen that a strong philosophical foundation for middle years and prominent voice from advocates is not enough. Policy drives reform home, and we have seen policy makers overturn long-standing initiatives for middle years reform through their vision that is limited to broad generalisations of adolescence that do not particularize effectively for those learners in the middle years of schooling.

References

Australian Bureau of Statistics. (2009). *Australian and New Zealand Standard Classification of Occupations*, First Edition, Revision 1. Catalogue 1220.0. Australian Government: Canberra.

———. (2010a). *Population by Age and Sex, Australian States and Territories*, June 2010. Catalogue 3201.0. Australian Government: Canberra.

———. (2010b). *Schools*, Australia, 2010 Catalogue 4221.0. Australian Government: Canberra.

———. (2011). *Population Clock*. http://www.abs.gov.au/ausstats/abs%40.nsf/94713ad445ff1425ca25682000192af2/1647509ef7e25faaca2568a900154b63?OpenDocument

Australian Curriculum, Assessment and Reporting Authority. (2010). *The Shape of the Australian Curriculum*. Sydney, Australia: ACARA.

Bahr, N. (2010). The middle years learner. In D. Pendergast & N. Bahr (Eds), *Teaching Middle Years: Rethinking curriculum, pedagogy and assessment*. (2nd Edition). Allen & Unwin: Crows Nest, 50-67.

Caldwell, B., & Sutton, D. (2010a). *Review of Teacher Education and School Induction: First Report-Full Report* (18 August). Brisbane, Queensland: Queensland State Government.

———. (2010b). *Review of Teacher Education and School Induction: Second Report-Full Report* (29 October). Brisbane, Queensland: Queensland State Government.

Chadbourne, R. & Pendergast, D. (2010). The philosophy of middle schooling. In: D. Pendergast & N. Bahr (Eds.), *Teaching Middle Years: Rethinking curriculum, pedagogy and assessment* (2nd Edition). Allen & Unwin: Crows Nest, 23-49.

Middle Years of Schooling Association. (2008). *MYSA Position Paper: Middle Schooling: People, Practices and Places*. MYSA: Brisbane.

———. (2008). *MYSA Position Paper: Middle Schooling: People, Practices and Places*. MYSA: Brisbane.

Ministerial Advisory Committee for Educational Renewal (MACER) (2003), *The Middle Phase of Learning*. Queensland Government Press: Brisbane, Queensland.

———. (2008). Melbourne Declaration on Educational Goals for Young Australians.

Pendergast, D. & Bahr, N. (2010). *Teaching Middle Years: Rethinking Curriculum, Pedagogy and Assessment*. (2nd Edition). Allen & Unwin: Sydney.

Queensland College of Teachers (2011). *Program approval guidelines for preservice teacher education*. The State of Queensland: Brisbane. Retrieved October 1,2011 from http://www.qct.edu.au/PDF/PSU/QCTProgramApprovalGuidelines.pdf

Queensland State Government (2003). *The middle phase of learning state action plan*. Queensland Government Press Brisbane, Queensland. Retrieved August 25, 2011 from http://education.qld.gov.au/etrf/pdf/midaction03.pdf

Vagle, M. D. (this volume). Trying to poke holes in Teflon: Developmentalism; young adolescence; and contingent, recursive growth and change. In M. D. Vagle (Ed.), *Not a stage! A critical re-conception of young adolescent education* (pp. 11-38). New York: Peter Lang Publishing.

Chapter 12

'Particularizing' Young Adolescents in an Indian Context

Ajay Sharma

Introduction

Scholarship on educational issues is replete with generalized statements that serve as distillates of received wisdom from research and collective lore over the years. As Vagle's introductory chapter in this volume illustrates, canonical literature in middle grades education too supports and is, in fact, based upon some globalized characterizations of young adolescents. For instance, it is believed that generally speaking young adolescents are idealistic, lack sustained interests, and are unable to cope with complex moral and ethical questions. Like any other movement for widespread school reform, the middle school movement in the United States has depended on such generalized claims to make the case for middle schools as the appropriate institutional learning spaces for young adolescents. Thus, they have been immensely useful in policymaking contexts.

However, on close scrutiny one finds that many of these articulations about young adolescents are based on empirical research done in mostly middle class and American cultural contexts. These decontextualized global characterizations are, then, of little help to researchers and educators in interpreting and explaining life as lived by young adolescents both within and outside school boundaries. What is needed, in fact, is a dialogic response by researchers to Vagle's (this volume) theoretical plea of moving from "characterizing" young adolescenCE to "particularizing" young adolescenTS. Through close-grained empirical research they need to present the 'particularized' ways in which young adolescents instantiate the 'characteristic' generalizations about them in diverse sociocultural, economic and geographical settings. That is, what is needed is a multiperspective, multilocational, and ever enlarging portraiture of life as lived and experienced by young adolescents—a narrative ensemble that is as empirically grounded as it is theoretically rich.

In response to Vagle's plea, this chapter offers 'particularized' snapshots of life as lived by young adolescents in a village in central India. These snapshots are embedded in a socio-cultural theoretical framework that views 'people as actively engaged with the environment' (Holland et al., 1998). This engagement is mediated by cultural means, that is, tools and signs (Vygotsky, 1980). Meaning that each person is seen as possessing a cultural 'toolkit' of mediational means that act as a resource as well as constraint in her engagement with the world (Wertsch, 1991). This toolkit is acquired by young adolescents through their evolving participation in the local sociocultural and socioeconomic activities of their community. As a learning process, this contextualized acquisition of a cultural toolkit constitutes "an integral part of generative social practice in the lived-in world" (Lave & Wenger, 1991: 35). By engaging in local social practices either under adult guidance or in collaboration with more capable peers, young adolescents learn to be active members of their local community. Further, because of increasing penetration of local contexts by global discourses all over the world, many of these local social practices are informed by a dynamic and dialogic bricolage of local and glocalized global discourses (Bronwyn & Bansel, 2007; Fairclough, 2004; Lankshear, 1997).

These snapshots present young adolescents as participants in social practices occurring outside school at their homes and workplaces. Data reported in this chapter comes from my doctoral dissertation—an ethnographic study of science learning in the middle school of the village Rajkheda (a pseudonym) that was conducted in 2004-05[1].

Situated in the Narmada valley region of Madhya Pradesh, India, Rajkheda is a medium-sized (by Indian standards) village of 270 families. It is on the main road linking two towns, Hoshangabad and Pachmadhi, in the Hoshangabad district. Rajkheda is a relatively poor village, with 125 families (44.4 percent) officially classified, in 2001, as below the poverty line. The villagers' main occupation is agriculture, and one can see agricultural fields in all directions from the village. The village had one unpaved main street running through it. The government middle and primary schools were located on one campus, quite near the entrance of the village and next to this street. By the time I finished my fieldwork, this main street had been converted into a paved road. The government middle school is the only middle school for Rajkheda and seven other neighbouring villages in that region. There is no high school in Rajkheda and students graduating from the middle school have to attend high schools in neighbouring towns in order to continue their formal education.

During my fieldwork, I came to know, quite closely, many young adolescents studying at the local middle school. They let me hang out

Figure 8: Rajkheda Village

with them before and after school, took me to their cricket matches, and invited me into their homes and lives outside school. I spent time with their parents and had meals with their families. In the beginning, most of these kids were somewhat shy to share their experiences, ideas, and opinions with me. However, with time this reluctance gave way to more open and relaxed conviviality between them and me. Still, I must confess that till the end, my relationship with them remained remarkably fluid and contextual. Some years back I had worked with teachers in that region's schools. But since I had moved out of the country to pursue higher studies and had come back as a researcher, I had a constantly shifting positionality as an ex-native cum researcher-from-abroad that worked differentially in different contexts in terms of access and power-relations. The snapshots I present below are, then, embedded within an undefined mix of *emic* and *derived etic* perspectives (Rogoff, 1996), and hence are shaped both by my theoretical and political commitments and local participants' viewpoints.

Young Adolescents at Home

Numerous studies have shown that how young adolescents (YA) live their lives outside school varies widely with socio-cultural setting (Brown, Larson, & Saraswathi, 2002). Having worked in the region, I was generally aware that kids in Rajkeda led busy lives outside school as productive members of the family and local economy. However, it was only after I visited their homes and spent time with them outside school that I came to understand more fully that even within a village, characterizing a young adolescent's life with broad brush strokes can be facile and misleading. There were indeed some broad similarities in children's lives outside school that could be attributed to the local context, but because caste, class and personal history intersected differentially for each child, there were significant differences in their home lives. In this section, I highlight both the commonalities and differences in their lives at home so as to present a 'particularized' portrait of the young adolescents of Rajkheda.

Given the fact that the village had a high poverty rate (that was typical of that region actually), most YAs I met came from very poor families. Though by local standards, some families were much better off than others. Poorer families lived in single or two room houses, had few basic amenities and depended on their bicycles or public transport for moving around. Agriculture was the main occupation in the village. Most poor families had little or no agricultural land, and earned their livelihood by working on other people's farms. All families in the village had access to electricity, though, interestingly, many of them had an illegal connection tapped directly from transmission lines that supplied electricity to the village. A water tank to supply water to the village had been built some years ago. However, as the project ran out of money before supply lines could be built, no house in the village had access to running water. Better-off families either had their own wells or used motor pumps to draw water from underground aquifers. Poorer families depended on public handpumps for their water supply. Most families also maintained some cattle for tilling or dairy purposes.

With few modern amenities and general lack of disposable income, day-to-day functioning in most families was heavily predicated upon significant contribution from all members including children. Thus, when I asked Raj, a 15-year-old boy who came from a poor family of landless agricultural laborers, what he did at home after school ended at 4 PM, he responded, "After 4, I go home, sir. Then eat something, feed the cattle, give them water. Fill up water, sweep the floor and wash the utensils if there are any ... and by then in the evening mummy and papa return. I can cook food too. I can cook potatoes" (interview, 03/04/2005). Likewise, Sarla, a 15-year-old girl whose parents worked as agricultural laborers, was not only in charge of cooking food for the family, looking after the family cow and her calf, and general maintenance of the house, but also acted as the primary caregiver for her six younger siblings. However, her cousin, Chandani, who lived close, did not have to cook food at home as she had an elder sister who cooked food for the family. As she told me after returning from school she only had to "give water to the cows, wash dishes and sweep the floor".

Figure 9: Cooking Food at Home

However, as I spent more time in the field it became apparent that not much could be stated by way of broad generalizations beyond observing that YAs of the village generally helped their parents in household chores. For instance, Govind's parents had no agricultural land and worked as labourers on other farmers' fields. But unlike Raj he did not have to do as many household chores. When I asked him what he did after school the dialogue proceeded as follows:

Me: So you come to school... well, after that?

Govind: After school I eat dinner and then study again.

Me: Really?... Does "light" come at night?

Govind: Yes.

Yashwant (a friend and classmate of Govind): Sir, sometimes it comes and sometimes it doesn't?

Me: Then what do you do if there is no "light".

Govind: Sir, there is "chimney". We use that then.

M: Uhmm... Then? You sleep?

G: After that I sleep. (interview, 03/07/ 2005)

As is clear from the dialogue above, Govind spent considerable time studying for school while at home. He told me that he also studied in the morning before coming to school. Like him, almost all students told me that they spent significant time studying before and after school. As someone who grew up in India and did fine in his studies, I never worked that hard for school so it was all a bit surprising for me. So, I would often challenge them to tell me the truth. But they all stood their ground as is clear from the dialogue below:

> Me: You come to the school every morning. So what is your daily routine? For instance, when do you wake up? What all you do in the morning?
>
> Raj: These days when the studies are in full swing, I get up at 4 in the morning.
>
> Me: Are you telling the truth?
>
> Raj: Yes, I am telling the truth.
>
> Me: Come on. Tell the truth. Are you able to wake up so early?
>
> Raj: (smiling) Yes, I am able to wake up. You see, ever since this month of January started, I have been getting up very early in the morning, getting up at 4 in the morning. It was difficult for the first week. I used to tell my mother to wake me up, but I just wasn't able to open my eyes. But after a few days, it was possible to wake up so early. After getting up, I go to toilet. I wash my face and hands so that I don't fall asleep again. And then I sit separately on a bed to study. I study till about 6 o'clock. Then I again wash and freshen up again. Then I drink tea around 7, and then head for tuition classes.[2]
>
> Me: So where do you go for tuition?
>
> Raj: You know our teacher Chote Shrivastavji. His younger sister teaches. I go to their house.
>
> Me: And what after tuition?
>
> Raj: After I come back from tuition, I take bath and have my meals, and come to the school. (interview, 03/04/2005)

Of course, it is quite likely that such a punishing schedule was followed with some consistency only when the final annual examinations were near at the end of the academic year. Still, amidst the variations in these YAs' lives at home, regular home study was one feature that was reported to me by all students. As Raj mentions in the dialogue above, most male students also went for extra coaching classes before coming to school. Among all the female students I came across none who went for these classes. Though I did not ask the students or their parents why this was so, knowing the sociocultural context of that village, there are two plausible explanations: (a) coaching classes were held in a neighboring village. Some of the parents, especially from the high castes, may not have felt confident about letting their daughters go out for these classes on their own. In fact, this was the reason why 8th grade was the last year in school for some female students as they would go out of village to attend high school; (b) gender-based discrimination against girls is widespread in India. As a result, when faced by economic constraints, parents generally do not spend as many resources for their education as for boys. Thus, private coaching was an extra expenditure that some parents in the village may not have wished to incur for their daughters.

Figure 10: Hanging Out with Friends

As the next section will elaborate, many YAs also helped their parents in their profession. However, this sort of direct economic contribution was limited while school was in session. Of course, some YAs could also be seen hanging out in front of the only general provisions shop (a tiny tin-roof shack) in the evenings (see Figure 10) and at a couple other places for public gathering. I heard complaints from some parents that their kids wasted a lot of their time loitering around or playing a gambling game with coins. Many YAs also disclosed to me their fondness for watching TV. But given the sporadic supply of electricity to the village, it is unlikely that this leisure activity reached levels anywhere close to that of most United States YAs.

Thus, the local socioeconomic and cultural context engendered some commonalities in roles and responsibilities at home for these YAs. If one goes by the guiding assumptions of sociocultural theories, it can be said that these similarities molded their participation in social events in similar ways. However, when I looked closer within a given context, interesting complexities appeared that led to significant differences in what these kids did at home. The role of these 'particularizing' experiences in molding actions and perspectives of a YA differentially from those of her peers cannot be underestimated. Many factors, such as caste, family's socioeconomic status, number of siblings, and one's age rank among them, contributed to these differences. Further, the strength of any factor varied from individual to individual. As I illustrate in the following section, such 'particularizing' complexities also led to remarkable differences in their participation in local economic activities.

Young Adolescents at Work

Societal norms govern the nature and extent of participation of YAs in social practices. Among middle-class families in India, just as in the United States, YAs are not expected to indulge in economic activity besides doing some odd jobs now and then for neighbors. In Rajkheda, however, poverty as well as social traditions positioned most YAs as productive participating members in the local economy. Through apprenticeship and under guidance of a senior peer or an adult belonging to their family or professional community, they learned to perform a variety of economic roles.

For instance, below I present a snippet from an interview with Raj in which he explained to me how he was helping his family economically:

> Me: So in farming, how do you help your family? What all things you do?
>
> Raj: These days I am helping in digging of sweet potatoes. I go after school to help uproot sweet potato plants.
>
> Me: Like when you told me after the exams the other day that you would be going straight away to the farm to uproot sweet potatoes.
>
> Raj: Yes. We uproot plants, and also do digging (with the help of tractor). We clean them, and fill it in baskets.
>
> Me: So this all you do.
>
> Raj: Yes, I do everything.
>
> Me: And in wheat, what all things do you do?
>
> Raj: With wheat, during harvest time, we cut it. Then use the thresher to get the wheat, and then pack it in bags after separating it from the chaff.
>
> Me: You had told me that you have done the work of making earthen tiles. Is this something that is done in your family or something that only you did?

Raj: No. My uncle also used to do this work. The younger uncle. He put me in this work with him. I have worked there for 5 years. You know these vacations in the summer. I work then.

Me: So now when there are vacations this summer, will you go this time too?

Raj: Yes, when the school breaks I'll go there to work.

Me: Where do you go?

Raj: You know this ( ) factory, the one that you get to see when you are coming to the school – falls on this side[3].

Me: So you must be going every morning and coming back in the evening.

Raj: No, I go early in the morning at 8. We work from 8 to 12, and then from 2 to 6. So we work for 8 hours every day.

Likewise, Mahesh helped his ironsmith father in making small farm implements (see Figure 11). Mahesh's father moonlighted as an agricultural labour. Following his father's lead, Mahesh also worked as a hired labourer occasionally.

Figure 11: Working as a Part-Time Ironsmith

However, Amaresh, a classmate of Raj and Mahesh and resident of Rajkheda, did not participate in any economic activity. His family had moved to Rajkheda some years back from another district, and they lived as tenants in the house of a big local farmer. Amaresh belonged to a family (and caste) of traditional goldsmiths. Not being traditional farmers and not owning any agricultural land, his father worked as a night guard in a factory close by. Because Amaresh could not participate in his family's traditional profession or his father's current profession, he did not participate in any local economic activity. Amaresh's family was very poor. However, like students from middle- and upper-class backgrounds, Amaresh just went to school, and spent rest of the day at home or in the neighborhood.

As the aforementioned examples of Raj and Mahesh show, many YAs who came from farming families helped cultivate crops and vegetables. However, data analysis revealed many interesting variations and exceptions to this overall theme. For instance, Yashwant came from an extended family of farmers. But he helped them in farming only on Sundays. On the other hand, Davendra and Deepak, whose fathers were farmers too, confessed that they never helped their family in farming[4]. Praveen too did not work on agricultural land like his parents. However, he worked at a grocery store in a neighboring town during summer vacations. Praveen told me that he was planning to drop out of school after eighth grade and start working at his cousin's general merchandise shop in the state capital Bhopal.

As a result of their active engagement with paid and unpaid work at home and the workplace, most YAs I met had either accumulated years of rich experience working as legitimate participants or by observing adults engaged in local socioeconomic practices. As a result, their conversations and participation in classroom often revealed a rich and nuanced knowledge and understanding about the local social and material world. But, again, owing to significant differences amidst overall similarities in their immersion in local socioeconomic practices, each YA's knowledge and understanding about the local world was similar and yet different. For instance, almost all YAs of the village knew that one can directly tap electricity from a high-voltage AC electric line for a house, but only some (all boys) had actually done so. Similarly, most YAs knew how to feed and take care of cattle at home, but only a few could go into detail on their typical ailments and how to treat them. While planning this study, I had made some assumptions about the YAs I was likely to meet on the basis of reference literature and my prior experiences with schools in that region. Close interaction with these children made me realize how different each one of them was. But do such differences really matter if our objective is to understand YAs in terms of their behavioural characteristics, attitudes and abilities? This is the question I turn to next in the concluding section wherein I argue in favour of moving away from broad characterizations of YAs and, instead, paying close attention to the particularizing nature of different contextual influences upon individual YAs.

Conclusion

It is clear that YAs of Rajkheda had strikingly different experiences and societal roles than most middle-class YAs in the United States—a population group most frequently used to characterize YAs in dominant middle grades policy and school reform documents. Because of these differences, the behavioural, intellectual and emotional categories appropriate for describing YAs of Rajkheda would be very different from those useful for middle-class YAs of America. As Rogoff (2003) said, "people develop as participants in cultural communities. Their development can be understood only in light of the cultural practices and circumstances of their communities which also change" (pp. 4–5). In her study of children's lives in different cultural communities Rogoff (2003) too found significant differences in the extent to which children are allowed to observe and participate in adult activities. For instance, comparing children from a farming community in East Africa with middle-class American children, she found that 4-year-old children from the African farming community "spent 35% of their time doing chores, and 3 year-olds did chores during 25% of their time.... In contrast, middle-class US children of the same ages spent none to 1% of their time doing chores, though they did spend 4% to 5% of their time accompanying others in chores (such as helping the mother peel a carrot or fold laundry)" (p. 136). Rogoff further reports that by the time they are between 7 and 12 years old, the Aka kids of Central Africa can hunt and butcher large game animals, trap porcupines and grow food plants. In contrast, most middle-class American kids may not even know how to hold a butcher's knife properly and safely, though they may know a lot about manipulating symbols and images on a computer screen or understanding a subway map.

For Rogoff, culture is the determining factor in an individual's development. Further, culture is assumed to influence the development of all children within a cultural context in a similar fashion. This makes it possible for her to describe the development of children in a particular culture in broad general terms. However, as I discovered during my fieldwork, even within one cultural context, each individual finds herself positioned uniquely in terms of experiences and societal roles depending upon how her personal history intersected with other determining factors, such as caste, gender, socioeconomic status, material conditions and family situation. So while the cultural-material context of Rajkheda put these particular YAs in similar sets of social events and practices, each YA experienced and responded to them differently. This led me to question the "lone ethnographer's guiding fiction" of culture as a homogenous, well-bounded, discrete entity (Rosaldo, 1989). More importantly, fieldwork with YAs in Rajkheda also showed me that even within a cultural context, generalized claims about YAs (or any age-defined population group) are deeply problematic in terms of their ability to represent lives as lived and experienced by these kids. I realize that for policymaking and school reform purposes, we need a shared understanding of YAs. This chapter then makes a plea for abandoning efforts to build this shared understanding on the basis of some broad generalizations of YAs, even if they are posited in cultural terms. It argues, instead, for responding to Vagle's plea to "move from characterizing young adolescen(CE) to particularizing young adolescen(TS)" (p. 25) by situating representations of YA in a rich and diverse portraiture of life as lived and experienced by young adolescents.

References

Brown, B. B., Larson, R. W., & Saraswathi, T. S. (Eds.). (2002). *The world's youth: Adolescence in eight regions of the globe*. New York: Cambridge University Press.

Davies, B., & Bansel, P. (2007). Neoliberalism and education. *International Journal of Qualitative Studies in Education (QSE), 20*(3), 247-259.

Fairclough, N. (2004). Critical discourse analysis in researching language in the new capitalism: Overdetermination, transdisciplinarity and textual analysis. In L. Young & C. Harrison (Eds.), *Systemic functional linguistics and critical discourse analysis* (pp. 103-122). London: Continuum.

Holland, D., Lachiotte, W., Skinner, D., & Cain, C. (1998). *Identity and agency in cultural worlds.* Cambridge, MA: Harvard University Press.

Lankshear, C. (1997). Language and the new capitalism. *The International Journal of Inclusive Education, 1*(4), 309-321.

Lave, J., & Wenger, E. (1991). *Situated learning: Legitimate peripheral participation.* Cambridge, UK: Cambridge University Press.

Rogoff, B. (2003). *The cultural nature of human development.* New York: Oxford University Press.

Rosaldo, R. (1989). *Culture and truth: The remaking of social analysis.* Boston: Beacon Press.

Vagle, M. D. (this volume). Trying to poke holes in Teflon: Developmentalism; young adolescence; and contingent, recursive growth and change. In M. D. Vagle (Ed.), *Not a stage! A critical re-conception of young adolescent education* (pp. 11-38). New York: Peter Lang Publishing

Vygotsky, L. (1980). *Mind in society*. Cambridge, MA: Harvard University Press.

Wertsch, J. W. (1991). *Voices of the mind.* Cambridge, MA: Harvard University Press.

Chapter 13

Locked into Place through Teacher Education: The Discursive Construction of Young People in the Middle Years of Schooling

Barbara Garrick, Jayne Keogh, Donna Pendergast, & Shelley Dole

Introduction

In Australia, over the last decade, there has been a proliferation of teacher education programs with specialist 'middle years' components. This reflects a wider interest in the young adolescent years that is evident in the broader education environment. This chapter uses a broad analytic approach to explore the discursive positions that preservice middle years teachers take up, what they say, who is speaking, and what is being said about the middle years and young people in the middle years; as they journeyed through a specialised teacher education program. We focus on what constitutes 'middle years teachers' and 'middle years students' using responses gathered in a longitudinal study of student teachers. The chapter points to the importance of one of the pleas in this volume in particular, and we similarly urge a move from characterizing young adolescenCE to particularizing young adolescenTS.

In this chapter we show how particular discourses about middle schooling in Australia appear to be locked into place as the preservice teachers learn and develop within and through the text available to them. However, it seems that text is at one and the same time 'innovative' and 'constrained' by the institutional world of middle schooling in Australia. The preservice teachers were enabled as middle years teachers in ways that reproduce and reflect the dominant values and interests of current educational thought regarding the need for a unique middle years of schooling philosophy, with concomitant changes in ways of doing pedagogy, curriculum and assessment for teaching middle years students in the new millennium. Furthermore they produced multiple readings and contesting discourses within the field of middle schooling.

The Program and the Research Agenda

This chapter is informed by a longitudinal study of a distinctive and specialised pre-service middle years' dual degree teacher education program. The model involves students completing two years in an approved non-education program then moving into a two-year specialist middle years teacher education program. The program ran for 6 years and a longitudinal study gathered data from 276 students in the six cohorts enrolled in the program. They were surveyed using a written questionnaire and participated in interviews. The same survey questions were repeated each year, both on the written form and in the face-to-face interviews. Responses to three questions and how they contribute to the notion of adolescents/adolescence will be considered in this chapter:

1. Question 1: What is your understanding of the 'middle years'?
2. Question 2: In what ways do you consider yourself to be a developing middle years' teacher?
3. Question 3: What is your understanding of a young person in the middle years?

The conceptual foundations of the program under investigation have been the focus of research in the past (see, for example, Mitchell et al., 2003; Hunter et al., 2004; Keogh et al., 2004; Garrick et al., 2008), as the program purports to be innovative in the field of middle years teacher education in Australia. Smith (1991, pp. 124–125) has argued that professionals need to learn how to relate to other professionals *as* professionals so as to be able to talk and write *to* professionals *about* professionals. Teacher education programs enable new and beginning teachers to develop these capacities.

The teacher education program from which these data were derived emphasised and embedded a range of key signifying educational and professional middle years of schooling practices pertaining to effective teaching and learning throughout the program including, for instance, the need for middle years teachers to be reflective practitioners and lifelong learners, and the need for middle years students to be engaged in their learning through classroom strategies such as inclusive curriculum, hands-on learning and authentic assessment. Analysis of the data reveals the ways in which the preservice teachers were enabled to write and talk *about* teachers and students, *as* teachers, *to* and *for* teacher educators. Sharing this information will go some way to building a greater understanding of middle years' teacher and middle years' student identities as connected to teacher training and teacher practice.

We employ textual and discourse analysis to investigate the survey and interview data. Two broad analytic approaches are used as different lenses to interrogate the data. First, strategies pertaining to membership categorisation analysis (MCA) are used to unpack the categories 'middle years' students', and 'middle years' teachers' and their associated attributions that were written into being within and through the survey text (cf. Baker & Keogh, 1995, p. 265; Heritage, 1984, p. 283). A method from the field of Critical Discourse Analysis (CDA) is then used to interrogate the data. The semiotic concept of intertextuality is used to examine the relationship between the comments made by the pre-service teachers who undertook the survey and the literature on middle schooling, which defines the available discursive terrain.

Intertextuality is the process whereby one text refers endlessly to other texts (their intertexts) and to their processes of social and cultural production (Fox, 1995). Intertextual analysis is the process whereby the analysis of one text is initiated into the processes and history of that text's production. Agger (1990, p. 3) observes that intertextuality is a "concept that indicates that various dialogues and negotiations are going on between texts and authors." The pre-service teachers who completed the longitudinal study's survey engaged in this process of negotiation when they completed this survey. It is possible to assume that their answers to the survey questions were mediated for example, by the texts that they had access to, the dialogues they had engaged in with lecturers in the course, dialogue with students and teachers during the practicum experience and with the general and available discursive terrain of middle schooling in Australia. Bakhtin (1981, pp. 42–49) observes that text is always part of a much greater system than the word or sentence alone and that the use of a word or sentence is always re-articulated and re-shaped at the moment of utterance.

Given the discursive terrain used by the pre-service teachers involved in the survey and the language available to them to describe themselves, we argue that middle school students and middle school practices and pedagogy have material effects which will permeate newer pre-service teacher education programs in this area.

Researching Middle Years' Teacher Education: Multiple Readings and Analysis

We considered the data with two questions in mind, namely:

1. Who is speaking to/for pre-service teachers and what is being said? What is the authority of each individual when speaking on the subject?
2. What discursive positions/resources are available for pre-service teachers to take up? What is available to say? What is the dominant discourse?

Membership Categorisation Analysis: Who Is Speaking and What Is Being Said?

Our first analysis focuses particularly on the students' responses when they describe their notions of what it is to be a 'middle years teacher' (question 2), and what it is to be a 'middle years student' (question 3). This analysis begins to answer the question: *Who is speaking to/for pre-service teachers, and what is being said? What is the authority of each individual when speaking on the subject*?

Membership categorisation analysts show how membership categorisation devices (hereafter MCDs) work to textually constitute social roles and relationships, including the organisation of institutional discourses and power (Baker, 1997, p. 131). Sacks (1992, pp. 113–125) suggests that people textually and conversationally constitute themselves and others in certain categories based on their extra-local knowledges which are constituted within particular contexts. Often categories within particular MCDs imply a second term to a standard relational pair (hereafter SRP) such as, for example, teacher-student within the device 'school' (cf. Baker, 2000). Within talk and text, membership of one SRP excludes membership of any other SRP within any one MCD. In the data, participants write of themselves as being members of the category 'middle years' teacher', and write of the SRP category 'middle years' students'. Both these categories are subsumed within the broad MCD 'school' as members of this community. Categories and categorisation work to 'lock discourses into place'. In this way MCA reveals 'the organisation of social relations and other micro-politics of everyday and institutional life' (Baker, 2000, p. 99).

Understandings of categorical work revealed through MCA allow inferences to be made about what people are or should be like if they belong to certain categories or classes, and what is appropriate or 'normal'. For example, we know that teachers 'teach', and students 'learn'. Such categorical associations have been termed 'category-bound activities', 'category-tied activities' and 'predicates' (Baker, 2000, p. 103). It may come as no surprise, therefore, to see such taken-for-granted associated activities and attributions being actively constituted and presented within and through this set of research data.

Analysis reveals the research participants' versions of what members of this categorical standardised relational pair (*persons*) do, in what ways, and how (*practices*). It is shown that the school and sites within the school, such as classrooms (*place*) are also invoked within and through the data. Analysis of the responses by the pre-service teachers themselves shows how the survey and interview data actively constitute particular versions of 'middle years students', and themselves as 'developing middle years teachers', and their associated activities and attributions. As 'developing middle years' teachers' the participants present themselves within and through their responses as having the authority to speak on or about middle school pre-service education in Australia.

Analysis of the participants' responses to the survey questions illustrates this point. In Survey Question 2—*In what ways do you consider yourself to be a developing middle years' teacher?*—there were a variety of responses in the pre-service teacher education (MYS) program cohorts. One typical response consisted of a fairly simple and concise description,

> ...understanding about adolescents. (Student 3, Cohort 1, 2003)

Others were very much more complex, revealing and problematising the categorical construction of what it is to be a 'middle years teacher', and themselves as 'middle years teachers', as in this example:

> I consider myself to be a developing middle years' teacher in respect to my understanding of adolescent's basic needs, educational strategies and productive pedagogies. I am learning dramatically that the global and social influences have changed what teaching means to me. I like the idea of being this type of teacher, because it is more facilitatory [sic] as opposed to lecture driven. (Student 13, Cohort 1, 2003)

In this text, the pre-service teacher education student uses a broad characterization of young adolescents by using the collective 'adolescent basic needs' to describe their understanding, rather than particularizing for the individual adolescenTS' needs. This directly aligns with Vagle's (this volume) plea, which urges a move from characterizing young adolescenCE to particularizing young adolescenTS.

So, what particular categorical attributions are found within the details of the data? First, as expected, constructions of middle years' teachers as those who 'teach' were evidenced across the entire data set. However, these teacher categories and their associated attributions were presented in a variety of ways to produce this main discourse of *practice*, as evidenced in the following examples:

> Learning different strategies of how to teach, ways of teaching, etc. My confidence has grown and cannot wait to start teaching!! (Student 15, Cohort 1, 2003)

> I believe that my pedagogy, behaviour management techniques and assessment will need to be adapted, updated and reflected upon to cater for the needs of ALL students. (Student 51, Cohort 4, 2006)

As well as constituting themselves as teachers who teach, constructions of themselves as middle years teachers who know about adolescents and adolescent needs (*persons*) was also constituted across the data, as, for example, in the following:

> I feel that at this point I have a fairly good understanding of *adolescents in regards to their behavioural, social and cognitive development and turmoil this can*

> *create*. As a result I feel this understanding and interest in the development of this age group enhances my ability to educate them in a meaningful and engaging way. (Student 9, Cohort 1, 2003, our emphasis)

Again, the italicized text in this data reveals a normalising of adolescenCE rather than a particularizing of adolescenTS. It is noteworthy that although the data of teaching practice is made omnirelevant across the data, the participants construct themselves not just as 'teachers who teach', but, simultaneously, as particular sorts of teachers, specifically as teachers who are beginners. As such, versions of themselves as student teachers who are also learners are also invoked in various ways within and through the data, such as, for example, in the following excerpts:

> I am still learning yet feel I know a lot more than I did at the beginning of the year. (Student 23, Cohort 1, 2003)

> I will always be developing as I will always be dealing with different individual needs. I will continually be developing in areas of behaviour management, pedagogy, lesson planning, unit planning. (Student 56, Cohort 4, 2006.

Such categorical constructions might be viewed as part of the discourse *place* in that these are constructions of teacher positional *place*ment within the teacher education program, and in relation to their positional *place* as lifelong learners.

Although the details of the responses to question 2 varied across the data set, it seemed as though three major discourses were evidenced both in and through the written and spoken categorical constructions of what it is to be a middle years' teacher. The first major discourse was that of *practice*. Constructions of themselves as teachers who teach were constituted through the use of terms and phrases such as 'teaching', 'pedagogy', and 'strategies'. The second major discourse was that of *person*. Participants constructed themselves as persons who knew about adolescents and adolescent needs by the inclusion of terms and phrases such 'understanding', 'adapting to their needs', and 'awareness of needs of young people'. The third major discourse, that of *place/placement*, included constructions of themselves using descriptors and terms such as 'lifelong learner', 'developing' and 'experimenting'. As such, the versions of what it is to be a middle years teacher that were textually and conversationally written and talked into being within and through the data produced dominant versions of the category 'middle years teacher' that were foregrounded and emphasised within the teacher education program of which they were a part.

Similarly, in response to question 3—*What is your understanding of a young person in the middle years?*—the participants' responses included versions that constituted students as persons who have particular attributes (*persons*) that signify the need for particular *practices* that are particular to their stage of development (*place/place*ment). The typical responses very strongly reinforced the constitution of the students they would teach as having a range of characteristics in common, rather than recognition of the individual adolescenT. One example of these constructions includes:

> These young people are very vulnerable, easily lead [sic], rebellious and self-absorbed (although not all young people go through this). They need to be constantly stimulated and engaged by innovative teachers. School should not be a battleground for them, they need to be helped through this period. (Student 68, Cohort 2, 2004)

This entire text relies on taken-for-granted generalisations of young adolescents. However, the complexities and recognition of the need to particularise middle years' students was also evident in some responses, such as:

> Varied. Not all these students are the same and all have different needs. They are truly vibrant people who have a lot to offer (Student 15, Cohort 1, 2003)

> I don't think there is a typical answer to this question. There may be certain characteristics e.g. trying to find out who they are, trying to establish their own identity, trying to discover their place in the world. However it is still important to realise that everyone is an individual and it is important to know your students. (Student 83, Cohort 6, 2008)

As such, the participants' responses constituted commonsense versions of middle years' students that both reflected and reproduced the sorts of dominant discourses to which they were exposed as part of this middle years' teacher education program.

The use of MCA as an analytic tool to interrogate the construction of the categories 'middle years teachers' and 'middle years students' as members of the device 'school' has revealed a range of key signifying categorical attributes and associated educational and professional practices pertaining to the MYS signifying practices that had been foregrounded and emphasised throughout the teacher education programs in which the participants were enrolled. As such, the data both constitute and mirror the participants' worlds, revealing the invisible workings of the institutional world of the MCD 'school' of which they are a part. These data evidence some of the ways in which the research participants were enabled to write and talk *about* middle years' teachers and students, *as* middle years teachers, *to* and *for* middle years' teacher educators, evidencing their development as reflective practitioners and lifelong learners.

Having analysed how the actual textual data produced by the research participants in response to the survey questions worked to construct particular versions of what it is to be a 'middle years student', and what it is to be a 'middle years teacher', the chapter now moves to a different analytic lens. This approach goes beyond the level of the text and has the capacity to enrich understandings of the research participants' discursive construction of the middle years of schooling.

Intertextuality: What Was Available to Say?

The second part of this chapter provides an insight into the possible influences on the responses just considered. Critical Discourse Analysis (CDA) looks at the ways in which texts construct representations of the world particularly with an emphasis on the manner in which texts are ideologically shaped by relations of power (Janks, 1997). One method of CDA is used in this paper to investigate this claim further. Intertextuality is the process whereby one text refers endlessly to other texts (their intertexts) and to their processes of social and cultural production (Fox, 1995). Intertextual analysis, then, is the process whereby the analysis of one text is initiated into the processes and history of that text's production. Intertextuality is a linguistic and semiotic feature of all texts, which permits the analyst to see the "interdiscursive work" between texts, in this case between the survey data and the literature that surrounds it. This method can suggest that the latter texts exercise power over the former through a judgment as to what is available to be said.

In terms of this chapter, the method applies to what is available to be said in relation to middle schooling, middle school teachers and students and middle school teaching practices and pedagogy. In this way the method provides a mini-literature review each time it is marshalled within an analytic framework. Because signifiers refer endlessly and more importantly because signifiers show the manner in which human subjects are created in ways which "supersede earlier versions of rationality" (Fox, 1995, p. 4), this method permits the researcher to investigate the intertext using whatever texts are similar or different.

In the case of the data under review the intertexts chosen were some of the texts which appear in any description of the movement towards middle schooling in Australia and reports of the middle schooling movement which claim that the innovation often derives from a concern that students in this period of life become disengaged and disaffected by the schooling system. For example, the national professional body responsible for promoting middle years education in Australia, the Middle Years of Schooling Association (MYSA) in 2008 released the *Middle Schooling: People, Practices and Places Position Paper* (MYSA, 2008, p.1) which justifies the need for specialist middle years teachers in the following way:

> The middle years, from around age ten to fifteen, span the years from childhood to adolescence. Young adolescents in the middle years experience a range of significant physical, cognitive, emotional, social, and moral changes. During puberty, young adolescents experience more rapid and dramatic hormonal and structural changes than at any other period in their life. The sequence of physical change is generally similar from one person to another, although the onset, rate, and timing of these changes are highly individual, often creating stress and feelings of insecurity for the adolescent. Changes to brain and cognitive development peak during this period. Apart from the first five years of life, at no other time does the capacity and functioning of the brain undergo such an overhaul. This affects the learning ability of young adolescents and their success in managing the emotional, social and

> moral challenges of this stage. Disengagement, alienation and boredom in school often peak in the middle years and this may lead to a decline in achievement. Hence the middle years, particularly with respect to the productive engagement of young people in schooling and other contexts, is a priority for educators.

While the Position Paper does recognise difference, it is within a framework of commonality, and many teacher education students have drawn their understandings from such dominant discourses that they were exposed to during their preservice program of study.

Intertextuality works as a method for this paper because it seeks to show the history of reform in middle school education and the points of view of pre-service teachers engaged in such programs. The next section describes the method of intertextuality applied in this paper in more detail.

The Construction of the Middle Schooling Movement in Australia: The Text's Intertext

Several intertexts were called upon to examine the data. The method requires that the researcher examines the chosen text of study in light of the texts which exist alongside the studied text. McWilliam (1992) refers to these as the resources that are drawn upon by those studied when speaking to and for another. The texts that sat alongside the data are discussed in this chapter. They include the *Delors Report* (UNESCO, 1996) as representative of the education of students in 'new times', the era when the program was first mooted. There are also texts that have set the national agenda and include texts such as *In the Middle or at the Centre?* (Australian Curriculum Studies Association, 1993) which began a national debate on middle schooling and *From Alienation to Engagement* (Australian Curriculum Studies Association, 1996), which called for national middle schooling reform. In Queensland, texts such as the then Queensland Board of Teacher Registration's Working Party report entitled *Teachers Working with Young Adolescents* (1996) were accessed. This text recommended better ways to address the learning needs of young adolescents and the professional development needs of schools and teachers in this area. The Board of Teacher Registration accredited the teacher education program under review in this paper in 2001 (School of Education).

Queensland the Smart State: Education and Training Reforms for the Future (2002); *See the Future: the Middle Phase of Learning State School Action Plan* (2003); and the *Brisbane Catholic Education, Pathways in Middle Schooling* (2004) were also accessed.

To then examine the question as to the existence of a dominant discourse the authors relied on an analysis of middle schooling reform provided in a research paper written by Stevens et al. (2007). This paper summarised the available middle schooling literature in the period of the program under review in relation to pre-service teacher education programs. With the exception of the Stevens et al. (2007) paper, each text was available to the students through direct reading of the content of the texts or through discussion with lecturers during their coursework.

Pre-service Teachers' Text, Speaking through Discourses of Their Experiences in a New Program

The first set of intertexts chosen to review are those which confirm that pre-service teachers in the longitudinal study could speak on behalf of middle schooling teacher education programs in Australia during their cohort's experience of such. Their authority to speak seems to derive from the 'newness' of an 'innovative' program and the fact that many of the respondents were the 'first' members of this program.

Applying the concept of intertextuality, the authority of the pre-service teachers to speak in the first instance seems to derive from texts that state that pre-service education for middle schooling in Australia is 'new' and at the time of many of the surveys the 'first' program of its kind. Here Pendergast (2002) argues that:

> the establishment of the program under investigation in this study was a milestone for exponents of middle schooling in Australia. The *first* [my emphasis] of its kind (Pendergast, 2002), its existence served as a kind of affirmation that the two-tiered model of teacher education (primary and secondary) which has dominated pre-service teacher education may not be the best model for preparing teachers for the middle years. (p. 1)

In Western cultures the act of being 'first' and therefore 'before' implies authority and a situated position of increased sense of selfhood (Mansfield, 2000, p. 3). Of the 14 graduates who were respondents in the first cohort, two students spoke specifically about the nature of the 'new' program and described themselves as 'new age teachers'. One student aligned their developing knowledge with the developing university preparation program and said

> I consider myself as developing because we are still learning along with our uni[versity] program and middle schools as developing sub-schools. (Student 7, Cohort 1, 2003)

Although numerically inconclusive, it is feasible to suggest that all students in the first and second cohort knew that the program of study they were undertaking was in fact 'new'. The following section explains this claim further.

There are other texts that would have impacted the survey responses. For instance, the program under investigation existed in an era of 'new times', a linguistic construction particular to the last four decades of the late twentieth century which attempted to understand the social, cultural, political and economic changes the world was experiencing, such as the shift from analog to digital technology and the proliferation of computers which in effect removes boundaries in society; the shift from a limited period of formal education (e.g., compulsory schooling to age 15) to the expectation of lifelong learning. These fundamental changes presented educators with a set of challenges, particularly in relation to the needs of early adolescents and caused educators to respond effectively to young people's needs for self-definition and delineation in the creation of their own futures. The *Delors Report* (1996), the research of Darling-Hammond (2000) and of the *Queensland School Reform Longitudinal Study* (Education Queensland, 2001) was each aired in the period from 2000 to 2006 when the program under review was implemented. Each of these reports framed the environment for the pre-service teachers in this survey. Within this context, the application to the then Board of Teacher Registration to register the middle years pre-service education program, observed that this:

> *new* [our emphasis] Middle Years of Schooling teacher preparation program...aims not only to respond to the specific developmental needs of young adolescents but also focuses on the inequities in the provision of

> schooling within Australia, new technologies, new economies and work places and practices, and globalization. (School of Education, 2001, p. 8)

Further the application argued that there

> is strong evidence that those who have completed significant teacher education programs in higher education institutions cope better in the professional context and are more confident and successful with students than those who have not completed these programs. (School of Education, 2001, p. 8)

It seems that the resources available to the pre-service teachers under review in this paper are those of 'new' pedagogies and programs related to 'innovative' reform. This is evident in the following response, which is typical of much of the data set.

> I am learning and trying to incorporate all of the above and become an innovative teacher unlike the traditional running of classroom. (Student 12, Cohort 1, 2003)

The program existed before the full rollout to schools of middle schooling initiatives in Queensland through Education Queensland's *Queensland the Smart State: Education and Training Reforms for the Future* (2002) via *See the Future: The Middle Phase of Learning State School Action Plan* (2003) and alongside the Brisbane Catholic Education, *Pathways for Middle Schooling* (2004). The program also existed chronologically before the renewed support for middle years' education Australia wide around 2008 and reaffirms the important role of teachers as the most valuable pedagogical resource a school can have in relation to middle year's education (Jackson & Davis, 2000; Pendergast et al., 2005). In 2008 the Middle Years of Schooling Association (MYSA) launched its first national Position Paper on Middle Schooling as a platform for advocacy and innovation. MYSA frames middle schooling through the interconnected concepts of *People, Practices* and *Places.* Research by Pendergast, Keogh, Garrick, and Reynolds (2009) affirms the synergy between the MYSA Position paper and the responses of pre-service educators in the survey.

It would seem that the pre-service teachers who trained in the program were speaking to and on behalf of the first cohorts of specifically trained teachers in the middle schooling movement of the late twentieth and early twenty-first century. The pre-service teachers surveyed spoke through the language that was available to them. The next section explores this language and in particular the dominant discourse used for the purpose of communicating ideas of middle schooling and of middle years teachers and students.

Available Discursive Positions

The literature suggests that pre-service teachers undertaking teacher preparation programs form their own beliefs about teaching from their own biographies, from conflict/experience during the practicum and from information they receive through the duration of their course of study (see Britzman, 1986, 2003; Huberman, Thompson, & Weiland, 1997; Lortie, 1975). Of particular interest is the dominant discourse about middle schooling, and middle school students and their teachers, which appears in the literature and in the survey comments, such as adolescence being a phase or stage; a time of rapid change; and a period where disengagement is a concern.

Stevens et al. (2007) undertook a review of middle schooling literature and analysed the available discursive spaces of adolescence in relation to pre-service teacher education programs. They suggest that teacher programs around middle schooling currently hold that middle school students are neither young nor old but "in-between" and that these students are flawed and somehow "incomplete". They argue that there are four discursive traditions at work in this objectification where students are either seen as hormonal (developmental cognitive psychology), unfinished (biomedical pathological perspectives), oppressed (critical/conflict theorists) and/ or unruly (postmodernist perspective). Stevens et al. (2007) claim that such linguistic constructions require teachers to intervene in middle schooling programs in inappropriate ways. Instead these authors call for pre-service education programs that acknowledge that constructions of middle school students need to capture their lived experience in more fluid and multiple ways. Both the dominant age/stage model of understanding middle school students and the interventionist tenor of teachers and their training is evident in the survey data. However, there is also evident some shift in the data towards Stevens et al.'s

(2007) preferred model. That is, change is occurring within and through the pre-service teachers' descriptions of middle schooling and middle school students.

First the survey data is replete with concepts of at risk and unruly youth. For Question 1 of the survey—*What is your understanding of the 'middle years?*—responses included subthemes of adolescent terminology that the middle years were 'special' years, and that it was a time of 'disengagement'. The following typical example shows the interdiscursive work at play between the available literature around middle schooling and the program of study.

> That it's somewhere between grades 4–6 to about grade 9 or 10. That it's supposedly when students are young adolescents and have all these special and particular needs. A transition between childhood and adolescence as well as primary and secondary. (Student 2, Cohort 1, 2003)

The data also confirms the four dominant discursive middle schooling traditions uncovered by Stevens et al. (2007). Question 3 of the survey for instance asked students to answer the question: What is your understanding of a young person in the middle years? The three main sentiments that emerged were that a person in the middle years of schooling was (1) changing, (2) challenging, and/or (3) confused. For example, students made comments such as:

> A diverse person who is stuck between childhood and adulthood (changing). (Student 4, Cohort 1, 2003)

> Going through puberty, diff moods – diff days. Active yet need motivating at the same time? (challenging) Developing sense of self. Want to know how school content links to real-world. (Student 27, Cohort 1, 2003)

> A young person in the middle years is undergoing a great deal of change in their lives. As a result this can sometimes lead to confusion, angst and frustration. (confusing) Middle years' students need support and freedom within reasonable limits. (Student 9, Cohort 1, 2003)

But within this interdiscursive construction of middle school students, there are postmodern moments where pre-service teachers argue for the fluidity Stevens et al. (2007) suggest should occur. The comments below are drawn from data in the first and last years of the program. The final comment in this data set suggests a tension between the fluidity of adolescent experience now and the more dominant and modernist constructions of adolescence.

> Cannot essentialize too much due to extreme diversity. But young people need support that is appropriate to their needs at particular times. They need space but also guidelines. (Student 28, Cohort 1, 2003)

> A young person in middle years has a very challenging and competitive future. Their present lived reality is complex yet through it they must develop into round, valuable and productive citizens. (Student 44, Cohort 4, 2006)

Conclusion

The study of this particular data set from the longitudinal survey data and a study of reports of and about the program begin to suggest future possibilities available to educators in the area of middle schooling. Stevens et al. (2007) argue that programming for pre-service teachers in the middle years of schooling and for their students has tended to be one of objectification where the teacher is seen as the "fix" to the difficult conditions of the middle years' student. They call instead for teacher education programs that imagine the process as far more fluid and complex. This is consistent with Vagle's pleas, particularly his plea to move from characterizing young adolescenCE to particularizing young adolescenTS.

There are the beginnings of this construction in the survey data. The discourse around middle schooling that is being 'locked into place' by the data provided in this paper is that of pre-service teachers learning and developing within and through the text and talk available to them. Both text and talk are at one and the same time 'innovative' and 'constrained' by the institutional world of middle schooling in Australia. Further, a review of the data does make it clear that discussion about and analyses of the discursive constructions of the issues raised in this paper are valid and important. Two different analytic approaches have revealed that the participants of this longitudinal research study were enabled to write and speak as middle years teachers in ways that both reproduced and reflected the dominant values and interests of current educational thought regarding the need for a unique middle years of schooling philosophy, with concomitant changes in ways of doing pedagogy, curriculum and assessment for teaching middle years students in the new millennium.

References

Agger, B. (1990) The decline of discourse. *Reading, writing and resistance in postmodern capitalism*. London: The Falmer Press.

Australian Curriculum Studies Association (ACSA). (1993). *In the middle or at the centre? A report of the national conference on middle schooling*. Belconnen, ACT: Australian Curriculum Studies Association.

Bahktin, M.M. (1981). *The dialogic imagination: Four essays*. Austin: University of Texas Press.

Baker, C. (1997). Membership categorisation and interview accounts. In D. Silverman (Ed.), *Qualitative research: Theory, method and practice*. London: Sage, 130–143.

———. (2000). Locating culture in action: Membership categorisation in texts and talk. In A. Lee & C. Poynton (Eds.), *Culture and text: Discourse and methodology in social research and cultural studies* (pp. 99-113). New York: Rowman & Littlefield Publishers.

Baker, C., & Keogh, J. (1995). Accounting for achievement in parent-teacher interviews. *Human Studies, 18*(2/3), 263–300.

Brisbane Catholic Education. (2004). *Pathways for middle schooling walking the talk: A position paper and self-audit process*. Brisbane: Brisbane Catholic Education.

Britzman, D. (1986). Cultural myths in the making of a teacher: Biography and social structure in teacher education. *Harvard Educational Review, 56*(4), 442–457.

———. (2003). *Practice makes practice: A critical study of learning to teach*. Albany: State University of New York Press.

Darling-Hammond, L. (2000). How teacher education matters. *Journal of Teacher Education, 51*(3), 166–173.

Education Queensland. (2001). *The Queensland school reform longitudinal study* (Vols. 1 & 2). Brisbane: Author.

Fox, N. J. (1995). Intertextuality and the writing of social research. *Electronic Journal of Sociology, 1*(2), 1–16.

Garrick, B., Pendergast, D., Bahr, N., Dole, S., & Keogh, J. (2008). *Researching the construction of middle years' teacher identity: A study of graduates*. Conference proceedings, Australian Teacher Education Association, Sunshine Coast, 2008.

Heritage, J. (1984). *Garfinkel and ethnomethodology*. Cambridge, UK: Polity Press.

Huberman, M., Thompson, C. L., & Weiland, S. (1997). Perspectives on the teaching career. In B. J. Biddle, T. L. Good, & I. F. Goodson (Eds.), *International handbook of teachers and teaching*. Dordrecht, The Netherlands: Kluwer Academic, 11-78.

Hunter, L., Stevens, L.P., Pendergast, D., Mitchell, J., Bahr, N., Carrington, V., & Kapitzke, C. (July, 2004). *Finding sustainable spaces for young people in middle schooling: An historical and theoretical enquiry into adolescence*. Conference Proceedings: The Australian Teacher Education Association (ATEA) Making Spaces: Regenerating the Profession, Annual Conference, Bathurst.

Jackson, A. W., & Davis, G. A. (2000). *Turning points 2000: Educating adolescents in the 21st century*. New York: Teachers College Press.

Janks, H. (1997). Critical discourse analysis as a research tool. *Discourse: Studies in the Cultural Politics of Education, 18*(3), 27-48.

Keogh, J., Bahr, N., Hunter, L., Stevens, L., Wright, T., Kapitzke, C., Pendergast, D., & Rohner, C. (November, 2004). *Three years on: Growing teachers for the middle years*, Australian Association for Research in Education [AARE] 2004 International

Education Research Conference, Doing the Public Good: Positioning Education Research.
Lortie, D. C. (1975). *Schoolteacher: A sociological study.* Chicago: University of Chicago Press.
Mansfield, N. (2000). *Subjectivity: Theories of the self from Freud to Haraway.* St Leonards, NSW: Allen and Unwin.
McWilliam, E. (1992). Towards advocacy: Post-positivist directions for progressive teacher educators. *British Journal of Sociology of Education, 13*(1), 3–17.
Middle Years of Schooling Association (MYSA) (2008). *MYSA position paper: Middle schooling: People, practices and places.* Brisbane.
Mitchell, J., Katitzke, C., Mayer, D., Carrington, V., Stevens, L., Bahr, N., Pendergast, D., & Hunter, L. (2003). Aligning school reform and teachers education reform in the middle years: An Australian case study. *Teaching Education, 14*(1), 69–82.
Stevens, L.P., Hunter, L., Pendergast, D., Carrington, V., Bahr, N., Kapitzke, C., & Mitchell, J. (2007). Re-conceptualizing the possible narratives of adolescence. *The Australian Educational Researcher, 34*(2), 107–127.
Pendergast, D. (2002). Teaching in the middle years: Perceptions of real versus ideal teachers. *Australian Journal of Middle Schooling, 2*(1), 1–6.
Pendergast, D., Flanagan, R., Land, R., Bahr, M., Mitchell, J., Weir, K., Noblett, G., Cain, M., Misich, T., Carrington, V., & Smith, J. (2005). *Developing lifelong learners in the middle years of schooling.* Brisbane: The University of Queensland. Retrieved October 1, 2011 from http://www.curriculum.edu.au/verve/_resources/lifelonglearn_midyears.pdf
Pendergast, D., Keogh, J., Garrick, B., & Reynolds, J. (2009). The MYSA position paper and preservice teacher education: Surprisingly serendipitous synergies. *Australian Journal of Middle Schooling, 9*(2), 20-25.
Queensland Board of Teacher Registration, Working Party on the Preparation of Teachers for the Education of Young Adolescents (1996). *Teachers working with young adolescents.* Toowong, Queensland: Queensland Board of Teacher Registration.
Queensland Government. (2002). *Education and training reforms for the future: Queensland the smart state.* Brisbane: Queensland Government.
Queensland Government (2003). *See the future: The middle phase of learning state school action plan.* Brisbane: Queensland Government.
Sacks, H. (1992). *Lectures on conversation,* (Volumes 1 & 2). In G. Jefferson (Ed.). Oxford: Basil Blackwell.
School of Education. (2001). *Bachelor of education (middle years of schooling): Submission to the Queensland Board of Teacher Registration.* Faculty of Social & Behavioural Sciences, St Lucia: University of Queensland.
Smith, D.E. (1991). *The conceptual practices of power: A feminist sociology of knowledge.* Boston: Northeastern University Press.
UNESCO. (1996). *Learning the treasure within: Report to UNESCO of international commission on education for the twenty- first century.* Paris: United Nations Educational, Scientific and Cultural Organization. Retrieved October 1, 2011 from http://www.unesco.org/education/pdf/15_62.pdf
Vagle, M. D. (this volume). Trying to poke holes in Teflon: Developmentalism; young adolescence; and contingent, recursive growth and change. In M. D. Vagle (Ed.),

Not a stage! A critical re-conception of young adolescent education (pp. 11-38). New York: Peter Lang Publishing.

Acknowledgement

We wish to acknowledge the contribution of Joy Reynolds as Research Assistant on this and the wider project from which it was drawn.

Closing

Some Messy Hopes

Mark D. Vagle

As you may recall, I closed the introduction to this volume with the following paragraph:

> Consider yourself formally invited to a messy conception. Come on in, find a chair, move some piles of paper around and let's talk about contingent, recursive relationality, particularizing young adolescen(TS), and a difference curriculum. I promise you the messiness will not distract from learning or become unprofessional—in fact, I cannot think of a better way to act as a professional learner than to resist clean explanations and get after the messy stuff. (Vagle, this volume, p. 8)

Although I want to be careful not to do much tidying up here either, I do close this volume with a set of messy hopes:

1. Beginning in my doctoral work and extending to the present, I have been consistently pressed (by people I respect) to "tie my ideas down"—to "make them" practical. I do want theoretical ideas to make a difference in the day-to-day lives of those living through and with the theories I and others propose. However, I think theorizing is an active, living project in and of itself. So, my first hope is that others find contingent, recursive conceptions of young adolescent growth and change something that prompts some active theorizing about what the schooling of young adolescents should be like.

2. There are innumerable microcontexts to open up and explore. The idea of creating contingent, recursive conceptions of growth and change is more of a process than it is a destination. There is no way to arrive at the end of this conception. Rather, this conception of growth and change, literally grows and changes. Although moving targets can be frustrating, this is precisely what we are dealing with when we talk about how people live and learn through their lives.

3. So what might we "do" with contingent, recursive conceptions of growth and change? How might they influence policy and classroom practice? My first thought is that we need to create contingent, recursive policies. We need to be more fluid in our policies. The policies need to be agile and mobile. The high-stakes testing regime in the U.S. (and

throughout the world) has done the opposite. The current policy context has narrowed the curriculum toward unprecedented sameness. We need policies that are responsive to changing, shifting contexts. The aspects that are the "same" in the curriculum need to be broad overarching ideas that can take lived shape in particular contexts. This is by no means a new idea. Prior to NCLB, the standards movement seemed to be headed for these sorts of commitments—but it got hijacked by the accountability movement (Ravitch, 2010). I hope we can redefine the policy context contingently and recursively.

4. To those who have been doing *critical* work for some time—maybe the entire 40 years for which Pinar (2009) describes—I hope you understand that over this same 40 years (and more) most scholars and educators interested in the education of 10-15 year olds have not. Developmentalists have dominated the study of young adolescence and the mainstream schooling of young adolescents—all the while critical theorists have been at work. Some critical theorists for whom I have the utmost respect, have wondered (to me) why it is necessary to make so many arguments here that are, for lack of a better phrase, "old news" in critical theory circles. I wholeheartedly agree with this wondering. However, as I discuss in the anchor essay, I find it necessary to bring critical theories to bear on these fields, precisely because it is really new news in these fields. So, I hope critical theorists can see the value in breathing new life (using old critical theory arguments) into fields associated with young adolescent education.

5. Finally, and perhaps most idealistically, I have an image in my head that I cannot (and do not want to) shake—it is my biggest messy hope. I hope that we can get to the point in the education of young adolescents that we cannot help but see the inherent value in each and every young adolescent. That we do not worry so much about whether they are developing on pace or not; but that we worry a lot about how they find themselves living in the world in relation to others. That we turn to them (really turn to them) to help us see structural inequities in the policies and practices that govern and control their lives. That we prepare teachers of young adolescents to be critical theorists who are highly attuned to who is privileged and who is marginalized by their (and their colleagues') pedagogies and curriculum. And relative to the contingent, recursive relationality proposed throughout this volume, I hope that schools and classrooms scratch and gnaw their way through superficial (obvious! Of course!) explanations in order to open up the beautifully complicated, messy micro-contexts that are constantly shifting and changing the very theoretical and practical ground we stand on.

References

Pinar, B. (2009). The unaddressed 'I" of ideology critique. *Power and Education, 1*(2), 189-200.
Ravitch, D. (2010). *The death and life of the great American school system: How testing and choice are undermining education*. New York: Basic Books.

Contributor Bios

Mark D. Vagle is an Associate Professor in the Department of Elementary and Social Studies Education at The University of Georgia. Before working in higher education, Mark taught in elementary and middle schools and was a middle school assistant principal. His current research and teaching can be broadly described as a continual pursuit of the dynamic interaction (tension, struggle) between relational and technical dimensions of pedagogy, especially as such dimensions are lived in context and over time. To this end, Mark draws on critical perspectives and uses phenomenology in his research. Mark is co-editor of a book (Palgrave Macmillan) entitled *Developmentalism in Early Childhood and Middle Grades Education: Critical Conversations on Readiness and Responsiveness*. He has published a number of scholarly works in journals and handbooks such as the *International Journal of Qualitative Studies in Education, Teaching Education, Teachers and Teaching: Theory and Practice, Journal of Adolescent and Adult Literacy, Handbook of Research in Middle Level Education (volume 6), Research in Middle Level Education Online, National Reading Conference Yearbook, Education and Culture,* and *Pedagogies: An International Journal.*

Nan Bahr is Professor and Assistant Dean, Teaching & Learning, Faculty of Education, Queensland University of Technology, Australia. She has oversight of the teaching quality in the faculty, and the readiness of graduates for the profession as beginner teachers or as leaders. She researches middle years of schooling, the nature of adolescence, resilience, and learning development. She has received several national and institutional awards for excellence in teaching and program design, and has published widely. Bahr has co-authored two important books on teaching young adolescents *Teaching Middle Years: Rethinking Curriculum, Pedagogy and Assessment* (Allen & Unwin) and *The Millennial Adolescent* (Australian Council for Educational Research).

Athene Bell is the district literacy specialist in Manassas City (VA) Public Schools where she works with teachers and students to support literacy initiatives within the school district. For 19 years she has taught English to adolescents, searching for innovative methods to promote and enhance literacy skills. She is also a doctoral student specializing in literacy at George Mason University. Her areas of interest include the study of visual and multimodal literacy among adolescents, teacher education, and formative design methodology.

Penny Bishop is Professor of Middle Level Education at the University of Vermont where she teaches future middle grades educators and conducts research on schooling for young adolescents. Having brought over $6 million to Vermont schools to improve the learning and lives of middle grades students, she serves as Director of the Tarrant Institute for Innovative Education, an organization dedicated to promoting student-centered, technology-rich learning. A former middle level English and Social Studies teacher, Penny serves on the National Middle School Association's Research Advisory Board and is Chair of the American Educational Research Association's Special Interest Group on Middle Level Education Research. She is author of four books and numerous articles on effective middle grades practice that have appeared in outlets such as *Research in Middle Level Education Online; Journal of Adolescent and Adult Literacy, Middle School Journal*, and, the *Reading Teacher*. She has also served for six months as policy advisor to the New Zealand Ministry of Education, providing research on effective schooling policies for students in the middle years in that country.

Enora R. Brown is an Associate Professor in the Department of Educational Policy Studies and Research in the School of Education at DePaul University. She has been in the field of education for the past 35 years, as a teacher in K-12, as a consultant and trainer for preschool teachers, as a researcher and program developer in social service related programs, and as a scholar and teacher in higher education. She received her Ph.D. from the University of Chicago in Developmental Psychology and a Master's in Social Work from Loyola University in Chicago. She teaches graduate and undergraduate courses in human development, middle school education, and youth identity for teacher educators and administrators. Her publications include *The Critical Middle School Reader*, coedited with Kenneth Saltman, published by Routledge in

2005. She has published a range of articles and book chapters on critical studies in human development, critical discourse analyses of children, youth, and adults, and in educational policy and reform and the politics of education, with an emphasis on identity, race, and social class. She is conducting an ethnography on the construction of youth identities in the context of divergent relational and sociocultural educational contexts. This research is the basis for a book and journal articles.

Leslie David Burns, Ph.D., is an Associate Professor of Literacy in the College of Education at the University of Kentucky. Dr. Burns served as the chief consultant for Kentucky's Model Curriculum Framework for all subject areas and grade levels, and currently serves as the higher education representative for English Language Arts in Central Kentucky to implement the state's Common Core Standards reforms. He served as the chair of The Conference on English Education's Task Force on Political Action in Education Reform, and co-authored the National Council of Teachers of English's standards for teacher education program accreditation. His research focuses on relationships between diversity, identity, social justice, teaching, learning, and adolescent literacies in contemporary schools. He has published in the *Harvard Educational Review, Research in the Teaching of English, English Education, English Journal,* and *Middle Grades Research Journal.* His most recent work, *Empowering Struggling Readers: Practices for the Middle Grades,* was published by Guilford Press.

Zan Crowder is a Doctoral Student at The University of North Carolina-Chapel Hill. Crowder's research interests tend toward a Humanities-based paradigm. While under the general rubric of Curriculum Theory, he seeks to incorporate elements of literary theory and history with educational policy and practice issues. Specifically, Crowder's current work seeks to use autobiographical sources to understand the role of the individual within a wider social and educational context. Juvenilia Studies offers one access point for witnessing these negotiations.

Hilary Conklin is an Assistant Professor in the Department of Teacher Education at DePaul University. Her research interests include studying the preparation of middle school social studies teachers, teacher learning, and the pedagogy of teacher education. She has published articles in journals such as *American Educational Research Journal, Harvard Educational Review, Theory and Research in Social Education,* and *Journal of Teacher Education,* and co-authored chapters with Ken Zeichner in *Studying Teacher Education: The Report of the AERA Panel on Research and Teacher Education* and the *Handbook of Research on Teacher Education: Enduring Issues in Changing Contexts (3rd edition).*

Shelley Dole is a senior lecturer in mathematics education at The University of Queensland. She teaches in the Bachelor of Education (Middle Years of Schooling) program and is the Program Director for the Bachelor of Education (Primary). She has been involved in several major research projects in a range of fields relevant to mathematics and numeracy education, including middle years literacy and numeracy for 'at-risk' students, connecting mathematics and science in the middle years of schooling, and numeracy across the learning areas. Her research interests focus particularly on promoting students' conceptual understanding of mathematics to encourage success and enjoyment of mathematical investigations in school. Dole is co-author of *Learning to Teach: New Times, New Practices* (Oxford University Press) and is a contributor in Pendergast & Bahr's *Teaching Middle Years: Rethinking Curriculum, Pedagogy and Assessment.*

Marriam Ewaida is currently working as a reading specialist in Manassas, Virginia. She has been teaching for the last seven years. Marriam has a BA in English Literature, a BEd in English and ESL from The University of British Columbia in Canada, and a Masters in Curriculum and Instruction/Literacy at George Mason University. She is currently a doctoral student in literacy at George Mason.

Barbara Garrick is a lecturer at Griffith University with a main research area of policy analysis. She is currently working on analyses of the recent federal government's Trade Training Centre Policies. She is working with a team of researchers to investigate the implementation of trade training in secondary schooling. Barbara has also analysed policies such as Queensland's Social Justice policies of the 1980s and the Victorian Government's school based reform programs in the mid-1990s. Her research interests are in understanding the knowledge economy and knowledge society, leadership, school based management and equity. Barbara also researches in the areas of middle years and diversity. Her research methodology includes policy analysis, critical discourse analysis and neo-Marxist, Foucauldian and post-structuralist methodologies.

Leigh A. Hall, Ph.D., is an Associate Professor of Literacy Studies in the School of Education at the University of North Carolina, Chapel Hill. Her research focuses on understanding how adolescents' identities shape their development as readers. Hall received the Literacy Research Association's (formerly National Reading Conference) prestigious Early Career Achievement Award in 2010. Her research has been published in journals such as *Harvard Educational Review, Teachers College Record, Reading Research Quarterly, The Journal of Adolescent and Adult Literacy, and Teaching and Teacher Education*. Hall's most recent book, *Empowering Struggling Readers: Practices for the Middle Grades* was published by Guilford Press.

Hilary Hughes-Decatur is an Assistant Professor of Teaching and Learning at Virginia Commonwealth University. Her research interests include young adolescent girls' experiences in and with their bodies, phenomenology and qualitative studies, equity-oriented teacher education practices, and young adolescent literacy. She has published articles in *English Journal, Middle School Journal,* and *Curriculum & Pedagogy*; has published chapters in books such as *Developmentalism in Early Childhood and Middle Grades Education: Critical Conversations on Readiness and Responsiveness,* and *Creating Organizationally Healthy and Effective Middle Schools: Research that Supports the Middle School Concept and Student Achievement*; and she has co-authored an article in *Field Methods*.

Jayne Keogh is a lecturer at Griffith University, Australia and qualitative researcher who uses a number of research approaches, including ethnomethodology, conversation analysis, membership categorisation analysis, discourse analysis and narrative theory. She takes an interest in the interactive co-construction of institutional relationships and structural arrangements, and has particular knowledge in the areas of parent-teacher (home-school) relationships, of workplace arrangements and positioning practices affecting casual (sessional) academic staff, of pre-service teacher relationships with their mentor teachers, and of the beginning teacher induction process into the profession.

Megan Lynch has been teaching high school English as a Second Language (ESL) at Osbourn Park High School in Manassas, VA for six years. She earned a Bachelor's Degree in Secondary Education from Indiana University and a Master's Degree in Education in Instruction and Curriculum from the University of Virginia. She is currently enrolled in the PhD in Education program at George Mason University. Her interests include education leadership, ESL policy, at-risk youth, and student achievement.

Shannon Moore is a PhD candidate in the Department of Curriculum and Pedagogy at the University of British Columbia. Her research interests include gender, masculinities in particular, youth and media. She has presented her work on masculinities and media at provincial, national and international conferences, including the annual conferences for the Canadian Society for the Studies in Education & the American Educational Research Association. In addition, she has co-authored a chapter, *Safe Schools, Sexuality and Critical Education*, in the *Routledge International Handbook of Critical Education*. Further, Moore has received a two-year Social Science and Research Humanities grant from the Canadian government in order to complete her research. Beyond her academic scholarship, Shannon has worked a classroom teacher in the public school system, and as a teaching assistant in Teacher Education program at UBC.

Bic Ngo is an Associate Professor of Curriculum and Instruction at the University of Minnesota. Her research examines "culture" and "difference" in the education of immigrant students, and the implications for theorizing immigrant identity, culturally relevant pedagogy, and critical multicultural education. Her research has appeared in journals such *Anthropology and Education Quarterly*, *International*

Journal of Qualitative Studies in Education, Education and Urban Society, and *Journal of Southeast Asian American Education and Advancement.* She is the author of *Unresolved Identities: Discourse, Ambivalence, and Urban Immigrant Students* (SUNY Press).

Donna Pendergast is Professor, Dean and Head, School of Education and Professional Studies at Griffith University, Australia. She has served as program director in pre- and in-service middle schooling teacher education programs and has conducted significant national research projects investigating literacy and numeracy, lifelong learning, resilience, and productive pedagogies in the middle years. She has published widely and is highly sought after as a consultant, school auditor, and speaker on issues related to middle schooling. In addition, she has been invited to provide policy advice at the Ministerial level on middle years education in several states in Australia. Pendergast has published widely, including two recent books related to the teaching of young adolescents *Teaching Middle Years: Rethinking Curriculum, Pedagogy and Assessment* (Allen & Unwin) and *The Millennial Adolescent* (Australian Council for Educational Research).

Ajay Sharma is an Assistant Professor in the Department of Elementary and Social Studies Education at the University of Georgia, Athens. His scholarship focuses on studying classroom discourse in K-12 science classrooms and science teacher education programs from the perspectives of justice and equity. He is also interested in exploring implications of climate change and neo-liberalism for science education and the democratic agenda of schooling. Sharma has published in education journals, such as *Science Education, Science & Education, Cultural Studies of Science Education* and *Education Dialogue.*

David C. Virtue is Associate Professor of Middle Level and Social Studies Education in the Department of Instruction and Teacher Education at the University of South Carolina. His areas of scholarly interest include social studies instruction, English language learners in the middle grades, and middle level teacher education and certification. His recent publications have appeared in *Middle Grades Research Journal, Research in Middle Level Education Online, Middle*

School Journal, The Clearing House, The Social Studies, Journal of Social Studies Research, and *Social Studies and the Young Learner*. Virtue has contributed to numerous edited volumes, including *Surviving the Storm: Creating Opportunities for Learning in Response to Hurricane Katrina, An International Look at Educating Young Adolescents, The Young Adolescent in the Middle School,* and *The Encyclopedia of Educational Reform and Dissent*. Virtue currently serves as editor of *Middle School Journal,* a publication of National Middle School Association. During the 2010-2011 academic year he served as a Fulbright roving scholar in Norway, giving workshops for teachers and students in *ungdomsskoler* (lower secondary schools) throughout the country.

Kristien Zenkov is an Associate Professor of Literacy Education at George Mason University and is the co-director of *Through Students' Eyes,* a project based in schools in Ohio, Virginia, Sierra Leone, and Haiti which asks high school and middle school youth to document with photographs and writing what they believe are the purposes of school. He received his PhD in Teacher Education from the University of Wisconsin-Madison, and was a faculty member at Cleveland State University for eight years before moving to George Mason. He has published more than seventy articles and book chapters concerning urban teacher education, language arts pedagogy, and curriculum standards in *School-University Partners, English Journal, Visual Studies, Journal of Adolescent and Adult Literacy, Educational Action Research, Journal of Urban Learning, Teaching, and Research,* and *School-Practitioner Quarterly*. Zenkov currently serves as the editor of *School-University Partnerships,* the official journal of the National Association for Professional Development Schools (NAPDS) and also serves on the editorial boards of the *Journal of Teacher Education, Urban Education,* and *Equity and Excellence in Education*. He is presently based in Port-au-Prince, Haiti, where he is continuing his literacy and teacher education work with middle school and high school youth and pre- and in-service teachers.

Notes

Trying to Poke Holes in Teflon: Developmentalism; Young Adolescence; and Contingent, Recursive Growth and Change

1 I have introduced a number of the theoretical arguments in this essay—namely, Lesko's contingent, recursive conception of growth and change and critical theoretical perspectives in early childhood education and adolescent literacy—elsewhere (Lee & Vagle, 2010; Vagle, 2011). However, this essay serves as a more comprehensive treatment of such arguments.

2 There is no single name for this field. Perhaps most common is *middle school*, as that is what people generally imagine—a school which "houses" young adolescents. Indeed, the field did grow out of a movement from a junior high school model in the 1960s and was termed middle school. National Middle School Association (NMSA) was founded in the early 1970s in the United States and has since gained considerable momentum, as there are affiliate organizations in most U.S. states and in Canada, Australia, New Zealand, and throughout Europe. Recently, NMSA changed its name to the Association for Middle Level Education (AMLE). Some, however, have started to use middle *grades* rather than middle school. This may seem like a subtle rhetorical shift. However, in this field it is my sense that researchers and practitioners are trying to re-identify themselves by moving to this nomenclature—away from a "school" structure and a particular grade configuration toward a specific time in life—young adolescence. For instance, a relatively new research journal, *Middle Grades Research Journal*, reflects this shift. To further complicate matters, National Middle School Association's (now *AMLE*) list of affiliate organizations in most U.S. states; in the Canadian provinces of Manitoba, Alberta, Ontario, and Saskatchewan; and in Europe, Australia, and New Zealand demonstrates a variety of names. Some affiliates use the term Middle School (e.g., Alabama, Minnesota, New Jersey), others Middle Level (e.g., European League of Middle Level Education; Indiana, Ontario), and others Middle Years (e.g., Australia's "Middle Years of Schooling Association"; Alberta's "Middle Years Council") (NMSA, 2008).

I am not sure why various organizations and journals around the world name themselves middle (school, level, grades, years). I do assume, however, that it does matter to those inside these contexts. Although I would prefer to move away from reference to "middle" in favor of *young adolescent education*, I felt that this would be too great of a departure at the beginning of this essay. So, I chose *middle grades* because I think it reflects a shift that is taking place in the United States. This also means that I locate my arguments in U.S. contexts. That said, the arguments I make in this chapter intend to interrogate any sort of static, fixed conception of a stage or school or grade configuration regardless of how it is named in the US and around the world. In other words, my interest is on the conception of young adolescent growth and change and its implications for a generous, critical education for young adolescents, not on grade levels and school structures.

3 A notable exception to this statement can be found in the work of Australian scholars Nan Bahr (Queensland University of Technology) and Donna Pendergast (University of Queensland)—contributors to this book. In two of their works, *Teaching Middle Years: Rethinking Curriculum, Pedagogy, and Assessment* and *The Millenial Adolescent*, Bahr and Pendergast seriously consider socio-historical constructions of adolescence and provide a rich description of the historical foundations of adolescence and middle schooling. Moreover, their texts provide a variety of perspectives (including developmentalist) and have a "wondering, questioning" quality that is a welcome addition to the literature.

4 It is possible that other countries throughout the world assume a developmental adolescence and have, in turn, designed their middle schooling policies and practices in response. I limit my reference to the aforementioned, because these countries/continents are listed on National Middle School Association's website as affiliate organizations. See National Middle School Association's website at http://www.nmsa.org/About NMSA/AffiliateOrganizations/AffiliateWebLinks/tabid/332/Default.aspx for a complete list of affiliate organizations across the U.S. and throughout the world.

5 Mollie Blackburn and Jill Smith (2010) provide a clear conception of heteronormativity when they say the following: "By heteronormativity we mean a way of being in the world that relies on the belief that heterosexuality is normal, which implicitly positions homosexuality and bisexuality as abnormal and thus inferior. It is often much more subtle than homophobia" (p. 625).

6 It is important to note that this particular text was written prior to the latest edition of *This We Believe* (NMSA, 2010), and therefore does not include the contextualizing and minoritizing moves seen in *This We Believe.* Again, however, my arguments here focus on foregrounding a contingent,

recursive conception of growth and change instead of a developmentalist conception.

Reappraising "Juvenilia" as a Means of Re-Conceptualizing "Adolescence"

1 It would be a mistake to read Byron's influence as appealing solely to a mythical and universal rebellious spirit inherent in adolescence. Shelley's *Zastrozzi: A Romance* (1810) presents a satanic Byronesque character whose final end may be read as an ambiguous judgment on the character. The Tennyson brothers explicitly emulate Byron's preface to his own juvenilia in prefacing their own. Chapter 1 of Anna Barton's *Tennyson's Name* explores the relationship. Charlotte and Branwell Brontë's Duke of Zamorna changes regularly over the course of their Angrian tales, at times, it seems simply according to Charlotte's moods. The reading of a cultural icon is contingent upon the reader.

2 The editors of the Juvenilia Press edition express the apprenticeship model succinctly. "Through them [her youthful plays], Alcott explored the literary world and began to develop a talent that would bring her great success. Because of the imagination she developed as a child, she became one of the most celebrated writers of juvenile fiction in nineteenth-century America. *Norna* deserves credit as a stepping stone in that direction"(p. v).

3 It should be made clear that my call for a reappraisal of "juvenilia" is not original. Many scholars have presented various ways in which to move beyond the apprenticeship model and to consider these writings in a different light. For example, see Showalters and Mahon's (1993) edition of Rossetti, Castle (2002), Doody (2005), Robertson (1998) and Alexander (2005).

4 Donzelot (1979) and Nissenbaum (1996) both detail the ways in which family structures and power dynamics shifted in the nineteenth century as a result of social forces. Chapter two of Grumet's (1988) *Bitter Milk* also provides excellent analysis of these relationships as they pertain to schooling.

5 The scholars whose work has been critical in reviving and sustaining and interest in "juvenilia", Juliet McMaster and Christine Alexander (2005) comment on this problem in their book *The Child Writer from Austen to Woolf.* Their point is that these texts are inherently a product of the privileged class. There are simply no available, extant writings from children who were uneducated or performing physical labor from an early age.

6 For more on Jane Austen's juvenilia, see Butler, (1975), Doody (2005), Gilbert & Gubar (1979), and Waldron (1999).

7 I am indebted to Beverly Taylor (2005) for introducing me to this autobiographical piece and to her thoughtful reading of it published in *The Child Writer from Austen to Woolf*.

Norwegian Perspectives on Educating Young Adolescen(TS)

1 The phrase "field of middle level education" refers here to the body of educators and researchers who focus on ideas, issues, policies, and practices associated with schools serving students age 10 to 15 and whose major academic affiliations are the Middle Level Education Research group of the American Educational Research Association, National Middle School Association (NMSA), and NMSA affiliates worldwide. Most of this work is conducted by scholars in the United States and other Anglophone countries, including New Zealand, Australia, and Canada.

2 The author gratefully acknowledges the U.S.-Norway Fulbright Foundation for granting the opportunity to work as a Roving Scholar in Norwegian lower secondary schools during the 2010 – 2011 academic year. More information about the Roving Scholars Program, which is unique to Norway, is available at http://www.fulbright.no/.

3 While the "middle school concept" as it is understood here has influenced schooling in many countries, the focus throughout the chapter is on the U.S. context.

4 The number of 15-year-olds in Norway reporting that they have at least three close friends of the same sex was 88% for girls and 87.2% for boys compared to, for example, 80.6% and 77.5% in the U.S., 85.1% and 82.7% in Canada, 70.7% and 79.7% in Germany, and 67.3% and 78.2% in France.

5 An earlier version of certain parts of this section on scheduling appeared in the January 2011 issue of *Middle School Journal* (Virtue, 2011).

'Particularizing' Young Adolescents in an Indian Context

1 All names are pseudonyms in this chapter.

2 By 'tuition classes' Raj was referring to coaching sessions run by private tutors after or before school. Most students in the local middle school attended such coaching sessions. This kind of extra help was expensive, but was considered an unavoidable, necessary educational expense by parents in the village.

3 According to the transcription convention adopted in this research, empty parentheses ( ) indicate unintelligible words or phrases.

4 Neither did they do any household chores while at home.

Index

D

E

F

G

H

I

U

V

W

Y

AC SS Adolescent Cultures, School & Society

Joseph L. DeVitis & Linda Irwin-DeVitis
GENERAL EDITORS

As schools struggle to redefine and restructure themselves, they need to be aware of the new realities of adolescents. Thus, this series of monographs and texts is committed to depicting the variety of adolescent cultures that exist in today's troubled world. It is primarily a qualitative research, practice, and policy series devoted to contextual interpretation and analysis that encompasses a broad range of interdisciplinary critique. In addition, this series seeks to address issues of curriculum theory and practice; multicultural education; aggression, bullying, and violence; the media and arts; school dropouts; homeless and runaway youth; gangs and other alienated youth; at-risk adolescent populations; family structures and parental involvement; and race, ethnicity, class, and gender/LGBTQ studies.

Send proposals and manuscripts to the general editors at:

Joseph L. DeVitis & Linda Irwin-DeVitis
Darden College of Education
Old Dominion University
Norfolk, VA 23503

To order other books in this series, please contact our Customer Service Department at:

(800) 770-LANG (within the U.S.)
(212) 647-7706 (outside the U.S.)
(212) 647-7707 FAX

or browse online by series at:

WWW.PETERLANG.COM

www.ingramcontent.com/pod-product-compliance
Ingram Content Group UK Ltd.
Pitfield, Milton Keynes, MK11 3LW, UK
UKHW022122230426
12048UKWH00011BA/656

9 781433 116346